CRIMINOLOGICAL THEORY

STUDIES IN CRIME, LAW, AND JUSTICE

Series Editor: James A. Inciardi,
Division of Criminal Justice, University of Delaware

Studies in Crime, Law, and Justice contains original research formulations and new analytic perspectives on continuing important issues of crime and the criminal justice and legal systems. Volumes are research based but are written in nontechnical language to allow for use in courses in criminal justice, criminology, law, social problems, and related subjects.

CRIMINOLOGICAL THEORY
Context and Consequences

BY

J. Robert Lilly
Francis T. Cullen
Richard A. Ball

STUDIES IN CRIME, LAW AND JUSTICE ■ Volume 5

 **SAGE** Publications
International Educational and Professional Publisher
Newbury Park   London   New Delhi

For
Our Parents

For information address:

SAGE Publications, Inc.
2455 Teller Road
Newbury Park, California 91320

SAGE Publications Ltd.
6 Bonhill Street
London EC2A 4PU
United Kingdom

SAGE Publications India Pvt. Ltd.
M-32 Market
Greater Kailash I
New Delhi 110 048 India

Printed in the United States of America

Library of Congress Cataloging-in-Publication Data

Lilly J. Robert.
    Criminological theory : context and consequences / by J. Robert
Lilly, Francis T. Cullen, Richard A. Ball.
      p. cm. — (Studies in crime, law, and justice ; v. 5)
    Bibliography : p.
    Includes index.
    ISBN 0-8039-2638-3. — ISBN 0-8039-2639-1 (pbk.)
    1. Crime and criminals. 2. Crime and criminals — United States.
3. Criminal behavior — United States. I. Cullen, Francis T.
II. Ball, Richard A., 1936- . III. Title. IV. Series.
HV6018.L55 1989
364'.973—dc 19   88-32684
                                                            CIP

93 94 15 14 13 12 11 10 9 8 7 6

Contents

1

The Context and Consequences of Theory

Crime is a complex phenomenon and it is a demanding, if intriguing, challenge to explain its many sides. Often, commentators (some, but not all, public officials come to mind) suggest that using good common sense is enough to explain why citizens shoot or rob one another and, in turn, to inform us as to what to do about such lawlessness. Our experience — and we trust this book, too — teaches that the search for answers to the crime problem is not so easy. It requires that we reconsider our biases, learn from the insights and mistakes of our predecessors who have risked theorizing about the causes of crime, and consider clearly the implications of what we propose.

But the task — or, as we see it, the adventure — of explaining crime is an important undertaking. To be sure, crime commentary frequently succumbs to the temptation to exaggerate and sensationalize, to suggest that crimes which are exceptionally lurid and injurious comprise the bulk of America's lawlessness, or perhaps to suggest that most citizens spend their lives huddled behind barricaded doors and paralyzed by the fear that local thugs will victimize them. There is, of course, an element of truth in these observations, which is why they have an intuitive appeal. Yet most Americans — particularly those living in more affluent communities — do not have their lives ripped apart by a brutal assault or tragic murder; and though many citizens lock their doors at night, install burglar alarms, and perhaps buy weapons for protection, they typically say they feel safe in and close to their homes (Cullen, Clark, and Wozniak, 1985; Scheingold, 1984).

These cautionary remarks, however, do not detract from the reality that crime is a serious matter which deserves, we believe, study and understanding. If most Americans escape the kind of victimization that takes their lives or destroys their peace of mind, too many others do not share this good fortune. Thus media reports of Americans killing Americans are sufficiently ubiquitous that many of us have become so desensitized to the violence in our communities that we give these accounts scarcely more attention than the scores from the day's sporting events. And it is likely that most of us have friends, or friends of friends, whom we know have been seriously assaulted or perhaps even murdered.

Statistical data paint an equally bleak picture. Each year, the FBI publishes the *Uniform Crime Reports*, in which it lists the number of crimes that have become known (mostly through reports by citizens) to the nation's police departments. For 1987 alone, over 20,000 Americans were murdered and nearly 1.5 million others were either robbed, raped, or seriously assaulted; an additional 12 million citizens, the FBI's figures revealed, had their houses burglarized or their property damaged or stolen (FBI, 1988:41).

It is disturbing that these statistics capture only part of the nation's crime problem. Many citizens, perhaps one in two, do not report crimes against them to the police and thus these acts do not appear in the *Uniform Crime Reports*. A study by the Bureau of Justice Statistics (1988), for instance, revealed that in 1984 one in four American households — 22.3 million altogether — were "touched" by a criminal victimization.

Further, the FBI's statistics include data only on serious street crimes. Yet we know that minor crimes — petty thefts, simple assaults — are even more widespread. "Self-report" surveys in which respondents (typically juveniles) are asked how many offenses they have committed consistently indicate that the vast majority of people have engaged in some degree of illegality. More important, however, there are other realms of criminality — not only quite prevalent but also quite serious — that have not traditionally come to the attention of police because they are not committed on the "streets." Domestic violence — child abuse, spousal assault; that is, the violence that occurs "behind closed doors" — is one of these areas (Straus, Gelles, and Steinmetz, 1980). Another such area is "white-collar crime," the crimes committed by affluent people in the course of their occupations (Sutherland, 1949). As recent revelations suggest, corruption in the business and political communities takes place regularly and has disquieting consequences (Cullen, Maakestad, and Cavender,

1987; Simon and Eitzen, 1986).

More statistics and observations could be added here, but this would only belabor the point: Crime is a prominent feature in our society. Indeed, as Elliott Currie notes, lawlessness — particularly violence — is higher in the United States than in any other industrialized Western nation. Making cross-cultural comparisons is difficult; for example, nations differ in what they consider to be illegal and in their methods of collecting crime data. Even so, Currie's (1985:25) review of available statistical information revealed that as of the late 1970s "about ten American men died by criminal violence for every Japanese, Austrian, West German, or Swedish man; about fifteen American men died for every Swiss or Englishman; and over twenty for every Dane."

But why is crime so prevalent in America? Why in some of our communities but not others? Why do some kinds of people break the law, while others are law-abiding? Why do the affluent, not just the disadvantaged, commit illegal acts? How can these varied phenomena be explained?

Over the years, theorists have endeavored to address one or more of these questions. In this book, we attempt to give an account of their thinking about crime — to examine its roots, its content, and its consequences. Before embarking on this story of criminological theorizing, however, it is necessary to discuss the framework which will inform our analysis.

THEORY IN SOCIAL CONTEXT

Most Americans have little difficulty in identifying the circumstances they believe cause people to engage in wayward conduct. When surveyors ask citizens about the causes of crime, only a small percentage of the respondents say they "have no opinion." The remainder of those polled usually remark that crime is caused by factors such as unemployment, bad family life, or lenient courts (Flanagan, 1987).

Most people, then, have developed views cn why crime occurs; that is, they have a "theory" of criminal behavior. But where do such views, such theories, come from? One possibility is that citizens have taken the time to read extensively on crime, have sifted through existing research studies, and have arrived at an informed assessment of why laws are disregarded. But, only the exceptional citizen develops his or her views on crime — or on any other social issue — this way. Apart from those who study crime for a living, criminologists, the rest of the people do not have the time, nor some the inclination, to investigate carefully the crime problem.

This observation may not seem particularly insightful, but it is important in illuminating that most people's opinions about crime are drawn less from rational thought and more from the implicit understandings they have come to embrace during their lives. Attitudes about crime, as well as about other social issues, can come from a variety of sources: parents, church sermons, how crime is depicted on television, whether one has had family or friends who have turned to crime, whether one has experimented with criminal activity oneself or perhaps been victimized. In short, social experiences shape the way in which people come to think about crime.

This conclusion allows us to offer three additional points. First, members of the general public are not the only ones whose crime theories are influenced by their life-experiences. Academic criminologists and government officials who formulate crime policy have a professional obligation to set aside their personal biases, read the existing research, and endorse the theory which the evidence most supports. To an extent, criminologists and policymakers let the data direct their thinking, but it is equally clear that they do not do so fully. Like the general public, they too live in society and are shaped by it. Before ever entering academia or public service, their personal experiences have provided them with certain assumptions about human nature and about the way the world operates (thus some will see themselves as liberals, others as conservatives). After studying crime, they often will revise some of their views. Nonetheless, few ever convert to a totally different way of thinking about crime; how they explain crime remains, if only in part, conditioned by the experiences they have had.

Second, if social experiences influence attitudes about criminality, then as society changes — as people come to have different experiences — views about crime will also change. We will illustrate this point throughout this book, but a few brief examples might help to clarify matters for immediate purposes.

It will not surprise many readers to learn that Americans' views on crime have changed markedly since the settlers first landed on the nation's shores. Indeed, at different times in our history, Americans have attributed the origins of crime to spiritual demons and the inherent sinfulness of humans, to the defective biological constitution of inferior people in our midst, to the denial of equal opportunity, and to the ability of the coldly rational to calculate that crime pays. As we will see, each of these theories of crime (and others as well) became popular only when a particular set of circumstances coalesced to provide people with the experiences that made such reasoning seem logical or "believable."

Thus for colonists living in a confined, highly religious society, it "made sense" for them to attribute crime to the power of demons to control the will of those who fell prey to the temptations of sin. For those in the late 1800s who witnessed the influx of foreigners of all sorts and learned from the Social Darwinists that natural selection determined where each individual fell in the social hierarchy, it "made sense" that people became poor *and* criminal because they were of inferior stock. For those of the 1960s, however, who were informed that systematic barriers had prevented minorities from sharing in the American dream, it "made sense" that people became criminal *because* they were poor — because they were denied equal opportunity. And in more recent times, as society has taken a turn in a conservative direction and it has become fashionable to blame social ills on a permissive society, it has "made sense" to more and more Americans that people commit crimes because they know they risk, if ever caught, only a slap on the wrist.

In short, social context plays a critical role in nourishing certain ways of theorizing about crime. If the prevailing social context changes and people begin to experience life differently, there will be a corresponding shift in the way they see their world and the people in it. Previous theories of crime will lose their appeal, and other perspectives will increasingly "make sense" to larger numbers of people. Note that all this can take place — indeed, usually does take place — without systematic analysis of whether the "old" theory was, in fact, wrong or if the new theory represents an improvement!

But does any of this relate to you, the reader? Our third point in this section is that your (and our) thinking about crime has undoubtedly been conditioned by your social experiences. When most of us look to the past, we wonder with a certain smugness how our predecessors could have held such strange and silly views about crime, or other things. In making this kind of remark, however, we not only fail to appreciate how their thoughts and actions were constrained by the world in which they lived but also implicitly assume that our thoughts and actions are unconstrained by our world. Our arrogance causes us to accept our interpretations, our theories, as "obviously" correct; we forget that future generations will have the luxury of looking at us and assessing where we have been strange and silly.

This discussion suggests the wisdom of pausing to contemplate the basis of your beliefs. How have your social experiences shaped the way you explain crime? Asking and seeking answers to this question, we believe, opens the possibility of lifting the blinders that past experiences often strap firmly around one's eyes. It creates, in short, the exciting opportunity to think differently about crime.

THEORY AND POLICY: IDEAS HAVE CONSEQUENCES

"Theory" is frequently dismissed as mere empty ruminations — fun, perhaps, but not something for which practical men and women have time. But this is a short-sighted view, for as Thomas Szasz (1987) has cautioned, "ideas have consequences." Theory matters.

When it comes to making criminal justice policy, there is ample evidence of this maxim (Sherman and Hawkins, 1981). Lawlessness is a costly problem; people lose their property, and sometimes their lives. The search for the sources of crime, then, is not done within a vacuum. Even if a theorist wishes only to ruminate about the causes of theft or violence, others will be ready to use these insights to direct efforts to do something about the crime problem. Understanding why crime occurs, then, is a prelude to developing strategies to control the behavior. Stephen Pfohl (1985:9-10) has captured nicely the inherent relationship between theory and policy:

Theoretical perspectives provide us with an image of what something is and how we might best act toward it. They name something this type of thing and not that. They provide us with the sense of being in a world of relatively fixed forms and content. Theoretical perspectives transform a mass of raw sensory data into understanding, explanations, and recipes for appropriate action.

This discussion also leads to the realization that different theories suggest different ways to reduce crime. Depending on what is proposed as the cause of illegal behavior, certain criminal justice policies and practices will seem reasonable; others will seem irrational and perhaps dangerously irresponsible. Thus if offenders are viewed as genetically deranged and untrainable — much like wild animals — then caging them would seem to be the only option available. But if offenders are thought to be mentally ill, the solution to the problem would be to give them psychotherapy. Or if one believes that people are moved to crime by the strains of economic deprivation, providing job training and access to employment opportunities would seem to hold the promise of diminishing their waywardness.

This is not to assert that the relationship between theory and policy is uncomplicated. Sometimes theories emerge and then the demand to change policy occurs; sometimes policies are implemented and then attempts are made to justify the policies by popularizing theories supportive of these reforms; often the process is interactive with the theory and policy legitimating one another. In any case, the important point is that support for criminal justice policies will eventually collapse if the theory on which they are based no longer "makes sense."

An important observation follows from this discussion: as theories of crime change, so do criminal justice policies. At the turn of the century, many Americans felt that criminals were "atavistic reversions" to less civilized evolutionary forms or, at the least, "feebleminded." The call to sterilize offenders so that they could not pass criminogenic genes to their offspring was widely accepted as prudent social action. Within two decades, however, citizens were more convinced that the causes of crime lay not within offenders themselves but in the pathology of their environments. The time was ripe to hear suggestions that efforts be made to "save" slum youths by setting up neighborhood delinquency prevention programs or, when necessary, by removing juveniles to "reformatories," where they could obtain the supervision and treatment they desperately needed. More recently, numerous politicians have climbed on the bandwagon which claims that crime is caused by the permissiveness that has crept into the nation's families, schools, and correctional system. Not surprisingly, they have urged that efforts be made to "get tough" with offenders, to teach them that crime does not pay by sending them to prison for lengthier stays and in record numbers.

We must remember, however, not to decontextualize criminological theory: the very changes in theory that undergird changes in policy are themselves a product of transformations in society. As noted above, explanations of crime are intimately linked to social context — to the experiences people have that make a given theory seem "silly" or "sensible." Thus it is only when shifts in society occur that theoretical models gain or lose credence and, in turn, gain or lose the ability to justify a range of criminal justice policies.

We hope as well that the reader will find the discussion of some personal relevance. We have suggested that thought be given to how your own context may have shaped your thinking; now we suggest that similar thought be given to how your thinking may have shaped what you have thought should be done about crime. The challenge we are offering is for you to reconsider the basis and consistency of your views on crime and its control — to reconsider which theory you should embrace and the consequences this idea should have. Hopefully, our book will aid you as you embark upon this adventure.

CONTEXT, THEORY, POLICY: PLAN OF THE BOOK

"Perhaps the clearest lesson to be learned from historical research on crime and deviance," Timothy Flanagan (1987:232) reminds us, "is that the approach to crime control that characterizes any given era in history is inexorably linked to contemporaneous notions about crime causation." These remarks are instructive because they capture the central theme of our book: the interconnection among social context, criminological theory, and criminal justice policy-making. As we progress through the subsequent chapters, this theme will form the framework for our analysis. We will not only discuss the content of a theoretical perspective, but also its context and consequences.

The scope of the enterprise, however, should be clarified. Our purpose here is to provide a primer in criminological theory — a basic introduction to the social history of attempts, largely by academic scholars, to explain crime. In endeavoring to furnish an accessible and relatively brief guide to such theorizing, we have been forced to leave out historical detail and omit discussions of the many theoretical variations each perspective on crime has typically fostered. As a result, this book should be viewed as a first step to understanding the long search for the answer to the riddle of crime. We hope that our account encourages you to take further steps in the time ahead.

Our excursion into the story of criminological theory commences, as most stories do, at the beginning. Chapter 2 discusses early efforts, to use Ysabel Rennie's (1978) words, "to search for the criminal man." Most of these attempts, as we shall see, argued that the causes of crime lay within men and women: in their soul, their will, or their bodily constitution. Chapter 3, by contrast, focuses on scholars who argued that the answers to crime were not to be found within people, but in the social circumstances in which people must live. Some of these scholars asserted that the seeds of crime were rooted in the fabric of slum life; others felt that the very nature of American society was criminogenic.

Chapters 4, 5, and 6 examine theoretical models that largely (though not exclusively) emerged and then gained force in the 1960s and 1970s. To some degree, each model was an attempt to move beyond previous sociological theories of crime. Thus in Chapter 4 we learn about "control" theorists, who suggested that the question was not so much why people's social environments motivated them to commit criminal acts — the traditional question criminologists asked — but why such circumstances *stopped* them from breaking the law. In Chapter 5 "labeling" theory is discussed. Scholars in this perspective offered the bold argument that the main cause of committed involvement in crime is not society per se, but rather the very attempts that are made to reduce crime by stigmatizing offenders and processing them through the criminal justice system. And in Chapter 6 we review theorists — often called "conflict" or "radical" scholars — who have gone so far as to suggest that the embrace of capitalism is what induces high rates of lawlessness among both rich and poor.

The seventh chapter brings our story up-to-date and to a close. Here we explore the theoretical trends that have gained in popularity during the last decade and which are having an increasing sway on the nature of criminal justice policy. We discover that many of these theoretical explanations are attempts to revitalize — dressed in new language and with more sophisticated evidence — the models of crime that were popular closer to the turn of the century. Thus we see that claims are being made once again that the sources of crime lie deeply within the individual and not within the social fabric. The ramifications of this theoretical shift are immense, and, we argue, merit our close assessment.

2

The Search for the Criminal "Man"

Before we examine the content of this chapter, it is important to remember a few of the cautionary comments offered in Chapter 1. By keeping these ideas in mind we will more than likely be successful in accomplishing the goal of introducing you to the context and consequences of criminological theory.

We want to remember that the search for explanations of criminal behavior is not easy because we must constantly guard against our biases, mistaken perceptions, and prejudices. Unless we maintain our intellectual guard against these problems, our learning will be severely limited, and that is unwanted. This will become obvious as we study the following chapters and learn that many theories of crime, which have experienced popularity with the public and professional criminologists, have also been criticized for having serious blind spots. Unfortunately, the "blind spots" often have contributed to the creation and implementation of official policies that have produced results as undesirable as crime itself. While it is impossible to develop perfect policies, we must keep in mind the fact that theories do influence the policies and practices found in criminal justice systems.

It is important to remember that the explanations of crime, whether they are created by the public or professional criminologists, are influenced by the social context from which they come. This means that the "social context" will consist of perceptions and interpretations of the past as well as the present. It may also mean that the explanations of crime include some thoughts about what crime and society will look like in the not-too-distant future. This is exactly what Bennett (1987) has recently offered in *Crimewarps*, a study of what crime will look like in the next 20 to 50 years. A brief examination of the social context which influenced her writing of *Crimewarps* will help illustrate what we mean by the importance of social context. As you will see, the context includes general sociological factors such as time and place. It also includes the author's career experiences and opportunities.

By the time Bennett began to work on *Crimewarps,* she had completed a Ph.D. in sociology (1972) and was an accomplished scholar, researcher, teacher, and journalist with more than 20 years of work on the topic of crime. In addition, she was an associate of the Center for Policy Research and the Center for Investigative Reporting. She had also worked as a network correspondent for NBC News, and she had been a talk show host for PBS television. In other words, we can say that Bennett was experienced and therefore prepared to study major "trends." In fact, her book was an outgrowth of having been asked by the Insurance Information Institution to be a consultant and media spokesperson on the topic of "the state of crime in the future" (Bennett, 1987:vii). Bennett's experiences and the consulting work for the Insurance Information Institution occurred within a shifting social context which she connected to crime by using the term "crimewarps." She used this term to refer to "the bends in today's trends that will affect the way we live tomorrow" (Bennett, 1987:xiii). Essentially her thesis is that much of what we have come to regard as basic demographic features of our society's population and crime trends are dramatically changing. She refers to these crimewarps as representing a "set of major social transformations" (Bennett, 1987:viii). Altogether she identifies six "warps." For example, she labels one warp "the new criminal." This refers to the fact that today's "traditional" criminal is a poor, undereducated, young male. By relying on demographic information and dramatic news accounts of current crimes, Bennett argues that the traditional criminal will be displaced by "older, more upscale offenders." These will include, among other trends, more women involved in white-collar crime and domestic violence. In addition she argues that teenagers will commit fewer crimes while senior citizens "will enter the crime scene as geriatric delinquents" (Bennett, 1987:xiv).

The importance of this example lies not in the accuracy of Bennett's claims, her career experiences, or the fact she was invited by the Insurance Information Institute to work on the future of crime at a time when our society is experiencing dramatic demographic transformations. Rather, the lesson to keep in mind is that all of these factors coalesced in such a manner as to allow Bennett to write a book on crime that "makes sense," because it is "timely" in view of what we know about society today and what we think it may look like in the future. Remember, writers — like ideas — are captives of the time and place in which they live. For this reason alone, it is impossible to understand criminological theory outside its social context (Rennie, 1978:5). It remains to be seen how Bennett's book will be evaluated in 20 to 50 years, and it remains to be seen if the criminal "man" of the future fits Bennett's predictions.

One more cautionary comment needs to be made. Just as today's social context has made a book like Bennett's possible, the context of previous historical eras made different kinds of theories about crime possible. Early theories of crime tended to locate the cause of crime not in demographic shifts as has Bennett, but within the individual: in their soul (spiritualism/demonology), their will (classical school), or their bodily constitutions (positive school). We will examine each of these theories in this chapter. We are now ready to begin our search for the criminal man. We start with the earliest explanation, spiritualism.

SPIRITUALISM

As an explanation of criminal behavior, spiritualism provides a sharp contrast to the scholarly explanations used today. Unlike today's theories, spiritualism stressed the conflict between absolute good and absolute evil (Tannenbaum, 1938:3). People who committed crimes were thought to be possessed by evil spirits, often referred to as demons.

While the genesis of this perspective is lost to antiquity, there is ample archaeological, anthropological, and historical evidence that this explanation has been around for many centuries. We know, for example, that primitive people explained natural disasters such as floods and famines as punishments by spirits for wrongdoings. This type of view was also used by the ancient Egyptians, Greeks, and Romans. Much later, during the Middle Ages in Europe, spiritualistic explanations had become well organized and connected to the political and social structure of feudalism.

One important reason for this particular development is that, originally, crime was a private matter between the victim or the family of the victim and the offender(s). Unfortunately, this means of responding to offenses had a tendency to create long blood feuds that could destroy entire families. There was also the problem of justice: a guilty offender with a strong family might never be punished.

To avoid some of these problems other methods were constructed for dealing with those accused of committing a crime. Trial by battle, for example, permitted the victim or some member of his or her family to fight the offender or some member of the offender's family (Vold and Bernard, 1986:7). It was believed that victory would go to the innocent if they believed and trusted God. Unfortunately, this arrangement permitted great warriors to continue engaging in criminal behavior, buttressed by the belief they would always be found "innocent." Trial by ordeal determined guilt or innocence by subjecting the accused to life threatening and painful situations. People, for instance, might have huge stones piled upon them. If they were innocent, it was believed that God would keep them from being crushed to death. If they were guilty, a painful death would occur. People were also tied up and thrown into a river or pond. If they were innocent, God would allow them to float; drowning meant they were guilty (Vold and Bernard, 1986:7).

Compurgation represents another means of determining innocence or guilt based on spiritualism. Unlike trial by battle or ordeal which involved physical pain and the threat of death, compurgation allowed the accused to have reputable people swear an oath that they were innocent. The logic was based on the belief that no one would lie under oath for fear of God's punishment (Vold and Bernard, 1986:7).

The same fear of God's punishment formed the explanation of crime and deviance for what Erikson (1966) has called the "wayward Puritans," citizens in the early American Massachusetts Bay Colony. And later when our penitentiaries were constructed they were thought of as places for "penitents who were sorry for their sins" (Vold and Bernard, 1986:8). Today we have many groups and individuals who believe crimes and other wrongs can be explained by the Devil. In early 1987, for example, when "prime time preacher" Jim Bakker of the famed "PTL Club"

(Praise the Lord and People That Love) confessed to an adulterous one-night-stand with a former church secretary, some of his followers said it was the result of the Devil's work (*Newsweek*, 1987a:16). And on one occasion when Internal Revenue Service auditors revealed that several millions of dollars were unaccounted for by the PTL organization, Bakker's wife Tammy Faye said the Devil must have gotten into the computer (*New York Times,* 1987a). Others who have been caught for criminal acts have turned to God for a cure for their behavior. Charles Colson of Watergate fame, for instance, takes the Christian message to prisoners as a solution to their problems.

It is important to remember that even though people may criticize "the Devil made me do it" argument as quaint or odd, it nevertheless makes sense for some people who try to understand and explain crime. In fact, it may even be argued that the public's interest in this type of explanation grows at the same rate as our population growth. According to the National Council of Churches, church membership grows gradually at approximately the same rate as the nation's population. Altogether nearly 70 percent of the population say they are involved with a church, a figure that has remain steady in recent years (*New York Times*, 1987b:13).

The major problem with spiritualistic explanations, nonetheless, is that they cannot be scientifically tested. Because the "cause" of crime according to this theory is otherworldly, it cannot be verified empirically. It is primarily for this reason that modern theories of crime and social order rely upon explanations that are based on this world. These theories are called natural explanations.

Naturalistic theories and spiritualistic explanations have in common their origin in the ancient world. Despite this common origin, the two perspectives are very different. Thus, by focusing on the physical world of facts, naturalistic theories seek explanations that are more specific and detailed than do spiritualistic theories. This approach to thinking and explanation was very much part of the Greeks, for instance, who early on in their search for knowledge philosophically divided the world into a dualistic reality of mind and matter. This form of thinking is still prevalent in the Western world as evidenced by reasoning that restricts explanations of human behavior to either passion or reason.

An early example of a naturalistic explanation is found in "Hippocrates' (460 B.C.) dictum that the brain is the organ of the mind" (Vold, 1958:7). Additional evidence of efforts to explain phenomena by naturalistic reasoning was present approximately 350 years later in the first century B.C. in Roman thought, which attempted to explain the idea of "progress" with little reliance on demons or spirits (Vold, 1958:7). The existence of this reasoning, however, does not mean that demonic and spiritualistic explanations had begun to wane by the time of the Roman Empire. In fact, these explanations reigned high well into the Middle Ages.

On the other hand, naturalistic explanations persisted in spite of the spiritualistic perspective's dominance, and by the sixteenth and seventeenth centuries several scholars were studying and explaining humans in terms known to them (Vold, 1958:7-8). Their efforts are collectively identified as the Classical School of Criminology. Later in this chapter, we will consider a second influential naturalistic theory, the Positivist School of Criminology.

THE CLASSICAL SCHOOL: CRIMINAL AS CALCULATOR

The most important feature of this school of thought is its emphasis on the individual criminal as a person who is capable of calculating what he or she wants to do. This idea was supported by a philosophy which held that human beings had free will and that behavior was guided by hedonism. Individuals, in other words, were guided by a pain and pleasure principle by which they calculated the risks and rewards they would receive for their actions. Accordingly, punishment should be suited to the offense, not to the social or physical characteristics of the criminal.

If this sounds familiar, you should not be surprised; one of the basic tenets of our legal heritage is that people should be given equal treatment before the law. People should not be punished or rewarded just because they happen to have the right name or be from a powerful family. Equality is one of the powerful ideas that was widely endorsed by the eighteenth and nineteenth century Enlightenment writers who influenced our Founding Fathers. Of particular interest here is the scholar most often identified as the leader of the classical school of criminology: Cesare Bonesana

Marchese de Beccaria (1738-1794), an Italian mathematician and economist. It is Beccaria who pulled together many of the most powerful eighteenth century ideas of democratic liberalism and connected them to issues of criminal justice.

While it is true Beccaria was born into an aristocratic family and had the benefit of a solid education in the liberal arts, there is little if any evidence in his background which would have predicted that his one small book on penal reform, *On Crimes and Punishments* (1764) would be eventually acknowledged to have had "more practical effect than any other treatise ever written in the long campaign against barbarism in criminal law and procedure" (Beccaria, 1963:ix). Indeed, one biographical overview of Beccaria indicates that his education failed to produce a modicum of enthusiasm for scholarship except for some attraction to mathematics (Monachesi, 1973:36-37). But this interest soon passed and what seems to have emerged is a discontented young man with strong arguments against much of the status quo, including his father's objections to his marriage in 1761 (Beccaria, 1963:xii). To understand Beccaria's great contribution we must examine the social context of his life.

Unlike America's concern for protecting its citizens through "equal protection," "due process," and "trial by one's peers," the criminal justice system of Beccaria's Europe, especially the ancient regime in France, was "planned to ruin citizens" (Radzinowicz, 1966:1), a characterization that applied to the police, criminal procedures, and punishment. The police of Paris, for example, were "the most ruthless and efficient police marching in the world" (Radzinowicz, 1966:2). They were allowed by the French monarchy to deal not only with criminal matters, but also with the morals and political opinions of French citizens. They relied heavily on spies, extensive covert letter-opening, and the state-approved capacity not only to arrest people without warrants but also to pass judgment and hold people in custody indefinitely on unknown charges.

Once arrested the accused had few legal protections. He or she was cut off from legal assistance, subjected to torture, and kept in secret from family and friends. Witnesses against the accused testified in secret. Once guilt was determined, punishments were severe, "ranging from burning alive or breaking on the wheel to the galleys and many forms of mutilation, whipping, branding and the pillory" (Radzinowicz, 1966:3). Death by execution in early eighteenth century London took place every six weeks, with five to 15 condemned hanged on each occasion (Lofland, 1973:35).

Beccaria became familiar with these conditions through the association and friendship of Alessandro Verri who held the office of Protector of Prisoners in Milan, Italy, where Beccaria lived. Outraged by these conditions and having recently become familiar with the writings of such scholars as Montesquieu, Helvetius, Voltaire, Bacon, Rousseau, Diderot, and Hume, Beccaria was encouraged by a small group of intellectuals to take up his pen in behalf of humanity. He was not eager to write, however, because he did not enjoy writing and because he worried about political reprisals for expressing his views. He so feared persecution from the monarchy for his views that he chose to publish the book anonymously (Monachesi, 1973:38). It took 11 months to write but once published, the volume excited all of Europe as if a nerve had been exposed. By 1767, when the book was first translated into English, it had already been through several French and Italian editions. But what did it say? What caused all of the excitement?

Beccaria's tightly reasoned argument can be summarized in relatively simple terms (Radzinowicz, 1966; Vold, 1958). First, in order to escape war and chaos, individuals gave up some of their liberty and established a contractual society. This established the sovereignty of a nation and the ability of the nation to create criminal law and to punish offenders. Second, because criminal laws placed restrictions on individual freedoms, they should be restricted in scope. They should not be employed to enforce moral virtue. To prohibit human behavior unnecessarily was to increase rather than decrease crime. Third, the presumption of innocence should be the guiding principle in the administration of justice, and at all stages of the justice process the rights of all parties involved should be protected. Fourth, the complete criminal law code should be written and define all offenses and punishments in advance. This would allow the public to judge how and if their liberties were being preserved.

Fifth, punishment should be based on retributive reasoning because the guilty had attacked another individual's rights. Sixth, the severity of the punishment should be limited and it should not go beyond what is necessary for crime prevention and deterrence. Seventh, criminal punishment should correspond with the seriousness of the crime; the punishment should fit the crime, not the criminal. Fines, for example, would be appropriate for simple thefts, while the harsher sanctions of corporal punishment and labor would be acceptable for violent crimes. Eighth, punishment must be a certainty and inflicted quickly. Ninth, punishment should not be administered to set an example; neither should it be concerned with reforming the offender. Tenth, the offender should be viewed as an independent and reasonable person who weighed the consequences of the crime. Offenders should be assumed to have the same power of resistance as non-offenders. Eleventh, for Beccaria, the aim of every good system of legislation was the prevention of crime. He reasoned it was better to prevent crimes than to punish them.

Beccaria was not, however, the only scholar in his time to consider these issues. Jeremy Bentham (1748-1832), an English jurist and philosopher, also argued that punishment should be a deterrent and he too explained behavior as a result of free will and "hedonistic calculus" (Bentham, 1948). John Howard (1726?-1790), also English and a contemporary of Beccaria and Bentham, studied prisons and advocated prison reform (Howard, 1929). His work is often credited with having influenced the passage of England's Penitentiary Act of 1779, which addressed prison reform.

The influence of these writers, however, went far beyond the passage of specific laws. Their ideas inspired revolutions and the creation of entirely new legal codes. The French Revolution of 1789 and its famous Code of 1791, and the United States Constitution, were each influenced by the Classical School. However, by the 1820s crime was still flourishing and the argument that bad laws made bad people was being seriously questioned (Rothman, 1971:61-62). Also, the argument that all criminal behavior could be explained by hedonism was weakening as the importance of aggravating and mitigating circumstances increased. Nor did the new laws provide for the separate treatment of children. Nevertheless, the classical school did make significant and lasting contributions. The call for laws to be impartial and specific and for punishment to be for crimes instead of criminals, as well as the belief that all citizens should be treated fairly and equally, have now become accepted ideas. But what caused crime remained a troubling question unanswered by the Enlightenment's "rather uncomplicated view of Rational Man" (Sykes, 1978:11), a view based primarily on "armchair thinking." The result was a new search for the criminal "man," with emphasis given to action being determined instead of the result of free will. The advocates of this new way of thinking created what came to be known as the "Positivist School of Criminology."

THE POSITIVIST SCHOOL: CRIMINAL AS DETERMINED

The most significant difference between the Classical School and the Positivist School is the latter's search for empirical facts to confirm the idea that crime was determined by multiple factors. This is a clear shift away from the reasoning of Beccaria and Bentham who thought crime resulted from the free will and hedonism of the individual criminal. As will become apparent, the nineteenth century's first Positivists wanted scientific proof that crime was caused by features within the individual. They primarily emphasized the mind and the body of the criminal, thus to some extent neglecting social factors external to the individual. (Later these factors became the focus of sociological explanations of crime; more about this type of explanation later.)

However, the search for causes of crime in fact did not begin with the nineteenth century Positivists. Early examples in literature, for instance, connect the body through the ideas of beauty and ugliness to good and evil behavior. Shakespeare's Tempest portrays a deformed servant's morality as offensive as his appearance, and Homer's Illiad depicts a despised defamer as one of the ugliest of the Greeks. This form of thinking is still present, as evidenced by contemporary female beauty contests in which contestants vie with one another not only by publicly displaying their scantily clothed bodies but also through rendering an artistic performance of some sort. A beautiful woman is expected to do good things. While an example of sexist thinking, the connection between physical features and behavior is less than scientific.

The Birth of the Positivist School: Lombroso's Theory of the Criminal Man

The modern search for multi-factual explanations of crime is usually attributed to Cesare Lombroso (1835-1909), an Italian often called "the father of modern criminology" (Wolfgang, 1973:232). A clue to his work and the social context of his life is gleaned from his self-description as "a slave to facts," a comment that could not have been made by writers of the Classical School. In the century that separates Beccaria's graduation (1758) from the University of Pavia, and Lombroso's graduation from the same institution (1858) with a degree in medicine, secular, rational-scientific thinking and experimentation had become increasingly more acceptable ways to analyze reality.

An essential clue to understanding Lombroso's work is to recognize that in the last half of the nineteenth century the answer to the age-old question, "What sort of creatures are human beings?" had begun to depart from theological answers to answers provided by the objective sciences, particularly biology. It was here that humans' origins as a creature were connected to the rest of the animal world through evolution (Vold, 1958:27-28). No other nineteenth century name is more often associated with this connection than Charles Darwin (1809-1882), the English naturalist who argued that humans evolved from animals. His major works, *Origins of the Species* (1859), *The Descent of Man* (1871), and *Expression of Emotion in Man and Animals* (1872), each predate Lombroso's. For Lombroso the objective search for explaining human behavior meant disagreement with free-will philosophy. He became interested in psychiatry "sustained by close study of the anatomy and physiology of the brain" (Wolfgang, 1973:234).

Lombroso's interest in biological explanations of criminal behavior developed between 1859-1863 when he was serving as an army physician on various military posts. During this time he developed the idea that diseases, especially cretinism and pellarga, contributed to mental and physical deficiencies "which may result in violence and homicide" (Wolfgang, 1973:236). He also used his position as a military physician to measure systematically approximately 3,000 soldiers in order to document the physical differences among inhabitants from various regions of Italy. From this study, Wolfgang (1973:235) tells us Lombroso made "observations on tattooing, particularly the more obscene designs which he felt distinguished infractious soldiers." Later Lombroso used the practice of tattooing as a distinguishing characteristic of criminals. He started to publish his research on the idea that biology could explain criminal behavior in a series of papers that first started to appear in 1861. By 1876 he published his findings in *On Criminal Man* (1876), a book that went through several Italian editions and foreign language translations.

The central tenet of Lombroso's early explanations of crime is that criminals represent a peculiar physical type, distinctively different from noncriminals. In general terms, he claimed that criminals represent a form of degeneracy which was manifested in physical characteristics reflective of earlier forms of evolution. He described criminals as atavistic, a throwback to an earlier form of evolutionary life. For instance, he thought ears of unusual size, sloping foreheads, excessively long arms, receding chins, and twisted noses were indicative of physical characteristics found among criminals.

Lombroso classified criminals into four major categories: (1) born criminals, people with atavistic characteristics; (2) insane criminals which included idiots, imbeciles, and paranoiacs, as well as epileptics and alcoholics; (3) occasional criminals or criminaloids, whose crimes are primarily explained by opportunity, though they too have innate traits which predispose them to criminality; and (4) criminals of passion who commit crimes because of anger, love, or honor. They are characterized by being propelled to crime by an "irresistible force" (Wolfgang, 1973:252-253).

To Lombroso's credit, he modified his theory throughout five editions of *On Criminal Man*, with each one giving attention to more and more environmental explanations, including climate, rainfall, sex, marriage customs, laws, the structure of government, the effect of church organization, and the effect of other factors. However, he never completely gave up the idea of the existence of a born criminal type, and although he is most often thought of as the person who connected biological explanations to criminal behavior, he in fact was not the first person to do so.

This idea, for instance, was developed in the 1760s by the Swiss scholar John Caspar Lavater (1741-1781), who claimed there was a relationship between facial features and behavior. Later, Franz Joseph Gall (1758-1828), an eminent European anatomist, expanded the idea and argued that the shape of one's head could explain an individual's personal characteristics. This explanation was called phrenology, and by the 1820s it was stimulating much interest in the United States. One book on the subject, for instance, went through nine editions between 1837-1840 (Vold, 1958:45-46). It is instructive to note that as phrenology increased in popularity, its explanatory powers were expanded; more and more different forms of human conduct, it was claimed, could be explained by the shape of the head. The importance of phrenology for us is that it indicates the popularity of biological explanations of behavior nearly fifty years before Lombroso received his degree in medicine in 1858, and long before he was ever called "the father of modern criminology." In fact, Ellis (1913) identifies almost two dozen European scholars who had pointed to the relationship between criminals' physical and mental characteristics and their behavior before Lombroso. So why should Lombroso be studied and remembered?

While his biological explanation of crime is considered simple and naive today, Lombroso nevertheless made significant contributions that continue to have an impact on criminology. Most noteworthy here is the attention he gave to a multi-factor explanation of crime that included not only heredity but social, cultural, and economic variables. The multiple factor explanation is common in today's study of crime. Lombroso is also credited with pushing the study of crime away from abstract metaphysical, legal, and juristic explanations as the basis of penology "to a scientific study of the criminal and the conditions under which he commits crime" (Wolfgang, 1973:286). We are also indebted to Lombroso for the lessons he taught regarding methods of research. He demonstrated the importance of examining clinical and historical records, and he emphasized that no detail should be overlooked when searching for explanations of criminal behavior.

Lombroso's Legacy: The Italian Criminological Tradition

Enrico Ferri. Lombroso's legacy of positivism was continued and expanded by the brilliant career and life of a fellow Italian, Enrico Ferri (1856-1929). Born into the family of a poor salt-and-tobacco shopkeeper, Ferri came to be one of the most influential figures in the history of criminology (Sellin, 1973:361). In the words of Thorsten Sellin — one of the world's most eminent criminologists who as a young man in November 1925 heard Ferri lecture at the age of 70 — "Ferri the man is as fascinating as Ferri the Scholar" (Sellin, 1973:362). He was a scholar with brilliant ideas and strong passions who believed that life without an ideal, whatever it may be, was not worth living. By the age of 16, Ferri was developing his life-long commitment to the "scientific orientation," having come under the influence of a great teacher who himself was of strong convictions. Ferri gave up the clerical robe for the study of philosophy.

Ferri was just 21 when he published his first major work, *The Theory of Imputability and the Denial of Free Will.* It was an attack on free-will arguments, and it contained a theoretical perspective that was to characterize much of Ferri's later work on criminality, as well as his political activism. Unlike Lombroso who gave more attention to biological than to social factors, Ferri gave more emphasis to the interrelatedness of social, economic, and political factors that contribute to crime (Vold, 1958:33). He argued, for example, that criminality could be explained by studying the interactive effects among physical factors (such as race, geography, and temperature), individual factors (such as age, sex, and psychological variables), and social factors (e.g., population, religion, and culture). He also argued that crime could be controlled by social changes, many of which were directed toward the benefit of the working classes. He advocated subsidized housing, birth control, freedom of marriage, divorce, and public recreation facilities, each reflective of his socialistic belief that the state is responsible for creating better living and working conditions. It is not surprising that Ferri was also a political activist.

He was elected to public office after a much publicized lawsuit in which he successfully defended a group of peasants accused of "incitement to civil war" after a dispute with wealthy land owners (Sellin, 1973:373). He was re-elected 11 times by the Socialist Party and stayed in office until 1924. Throughout his career Ferri attempted to integrate his positivistic approach to crime with political changes. For example, he tried unsuccessfully to have the new Italian Penal Code of 1889 reflect a positivistic philosophy instead of classical reasoning. And after Mussolini came to power in the early 1920s, Ferri was invited to write a new penal code for

Italy (Vold, 1958:35). It reflected his positivistic and socialistic orientation but it too was rejected for being too much of a departure from classical legal reasoning. After nearly 50 years as a socialist-liberal, Ferri changed his philosophy and endorsed fascism as a practical approach to reform. According to Sellin (1973:77), fascism appealed to Ferri because it offered a reaffirmation of the state's authority over excessive individualism, which he had often criticized.

While it is puzzling to try to understand Ferri's shift from socialism to fascism, some insight is provided by considering that he was living at a time of great social change, and as a person with humble origins, he wanted the changes to produce a better society. To accomplish this reform he felt that individuals must be legally responsible for their actions, instead of only being morally responsible to God. This approach to responsibility represented a radical departure from tradition because it was offered within a theoretical framework that called for "scientific experts" not only to explain crime, but also to write laws and administer punishment. In essence, it was a call for the state to act "scientifically" in matters of social policy.

Ferri's call for legal responsibility was offered when Italy was experiencing much unrest caused mostly by industrialization in the late 1800s and later by the social disorder stemming from World War I. Evidence of Ferri's response to the changing conditions in Italy is found in the fact that in the first four editions of *Sociologia Criminale*, he had only five classes of criminals: (1) the born or instinctive criminal that Lombroso had identified as the atavist; (2) insane criminals who were clinically identified as mentally ill; (3) the passion criminal who committed crime as a result of either prolonged and chronic mental problems, or an emotional state; (4) the occasional criminal who was the product of family and social conditions more than abnormal personal physical or mental problems; and (5) the habitual criminal who acquired the habit from the social environment. For the fifth edition of *Sociologia Criminale* (1929-1930) he added a new explanation of crime, the involuntary criminal. Ferri explained this phenomenon as "becoming more and more numerous in our mechanical age in the vertiginous speed of modern life" (Sellin, 1973:370).

We must also understand that Ferri's interest in fascism did not occur in a social void absent of pubic support. It took only five years

from the time Benito Mussolini formed the Fasci del Combatti-
mento in 1919 until the first elections in Italy under the fascists
in 1924, when he received 65 percent of the vote. When Mussolini
asked Ferri to rewrite the Italian code, Ferri's response was consistent with the mood of the times.

Raffaele Garofalo. After Lombroso and Ferri, Raffaele Garofalo
(1852-1934) was the last major contributor to the Positivist or the
Italian School of Criminology. Unlike Lombroso's emphasis on
criminals as abnormal types with distinguishable anatomic, psychological, and social features, or Ferri's emphasis on socialistic
reforms and social defenses against crime, Garofalo is remembered
for his pursuit of practical solutions to concrete problems located
in the legal institutions of his day and for his doctrine of "natural
crimes."

In many ways his work represents more clearly than either
Lombroso or Ferri late nineteenth century European currents of
interest. This is the result of three different phenomena, each
interconnected. First, Garofalo was born only six years before
Lombroso received his degree in medicine. Thus, by the time he
was an adult, enough time had passed since the publication of
Lombroso's and Ferri's major works to permit some degree of
reactive evaluation. Second, Garofalo was both an academician
and a practicing lawyer, prosecutor, and magistrate who daily
faced the practical problems of the criminal justice system. Accordingly, he was in an excellent position to be familiar with the
great attention Lombroso's and Ferri's work had received in both
academic and penal circles and with the practical policy implications of their writings. Third, at the time Garofalo published the
first edition of *Criminology* in 1885 at age 36, the Social Darwinian
era was at the peak of its existence, with numerous suggestions
from biology, psychology, and the social sciences on how society
could guarantee the survival of the fittest through criminal law
and penal practice (Hawkins, 1931).

Garofalo's theoretical arguments on the nature of crime and on
the nature of criminals were consistent with Social Darwinism. He
argued, for example, that because society is a "natural body,"
crimes are offenses "against the law of nature." Criminal action
was therefore crime against nature. Accordingly, the "rules of
nature" were the rules of right conduct revealed to humans
through their reasoning. It is obvious here that Garofalo's think-

ing also included some influence from the classical school and its emphasis on reasoning. For Garofalo the proper rules of conduct came from thinking about what such rules should allow or prohibit. He nevertheless identified acts which no society could refuse to recognize as criminal and repress by punishment: natural crimes. These offenses, according to Garofalo, violated two basic human sentiments found among people of all ages, namely the sentiments of probity and pity (Allen, 1973:321; Vold, 1958:37). Pity is the sentiment of revulsion against the voluntary infliction of suffering on others, while probity refers to the respect for the property rights of others.

The Social Darwinian influence on Garofalo's thinking is also apparent in his explanation of where the sentiments of probity and pity could be found. They were basic moral sensibilities that appear more or less in "*advanced form in all civilized societies*" (Allen, 1973:321; emphasis added), meaning that some societies had not evolved to the point of advanced moral reasoning. Similarly, the Darwinian influence is present in Garofalo's argument that some members of society may have a higher than average sense of morality because they are "superior members of the group" (Allen, 1973:321).

Garofalo's notion of the characteristics of the criminal also reveals a Darwinian influence, but less so than when he addresses the issue of punishment and penal policies. In developing this portion of his theoretical arguments, he first reconsidered the Lombrosian idea of crime being associated with certain anatomical and physical characteristics and concluded that while the idea had merit, it had not been proven. Sometimes physical abnormalities were present, sometimes not. He argued instead for the idea that true criminals lacked properly developed altruistic sentiments (Allen, 1973:326). True criminals, in other words, had psychic or moral anomalies which could be transmitted through heredity. However, the transmission of moral deficiencies through heredity was a matter of degree. This conclusion led Garofalo to identify four criminal classes, each one distinct from the other because of deficiencies in the basic sentiments of pity and probity.

Murderers were totally lacking in both pity and probity, and would kill or steal when given the opportunity. Lesser criminals, Garofalo acknowledged, were more difficult to identify. He divided this category based on whether criminals lacked sentiments of either pity or probity. Violent criminals lacked pity, which could very much be influenced by environmental factors such as alcohol or the fact that criminality was endemic to the population. Thieves, on the other hand, suffered from a lack of probity, a condition that "may be more the product of social factors than the criminals in other classes" (Allen, 1973:23). His last category contained cynics or sexual criminals, some of whom would be classified among the violent criminals because they lacked pity. Other lascivious criminals required a separate category because their actions stemmed from a "low level of moral energy," rather than from a lack of pity (Allen, 1973:329).

Garofalo's reliance on Darwinian reasoning is nowhere more obvious than when he considers appropriate measures for the social defense against crime. Here he again uses the analogy of society as a natural body which must either adapt to the environment or be eliminated. He reasoned that because true criminals' actions revealed an inability to live by the basic human sentiments necessary for society to survive, they should be eliminated. Their death would contribute to the survival of society (Barnes, 1930:586). For lesser criminals, he proposed that elimination take the form of life imprisonment or overseas transportation (Allen, 1973:330).

It is clear that deterrence and rehabilitation were secondary considerations for Garofalo. However, he favored "enforced reparation" and indeterminate sentences, which indicates that Garofalo's social defenses against crime were modeled to some extent on the psychic characteristics of the offender. In this regard his position on punishment is more in line with the free will reasoning of the classical scholars than Garofalo might admit. One conclusion about Garofalo is clear, however, and that is his position on the importance of society over the individual. To him the individual represented but a cell of the social body that could be exterminated without much, if any, great loss to society (Allen, 1973:338). By giving society or the group supremacy over the individual, Garofalo and Ferri were willing to sacrifice individual rights to the opinion of "scientific experts," whose decisions might not include the opinions of those they were evaluating and judging, nor the opinion of the public. Not surprisingly, their work was accepted by Mussolini's regime in Italy because it lent the mantle of scientific credence to the ideas of racial purity, national strength, and authoritarian leadership (Vold, 1958:39).

The work of the Italian positivists also suffered from serious methodological research problems. Their work, for instance, was not very statistically sophisticated. As a result, their conclusions about "real" or "significant" differences between criminals and noncriminals were in fact highly speculative.

This problem was addressed by Charles Goring's (1913) study on 3,000 English convicts and a control group of normal males. Unlike Lombroso, Ferri, and Garofalo, Goring employed an expert statistician to make computations about the physical differences between criminals and noncriminals. After eight years of research on 96 different physical features, Goring concluded that there were no significant differences between criminals and noncriminals except for stature and body weight. Criminals were found to be slightly smaller. Goring interpreted this finding as confirmation of his hypothesis that criminals were biologically inferior, but he did not find a physical criminal type.

The Continuing Search for the Individual Roots of Crime

Body Types and Crime. The search for a constitutionally determined "criminal man" did not stop with Goring's 1913 conclusions. Kretschmer took up the theme as the result of his study of 260 insane people in Swabia, a southwestern German town. He was impressed with the fact that his subjects had definite types of body builds which were associated, he thought, with certain types of psychic dispositions. First published in German in 1922 and translated into English in 1925, Kretschmer identified four body types: asthenic, athletic, pyknic, and some mixed, unclassifiable types. He found asthenics to be lean and narrowly built, with a deficiency of thickness in the overall body. These men were so flat-chested and skinny that their ribs could be counted easily. The athletic build had broad shoulders, excellent musculature, deep chests, flat stomachs, and powerful legs. They were the 1920s counterpart of the modern "hunks" of media fame. The pyknics were of medium build with a propensity to be rotund, sort of soft-appearing with rounded shoulders, broad faces, and short, stubby hands. The asthenic and athletic builds, Kretschmer argued, were associated with schizophrenic personalities, while the pyknics were manic-depressives (Kretschmer, 1925).

Four years after the English translation appeared in the United States, Mohr and Gundlach (1929-30) published a report based on 254 native-born, white male inmates in the state penitentiary at Joilet, Illinois. They found that pyknics were more likely than asthenics or athletics to have been convicted of fraud, violence, and sex offenses. Asthenics and athletics, on the other hand, were more likely to have been convicted of burglary, robbery, and larceny. However, Mohr and Gundlach were unable to demonstrate any connection between body build, crime, and psychic disposition.

Ten years later the search for physical types which caused crime was taken up by Ernest A. Hooton, a Harvard anthropologist. He began with an extensive critique of Goring's research methods and proceeded to a detailed analysis of the measurements of more than 17,000 criminals and noncriminals from eight different states (Hooton, 1939). In his three-volume study he argued that "criminals are inferior to civilians in nearly all of their bodily measurements" (Hooton, 1939, Vol.1:329). He also reported that low foreheads indicated inferiority and that "a depressed physical and social environment determines Negro and Negroid delinquency to a much greater extent than it does in the case of Whites'" (Hooton, 1939:388).

These and similar conclusions generated severe criticism of Hooton's work, especially the racist overtones and his failure to recognize that the prisoners he studied did not represent criminal offenders who had not been caught, or offenders who had been guilty but not convicted. His control group was also criticized for not being representative of any known population of people. They consisted of Nashville firefighters and members of the militia, each of whom could be expected to have passed rigorous physical examinations which would distinguish them from average males. He also included in his control group beach-goers, mental patients, and college students. He offered no explanation as to why these disparate categories of people represented "normal" physical types. Hooton was also criticized for treating some small difference in measurement as greatly significant and for ignoring other differences that were found.

It is important to notice that despite the stinging criticism received by Hooton and by others who were searching for biological explanations, the search nevertheless continued and expanded into the 1940s and 1950s. The work by William H. Sheldon, for instance, shifted attention away from adults to delinquent male youths. He studied 200 males between 15 and 21 years of age in an effort to link physiques to temperament, intelligence, and delinquency. By relying on intense physical and psychological examinations, Sheldon produced an "Index to Delinquency" which was used to give a quick and easy profile of each male's problems (Sheldon, 1949). A total score of 10 meant a lad's case was severe enough to require total institutionalization; a score of 7 meant the case was borderline, while a score of 6 was interpreted as favoring adjustment and independent living outside of an institution.

Sheldon (1949) classified the boys' physiques by measuring the degree to which they possessed a combination of three different body components. The three components were endomorphy, mesomorphy, and ectomorphy. Each could dominate a physique. Endomorphs tended to be soft, fat people; mesomorphs had muscular and athletic builds; ecotomorphs had skinny, flat, and fragile physiques. Sheldon also rated each of the 200 youths' physiques by assigning a score of 1 to 7 for each component. For example, the average "physique score" for the 200 males was 3.5-4.6-2.7, a rather husky male (Sheldon, 1949:727). Overall, Sheldon (1949) concluded that because youths came from parents who were delinquent in very much the same way that the boys were delinquent, the factors that produce delinquency were inherited.

Sheldon's findings were given considerable support by Sheldon Glueck and Eleanor Glueck's (1950) comparative study of male delinquents and nondelinquents. As a group, the delinquents were found to have narrower faces, wider chests, larger and broader waists, and bigger forearms and upper arms than the nondelinquents (Glueck and Glueck, 1950:33). An examination of the overall ratings of the boys indicated that approximately 60 percent of the delinquents and 31 percent of the nondeliquents were predominantly mesomorphic. They included this finding in their list of outstanding factors associated with male delinquency. As with each of the previous scholars who have attempted to explain criminal behavior by primarily relying on biological factors, their findings neglected the importance of sociological phenomena. It is unclear, for instance, if the Gluecks' mesomorphs were delinquents because of their builds and dispositions, or because their physiques and dispositions are socially conceived as being associated with delinquency. This in turn could create expectations about illegal activities which males might feel pressured to perform.

Psychogenic Causes of Crime. At this point we turn our attention to another form of positivism, one that places no emphasis on types of physiques as causes of crime. Here the search for the causes of crime are directed to the mind. Often these theories are referred to as the "psychogenic school" because they seek to explain crime by focusing attention on the personality and how it was produced. In this way, the analysis is "dynamic" rather than "constitutional," as was the emphasis from biological positivism. This school of thought developed along two distinct lines: one stressed psychoanalysis, the other placed emphasis on personality traits. We begin with Freud and the psychoanalytical approach.

Sigmund Freud (1859-1939), a physician, did not directly address the question of what caused criminal behavior. He was interested in explaining all behavior, including crime. If an explanation could be found for normal behavior, surely, he reasoned, it could also explain crime.

At the core of his and his colleagues' theories is the argument that all behavior is motivated and purposive. However, not all desires and behavior are socially acceptable, so they must be repressed into the unconsciousness of the mind for the sake of morality and social order. The result is that tensions exist between the unconscious id, which is a great reservoir of aggressive biological and psychological urges, and the conscious ego, which controls and molds the individual. The super-ego, according to Freud (1920, 1927, 1930), is the force of self-criticism that reflects the basic behavioral requirements of a particular culture. Crime, therefore, is a symbolic expression of inner tensions that each person has, but fails to control. It is an "acted out" expression of having improperly learned self control.

Franz Alexander, a psychoanalyst, and William Healy, a physician, both applied Freud's principles in their study of criminal behavior (Alexander and Healy, 1935). For example, they explained one male criminal's behavior as the result of four unconscious needs: (1) overcompensation for a sense of inferiority, (2) the attempt to relieve a sense of guilt, (3) spite reactions toward his mother, and (4) gratification of his dependent tendencies by living a carefree existence in prison (Alexander and Healy, 1935:16-76).

Freud's colleague, August Aichhorn, wrote that many children continued to act infantile because they failed to develop an ego and super-ego which would permit them to conform to the expectations of childhood, adolescence, and adulthood (Aichhorn, 1936). Such children, Aichhorn contended, continued to operate on the "pleasure principle," having failed to adapt to the "reality principle" of adulthood. Kate Friedlander, a student of Freud and Aichhorn, also focused on the behavior of children and argued that some children develop antisocial behavior or faulty character which make them prone to delinquency (Friedlander, 1949). Redl and Wineman (1951) advanced a similar argument which stated that some children develop a delinquent ego. The result is a hostile attitude toward adults and aggression toward authority, because the child has not developed a good ego and super-ego.

The search for personality traits, the second tradition of investigation that attempted to locate the cause of crime within the mind, was started by attempting to explain mental faculties biologically. Feeble-mindedness, insanity, stupidity, and dull-wittedness were thought to be inherited. This view was part of the efforts in the late nineteenth century to explain crime constitutionally. It became a popular explanation in the United States after 1877 when *The Jukes* was published (Dugdale, 1877). It described a family as being involved in crime because they suffered from "degeneracy and innate depravity."

Interest in explaining family-based mental deficiencies by heredity continued through the end of the nineteenth and well into the first quarter of the twentieth century. H.H. Goddard, for example, published *The Kallikak Family* in 1912, and a follow-up study on the Jukes appeared in 1916 (Estrabrook, 1916). Unfortunately, these studies were very general, each avoiding advanced and comparative statistics.

More exacting studies of the mind came from European research on the measurement of intelligence. French psychologist Alfred Binet (1857-1911), for example, first pursued intelligence testing in laboratory settings and later applied his findings in an effort to solve the problem of retardation in Paris's schools. Aided by his assistant, Theodore Simon, Binet revised his I.Q. tests in 1905, 1908, and 1911, and when the scale appeared in the United States it was once again revised. Common to each revision was the idea that individuals should have a "mental age" that could be identified with an "intelligence quotient," or I.Q. score.

H.H. Goddard, author of the famed Kallikak study, is usually credited as the first person to test the I.Q.'s of prison inmates. He concluded that while most inmates were feeble-minded, the percentage of feeble-mindedness ranged from 29 percent to 89 percent (Goddard, 1914, 1921). However, his research was plagued by the difficult issue of determining what score(s) should be used to define feeble-mindedness.

The legitimacy and practical value of I.Q. testing was given great support when the U.S. Army Psychological Corps decided to use this method to determine who was "fit" for military service in World War I (Goddard, 1927). The result was that at one point nearly a third of the draft army was thought to be feeble-minded. This conclusion was later modified, but faith in I.Q. testing as a means of explaining crime continued well past World War I and into the 1920s and 1930s. However, the increasing use of sophisticated research methods began to produce results that indicated that when inmates were compared to the general population, only slight differences in feeble-mindedness were found. Today very little if any research tries to explain crime as the result of feeble-mindedness.

THE CONSEQUENCE OF THEORY: POLICY IMPLICATIONS

The Positivist School and the Control of the Biological Criminal

The most obvious orientation displayed by positivists of the mid-nineteenth century through the first quarter of the twentieth century was their placement of the causes of crime primarily within individual offenders. This is not at all surprising once we recognize that the early positivists — especially Lombroso, Ferri, and Garofalo in Italy; Freud, Aichhorn, and Kretschmer in Austria and Germany; and Alexander and Healy in the United States — were each educated in medicine, in law, or in both fields. Each of these disciplines places great emphasis on individuals as the explanation of behavior. It is this flavor of emphasis that sheds much light on the policy consequences of their explanations of crime. But the disciplinary perspectives alone are inadequate for the purposes of understanding fully these consequences, because each discipline was influenced by the general "temper of the times." For the positivists considered in this chapter, the "temper of the times" was Darwinism strongly flavored by Victorianism.

The magnitude of the impact of the Darwinian argument is difficult to describe in a few paragraphs or pages, and, indeed, even in a score of books. Nevertheless, an effort must be attempted before we proceed. In the simplest of terms Darwin's evolutionary thesis represents one of the most profound theories of all times. It not only offered revolutionary new knowledge for the sciences, but it also helped to shatter many philosophies and practices in other areas. It commanded so much attention and prestige that the entire literate community felt "obliged to bring his world-outlook into harmony with their findings" (Hofstadter, 1955b:3). According to Hofstadter, Darwin's impact is comparable in its magnitude to the work of Nicolaus Copernicus (1473-1543), the European astronomer, and Isaac Newton (1564-1642), the English mathematician and philosopher, and Sigmund Freud (1859-1939), the Austrian psychoanalyst. In effect, all of the Western world had to come to grips with Darwin's evolutionary scheme.

While there was much discussion and controversy about the social meaning of Darwin's theory of "the struggle for survival" and the "survival of the fittest," Social Darwinists generally agreed that the theory's policy implications were politically conservative. It was argued that any policies which advocated government sponsored social change would, if executed, actually be an interference with nature. The best approach was minimum involvement. "Let nature take its course" became a frequent refrain uttered by Social Darwinists. It carried the clear message that accelerated social change was undesirable. Policies designed to accomplish "equal treatment," for example, were strongly opposed. Social welfare programs, it was argued, would perpetuate the survival of people who were negligent, shiftless, silly, and immoral; at the same time it would retard individual and national economic development. Hard work, saving, and moral constraint were called on as the solutions to individual and collective social and economic good fortune.

It is important to note an irony regarding the Social Darwinists.

While many of the nation's leaders in the late nineteenth and early twentieth century were opposed to programs of social change because they feared these programs would threaten the nation's survival, they were often the same people who were radically changing our economy and plundering our natural resources through speculation, innovation, and daring. They were also the same leaders who were introducing "new economic forms, new types of organization, new techniques" (Hofstadter, 1955b:9). Changes that benefited their interests were acceptable while changes for the less fortunate were not. The stage was set for "scientifically justified" forms of control that would contain or eliminate crime. This control came in the form of the genetics movement with the blessings of the Victorian concern for morality and purity (Pivar, 1973). Unfortunately the stage was also set for "scientifically justified" policies which in fact resulted in selective abuse and neglect.

When Social Darwinism was used to formulate crime control policies, major themes appeared. On the one hand, the "born criminal" legacy from Lombroso and his students, and especially Garofalo's policy of "elimination" for certain criminal offenders, produced a penal philosophy that stressed incapacitation. Clearly the emphasis was on removing criminals from the community so as to prevent them from committing any additional biologically determined harm. It was therefore inappropriate to attempt to reform or rehabilitate criminal offenders; warehousing convicted offenders was considered a sufficient socially responsible response to the problem of what to do with law-breakers.

On the other hand, the second means of controlling crime allowed for a type of rehabilitation. It was based on medical reasoning which viewed individuals as biological objects that needed treatment, and allowed some of the most repressive state policies in the history of American penology. The worst of these policies were justified by the study of genetics and what has been called the "eugenics movement" (Beckwith, 1985).

As a science in the early 1900s, the study of eugenics claimed that inheritance could explain the presence of simple and complex human behavioral characteristics. It thus reinforced the ideas of biological determinism and contributed greatly to the argument that many of the social problems of the late nineteenth century, such as the conflicts over wages and working conditions, could be traced to the genetic inferiority of foreigners who were working in the United States. The 1886 Haymarket bombings and riots in Chicago, for example, were thought to be caused by "inferior foreigners." This theme was advanced by industrialists and newspapers such as the *New York Times*, which described labor demonstrations as "always composed of foreign scum, beer-smelling Germans, ignorant Bohemians, uncouth Poles and wild-eyed Russians" (Beckwith, 1985:317).

With the support of leading industrialists such as the Carnegies and leading education institutions such as Harvard, centers for the study of eugenics were soon established, and efforts were undertaken to study the nation's "stock." Accordingly, many states passed laws designed to permit the application of the eugenicists' arguments. Between 1911 and 1930 more than 30 states, for example, established laws requiring sterilization for behavioral traits thought to be genetically determined (Beckwith, 1985:318). The laws targeted such behavior as criminality, alcoholism, sodomy, bestiality, feeble-mindedness, and the tendency to commit rape. The result was the sterilization of at least 64,000 people. Many of the same states also passed laws permitting psychosurgeries, including the now infamous frontal lobotomy. The total number of these types of operations is unknown.

The laws passed under the influence of the eugenics movement were not restricted to sterilization and psychosurgery, although these are the two most brutal and repressive measures they sponsored. They also endorsed miscegenation laws in 34 states which made it illegal for blacks and whites to marry each other; some states also forbade marriage between whites and orientals (Provine, 1973). They also vigorously called for the passage of immigration laws to be based on a quota system calculated on the proportion of people living in the United States from a specific country in 1890. And in 1924 the United States Congress, after hearing leading eugenicists testify that our stock was being weakened by the influx of people from southern and eastern European countries, passed the Immigration Restriction Act of 1924. It was explicitly directed to a population of people who were thought to be biologically inferior. As such, it was a racist law and a forerunner of the 1930s and 1940s eugenic policies of Nazi Germany.

Despite the clear implications of eugenic policies for repressing a targeted population, the practice of sterilization and psychosurgery continued in the United States until well into the 1970s. Between 1927 and 1972 in Virginia alone, more than 8,000 individuals were sterilized because they were identified as feeble-minded (Katz and Abel, 1984:232); more than 20,000 people were sterilized in California. However, as Katz and Abel point out, the real reason for sterilization was not feeble-mindedness: it was class. "The one characteristic that did have to be demonstrated was indigency. . . . Commitment papers had to certify that the individual was both without means of support and without any acquaintance who would give bond" (Katz and Abel, 1984:233). To allow the poor to propagate, it was claimed, would increase the number of feeble-minded offspring, the poor, alcoholics, criminals, and prostitutes.

The Positivist School and Criminal Justice Reform

In pointing out the worst effects of biologically-oriented theories, we are not unmindful that the positivist school also helped to usher in an approach to policy that was reformative rather than punitive in impulse. To be sure, the conclusion that offenders are characterized by unchangeable bodily or psychological characteristics leads logically to the conclusion that offenders should either be eliminated, caged indefinitely (incapacitation), or altered physically through intrusive measures. And "crime prevention," as we have seen, becomes a matter of not allowing the "defectives" to multiply. However, if one assumes that the causes determining crime are *changeable* — for example, unemployment or the emotional turmoil from family conflict — then the policy implications are much more optimistic. The challenge becomes diagnosing the forces that moved a person to break the law and then developing a strategy — perhaps job training, perhaps family counseling — to help the person overcome these criminogenic factors. In short, the challenge is to rehabilitate offenders so that they might rejoin society as "normal" citizens.

Notably, as America pushed into the twentieth century, the appeal of biologically-oriented theories eventually began to diminish. In their place, more optimistic positivist theories emerged, which drew their images of offenders from psychology and especially from sociology. These newer approaches argued that the troubles of criminals could be rectified through counseling or by fixing the social environments in which they lived.

This new way of thinking about crime had a large effect on policy. Indeed, in the first two decades of this century, this thinking helped shape a campaign that renovated the criminal justice system. Reformers, called "Progressives," argued that the system should not be arranged to punish offenders, but to rehabilitate them. Across the nation, state after state established a separate juvenile court to "save" children from a life in crime (Platt, 1969). Similarly, efforts were undertaken to make release from prison based on the extent to which a person had been rehabilitated, not on the nature of the crime (as the classical school would mandate). Accordingly, states passed laws that made sentencing more indeterminate (offenders were given sentences, for example, that might range from one to five years) and created parole boards to decide which offenders had been "cured" and should be returned to the community. Probation, a practice through which offenders were to be both supervised and helped by an officer of the court, also was widely implemented. More generally, criminal justice officials were given great discretion to effect the "individualized treatment" of offenders (Rothman, 1980).

We will return to these themes in the next chapter and later in the book as well. Even so, we need to emphasize two points. First, controversy still exists today on whether the policies instituted in the name of rehabilitation made criminal justice systems more humane or more repressive. Some criminologists believe that the discretion given to criminal justice officials allowed offenders to be abused (Rothman, 1980), while other criminologists insist that rehabilitation has helped to humanize a system that is punitive by nature (Cullen and Gilbert, 1982). Second, while the ideas of the early positivist theorists declined in popularity — though certainly they did not disappear as the Virginia sterilization example shows — we are now seeing a renewed interest in the idea that the origins of crime lie in unchangeable characteristics of individuals. As Chapter 7 will discuss, the 1980s have brought a revitalization of the view that criminals are wicked by nature, a view that has had questionable, if not disquieting, policy implications.

CONCLUSIONS

It should be clear that in order to understand the policies that are created to address the problems of crime, we must realize that they are greatly influenced by the theories that guide them. We must also remember to examine the social context in which theories and policies are constructed. This lesson is important because it points out that theories are neither value-free nor free from the times in which they are advocated. Theories also have an impact on people. Sometimes the "scientifically justified" policies are allowed to do great harm because the social context in which they are advocated and implemented is ignored. The consequences are often irrevocable.

3

Rejecting Individualism: The Social Roots of Crime

Although exceptions exist, most early theories located the sources of crime *within* the individual. These theories differed markedly on where precisely the source of waywardness lay: Was it in the soul? The mind? The body's very biological make-up? Even so, they shared the assumption that little insight on crime's origins could be gained by studying the social environment or context *external* to individuals. In one form or another, these early theories blamed individual offenders, not society, for the crime problem.

As America turned into the twentieth century, however, a competing and powerful vision of crime emerged: a vision suggesting that crime, like other behavior, was a social product. The earlier theories did not vanish immediately or completely — indeed, in important ways, they continue to inform current-day thinking — but they did suffer a stiff intellectual challenge that thinned greatly the ranks of their supporters. But this major theoretical shift — one which rejected individualistic explanations of crime in favor of social explanations — might have been expected. Society was undergoing significant changes, and people's experiences were changing as well. The time was ripe for a new understanding of why some citizens break the law.

By the end of the 1930s, two major criminological traditions had been articulated that sought, in David Matza's words (1969:47), to "relocate pathology; it was moved from the personal to the social plane." The first of these traditions — the "Chicago School" of criminology — argued that one aspect of American society, the city, contained potent criminogenic forces. The other tradition — Robert K. Merton's "strain theory" — contended that the pathology lay not in one ecological location, like the city, but in the broader cultural and structural arrangements that constitute America's social fabric. Though they differed in how they believed that society created law-breakers, these theories agreed that the key to unlocking the mystery of crime was in understanding its social roots. Taken together, therefore, they offered a strong counterpoint to explanations that blamed individuals for their criminality.

The effects of these two schools of thought have been long-lasting. Even today, a half century after their initial formulation, the Chicago School and strain theories continue to be of interest to criminologists and to shape correctional policies. They deserve careful consideration.

THE CHICAGO SCHOOL OF CRIMINOLOGY

What made it seem reasonable — why did it "make sense" — to blame cities for the nation's crime problem? Why would such a vision become popular in the 1920s-1930s and, moreover, find special attention in Chicago?

In part the answers to these questions can be found in the enormous changes that transformed the face of America and made the city — not the "little house on the prairie" — the nation's focal point. In the last half of the 1800s, cities grew at a rapid pace and became, as J. John Palen (1981:63) observes, "a controlling factor in national life." Between 1790 and 1890, for example, the urban population grew 139-fold; and by 1900, 50 cities existed with populations in excess of 100,000 (Palen, 1981:63).

Chicago's growth, however, was particularly remarkable. When the city incorporated in 1833, it had 4,100 residents; by 1890, its population had risen to 1 million and by 1910 the count surpassed 2 million (Palen, 1981:63). But such rapid expansion had a bleaker side. Many of those settling in Chicago (and in other urban areas) carried little with them; there were waves of immigrants, displaced farm workers, and blacks fleeing the rural south. For most newcomers, the city — originally a source of much hope — brought little economic relief. They faced a harsh reality: pitiful wages; working twelve-hour days, six days a week, in factories that jeopardized their health and safety; living in tenements, which "slumlords built jaw-to-jaw . . . on every available space" (Palen,

1981:64). Writing on the meat-packing industry in Chicago, Upton Sinclair (1905) gave this environment a disquieting label: "the jungle."

As did other citizens, criminologists in the 1920s and 1930s witnessed, indeed lived through and experienced, these changes that created bulging populations and teaming slum areas. It was only a short leap for them to believe that growing up in the city, particularly in the slums, made a difference in people's lives. In this context, crime could not be seen simply as an individual pathology, but made more "sense" when viewed as a social problem.

This conclusion, moreover, was reinforced by a broad liberal reform movement that arose early in the 1900s: the "Progressive movement." Although they believed in the essential goodness of America and thus rejected calls for radical change, Progressives were critical of the human costs wrought by America's unbridled industrial growth. They were particularly troubled by the plight of the urban poor, a mushrooming population of the system's casualties who had few prospects of a stable or rewarding life. They worried, as David Rothman (1980:51) writes, that the "promise" of the American system "did not extend evenly to all segments of the society; it did not penetrate the ghetto or the slum. Thus an understanding of the etiology of crime demanded a very close scrutiny of the conditions in these special enclaves."

Criminologists in the Chicago School would echo this conclusion. The Progressives rejected the social Darwinists' logic that the poor, and the criminals among them, were biologically inferior and had fallen to society's bottom rung because they were of lesser stock. They preferred a more optimistic interpretation: the poor were pushed by their environment, not born, into a life of crime. Accordingly, hope existed that changing the context that nurtures offenders would reverse the slum's negative effects and transform them into law-abiding citizens. In particular, the goal was to save the poor, particularly their children, by providing social services — schools, clinics, recreational facilities, settlement houses, foster homes, and reformatories if necessary — that would lessen the pains of poverty and teach the benefits of middle-class culture (Platt, 1969; Rothman, 1980).

The moral imperative, however, was to act on this belief — and the Progressives did, creating what came to be known as the "age of reform" (Hofstadter, 1955a, 1963). The lynchpin of their agenda was the assumption that the government could be trusted to create and administer agencies that would effect needed social reform. The Progressives campaigned to have the state guide the nation toward the common good by controlling the greed of industry and by providing the assistance the poor needed to reach the middle class. In the area of criminal justice, their efforts led to the creation of policies and practices that were intended to allow the state to treat the individual needs and problems of offenders: the juvenile court, community supervision through probation and parole, and the indeterminate sentence (Rothman, 1980).

Thus, in the first decades of the 1900s, the city became a dominant feature of American life and a pervasive movement arose warning that the social fabric of urban slums bred crime. Still, the question remains as to why Chicago became a hot-bed of criminological research. As suggested, part of the answer can be found in this city's status as an emerging economic and population center. But the other piece of the puzzle lies in the existence at the University of Chicago of the nation's oldest sociology program, established in 1892.

By the 1920s, "surrounded . . . with ever-present reminders of the massive changes that were occurring within American society," the department's faculty and students had embarked on efforts to study systematically all aspects of the urban laboratory that lay before them (Pfohl, 1985:143). Robert E. Park, a newspaper reporter-turned-sociologist, was particularly influential in shaping the direction of this work. "I expect I have actually covered more ground," he commented, "tramping about in cities in different parts of the world, than any other living man" (Madge, 1962:89). These journeys led Park to two important insights.

First, he concluded that like any ecological system, the city's development and organization were not random or idiosyncratic, but rather were patterned and could be understood in terms of basic social processes such as invasion, conflict, accommodation, and assimilation. Second, he observed that the nature of these social processes and their impact on human behaviors, like crime, could be ascertained only through careful study of city life. Accordingly, he urged students and colleagues to venture into Chicago and to observe first-hand its neighborhoods and diverse conglomeration of peoples (Madge, 1962:89-90). Importantly, several scholars, most notably Clifford R. Shaw and Henry D. McKay, embraced Park's agenda and explored how urban life shaped fundamentally the nature of criminal activity. In doing so, they laid the foundation for the Chicago School of criminology.

Shaw and McKay's Theory of Juvenile Delinquency

Shaw and McKay were not faculty members at the University of Chicago, but rather were employed as researchers for a state-supported child guidance clinic. Even so, they enjoyed close relationships with the sociology department and were profoundly influenced by its theorizing. In particular, they were persuaded that a model of the city formulated by Ernest Burgess, Park's colleague and collaborator, provided a framework for understanding the social roots of crime. Indeed, it was Burgess's model that led them to the conclusion that neighborhood organization was instrumental in preventing or permitting delinquent careers (Gibbons, 1979:40; Pfohl, 1985:149). Below we will first review this general model of urban growth and then consider how it guided Shaw and McKay's approach to studying delinquency in Chicago.

Burgess's Concentric Zone Theory. As cities expand in size, how do they grow? One answer is that the growth is haphazard, not according to any set pattern. Like Park, however, Ernest Burgess rejected this view in favor of the hypothesis that urban development is patterned socially. He contended that cities "grow radially in a series of concentric zones or rings" (Palen, 1981:107).

As Figure 3.1 shows, Burgess delineated five zones. Competition decided how people were distributed spatially among these zones. Thus commercial enterprises were situated in the "loop" or "central business district," a location that afforded access to valuable transportation resources (e.g., railroads, waterways). In contrast, most high-priced residential areas were in the outer zones, away from the bustle of the downtown, away from the pollution of factories, and away from the residences of the poor.

The "zone in transition," however, was a particular cause for concern and study. This zone contained rows of deteriorating tenements, often built in the shadow of aging factories. The push outward of the business district, moreover, led to the constant displacement of residents. And as the least desirable living area,

Figure 3.1 Urban areas

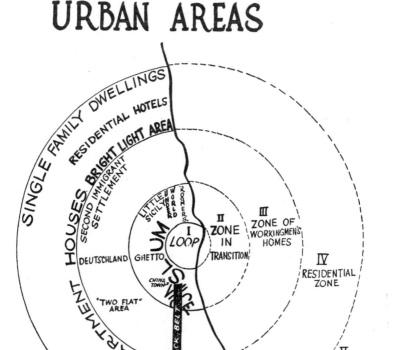

URBAN AREAS

the zone had to weather the influx of waves of immigrants and other migrants who were too poor to reside elsewhere.

These social patterns, Burgess observed, were not without consequences: they weakened the family and communal ties that bound people together and resulted in "social disorganization." This disorganization, Burgess and the other Chicago sociologists believed, was the source of a range of social pathologies, including crime.

Disorganization and Delinquency. Burgess's model was parsimonious and persuasive, but did it really offer a fruitful approach to the study of crime? Would it stand up to empirical test?

Shaw and McKay took it upon themselves to answer these questions. As a first step, they sought to determine if crime rates would conform to the predictions suggested by Burgess's model: highest rates in the zone in transition, with this rate declining progressively as one moved outward to the more affluent communities. Through painstaking research, they used juvenile court statistics to map the spatial distribution of delinquency throughout Chicago.

Their data analysis confirmed the hypothesis that delinquency flourished in the zone in transition and was inversely related to the zones' affluence and corresponding distance from the central business district. By studying Chicago's court records over several decades, they also were able to show that crime was highest in slum neighborhoods regardless of which racial or ethnic group resided there, and that as groups moved to other zones, their rates decreased commensurately. This observation led to the inescapable conclusion that it was the nature of the neighborhoods — not the nature of the individuals within the neighborhood — that regulated involvement in crime.

But what social process could account for this persistent spatial distribution of delinquency? Borrowing heavily from Burgess and the other Chicago sociologists, Shaw and McKay emphasized the importance of neighborhood organization in preventing or permitting juvenile waywardness. In more affluent communities, families fulfilled youths' needs and parents carefully supervised their offspring. In the zone in transition, however, families and other conventional institutions (schools, churches, voluntary associations) were strained, if not broken apart, by rapid urban growth, migration, and poverty; "social disorganization" prevailed. As a consequence, juveniles received neither the support nor the supervision required for wholesome development. Left to their own devices, slum youths were freed from the kind of social controls operative in more affluent areas; no guiding force existed to stop them from seeking excitement and friends in the streets of the city.

Shaw and McKay's focus on how weakening controls make possible a delinquent career allowed them to anticipate a criminological school that would eventually become known as "control" or "social bond" theory (see Chapter 4). As Ruth Rosner Kornhauser (1978:66-69) observes, however, they felt that another social circumstance also helped to make slum neighborhoods especially criminogenic. We turn next to this aspect of their thinking.

Transmission of Criminal Values. Shaw and McKay did not confine their research to the epidemiology of delinquency. Following Robert Park's admonition, they too "tramped" about Chicago. As we will see, they were activists who were involved in efforts to prevent delinquency. They also attempted to learn more about why youths become deviant by interviewing delinquents and compiling their autobiographies in a format called a "life-history." These efforts led to the publication of titles like *The Jack-Roller: A Delinquent Boy's Own Story, The Natural History of a Delinquent Career,* and *Brothers in Crime* (Shaw, 1930, 1931, 1938; see also Shaw and McKay, 1972:176-182).

These life-histories contained an important revelation: Juveniles were often drawn into crime through their association with older siblings or gang members. This observation led Shaw and McKay to the more general conclusion that disorganized neighborhoods helped produce and sustain "criminal traditions," which competed with conventional values and could be "transmitted down through successive generations of boys, much the same way that language and other social forms are transmitted" (Shaw and McKay, 1972:174). Thus slum youths grew up in neighborhoods characterized by "the existence of a coherent system of values supporting delinquent acts" (Shaw and McKay, 1972:173), and could readily learn these values in their daily interactions with older juveniles. In contrast, youths in organized neighborhoods — where the dominance of conventional institutions had precluded the development of criminal traditions — remained insulated from deviant values and peers; accordingly, for them a delinquent career was an unlikely option.

Summary. Shaw and McKay believed that juvenile delinquency could only be understood by considering the social context in which youths lived — a context which itself was a product of major societal transformations wrought by rapid urbanization, unbridled industrialization, and massive population shifts. Youths with the misfortune of residing in the socially disorganized zone in transition were especially vulnerable to the temptations of crime. As conventional institutions disintegrated around them, they were given little supervision and were free to roam the streets where they would likely become the next generation of carriers for the neighborhood's criminal tradition. Wilson ?

Later in this chapter, we will see how this vision of crime led Shaw and McKay to assert that delinquency prevention programs must be directed at reforming communities, not simply individuals. First, however, we will consider how their work laid the groundwork for Edwin Sutherland's classic theory of "differential association."

SUTHERLAND'S THEORY OF DIFFERENTIAL ASSOCIATION

In 1906 Edwin H. Sutherland departed his native Nebraska and travelled to the University of Chicago, where he enrolled in several courses in the Divinity School. He was also persuaded to register for Charles R. Henderson's course, "Social Treatment of Crime." Henderson took an interest in his new student — an interest that proved mutual. It was not long before Sutherland decided to enter the sociology program; he would devote the remainder of his career to exploring the social roots of criminal behavior (Geis and Goff, 1983, 1986; Schuessler, 1973).

After receiving his doctorate in 1913, Sutherland held a series of academic positions at midwestern institutions, including the University of Illinois and the University of Minnesota. In 1930, however, he was offered, and accepted, a professorship at the University of Chicago. His stay in Chicago proved short-lived. Apparently disenchanted with his position — he cited "certain distractions" as reason for his departure — Sutherland left five years later to join the sociology department at Indiana University, a post he held until his death in 1950. Even so, he maintained contact with his friends in Chicago, including, it should be added, Henry D. McKay (Geis and Goff, 1983:xxviii; Schuessler, 1973:xi-xii).

Though Sutherland spent most of his career away from the city and its university, the Chicago brand of sociology shaped intimately his thinking about crime. Indeed, as we will see below, much of his theorizing represented an attempt to extend and to formalize the insights found in the writings of Shaw and McKay and of other Chicago School scholars (see, for example, Thrasher, 1963 [1927]).

Differential Social Organization. Like most Chicago criminologists, Sutherland rejected individualistic explanations of crime. "The Neo-Lombrosian theory that crime is an expression of psychopathology," he claimed, "is no more justified than was the Lombrosian theory that criminals constitute a distinct physical type" (Sutherland, 1939:116). Instead, he was convinced that social organization — the context in which individuals are embedded — regulates criminal involvement.

Shaw and McKay had used the term "social disorganization" to describe neighborhoods in which controls had weakened and criminal traditions rivalled conventional institutions. At the suggestion of Albert Cohen, however, Sutherland substituted for social disorganization the concept of "differential social organization," a term which he felt was less value-laden and captured more accurately the nature of criminal areas. Thus Sutherland contended that social groups are arranged differently: some are organized in support of criminal activity, while others are organized against such behavior (Sutherland, 1973:21 [1942]). In turn, he followed Shaw and McKay's logic in proposing that lawlessness would be more prevalent in those areas in which criminal organization had taken hold and on a daily basis shaped people's values and actions.

Differential Association. Although Sutherland incorporated into his thinking the thesis that community or group organization regulates rates of crime, he built more systematically on Shaw and McKay's observation that delinquent values are transmitted from one generation to the next. For Sutherland, to say that the preference for crime was "culturally transmitted" was, in effect, to say that criminal behavior is *learned* through social interactions. To describe this learning process, Sutherland coined the concept of "differential association." Any person, he contended, may come into contact with "definitions favorable to violation of law" or with "definitions unfavorable to violation of law." The ratio of these definitions or views of crime — whether criminal or conventional influences are stronger in a person's life — determines if the person embraces crime as an acceptable way of life.

Sutherland held that the concepts of differential association and differential social organization were compatible and allowed for a complete explanation of criminal activity. As a social psychological theory, differential association explained why any given *individual* was drawn into crime. As a structural theory, differential social organization explained why *rates* of crime were higher in certain sectors of American society: where groups are organized for crime (such as in slums), definitions favoring legal violations flourish and thus more individuals are likely to learn — to differentially associate with — criminal values.

Sutherland's theory of differential association went through various stages of development, but by 1947 he was able to articulate in final form a set of nine propositions. These propositions comprise one of the most influential statements in criminological history on the causes of crime:

1. Criminal behavior is learned.
2. Criminal behavior is learned in interaction with other persons in a process of communication.
3. The principal part of the learning of criminal behavior occurs within intimate personal groups.
4. When criminal behavior is learned, the learning includes (a) techniques of committing the crime, which are sometimes very complicated, sometimes very simple; (b) the specific direction of motives, drives, rationalizations, and attitudes.
5. The specific direction of motives and drives is learned from definitions of legal codes as favorable and unfavorable.
6. A person becomes delinquent because of an excess of definitions favorable to violation of law over definitions unfavorable to violation of law. This is the principle of differential association.
7. Differential associations may vary in frequency, duration, priority, and intensity.
8. The process of learning criminal behavior by association with criminal and anticriminal patterns involves all the mechanisms that are involved in any other learning.
9. While criminal behavior is an expression of general needs and values, it is not explained by those general needs and

values since noncriminal behavior is an expression of the same needs and values (Sutherland and Cressey, 1970:75-76).

Theoretical Applications. Taken together, these propositions convey an image of offenders that departs radically from the idea that criminals are pathological creatures driven to waywardness by demons, feeble minds, deep-seated psychopathology, or faulty constitutions. Instead, Sutherland was suggesting that the distinction between law-breakers and the law-abiding lies not in their personal fiber but in the content of what they have learned. Those with the good fortune of growing up in a conventional neighborhood will learn to play baseball and to attend church services; those with the misfortune of growing up in a slum will learn to rob drunks and to roam the streets looking to do mischief.

But could the theory of differential association account for all forms of crime? Sutherland believed he had formulated a general explanation that could be applied to very divergent types of illegal activity. Unlike Shaw and McKay, therefore, he did not confine his investigations to the delinquency of slum youths. He compiled, for example, his famous life-history of Chic Conwell, a "professional thief" (Sutherland, 1937). This study showed convincingly that "differential association" with thieves was the critical factor in determining whether a person could become a pickpocket, a shoplifter of high-priced items, or a confidence man or woman. Such contact was essential because it provided aspiring professional thieves with the tutelage, values, and colleagues needed to learn and perform sophistical criminal roles.

More provocative, however, was Sutherland's (1949:9) claim that differential association could account for the offenses "committed by a person of respectability and high social status in the course of his [or her] occupation" — illegal acts for which Sutherland (1940) coined the term "white-collar crimes." His investigations revealed that lawlessness is widespread in the worlds of business, politics, and the professions. "Persons in the upper socioeconomic class," as he put it, "engage in much criminal behavior" (Sutherland, 1983 [1949]:7). Indeed, his own research into the illegal acts by large American corporations revealed that they violated legal standards frequently and that most could be termed "habitual criminals" (Sutherland, 1949).

This empirical reality, Sutherland observed, presented special problems for most theories of his day, which assumed that "criminal behavior in general is due either to poverty or to the psychophatic and sociopathic conditions associated with poverty." After all, most "white-collar criminals ... are not in poverty, were not reared in slums or badly deteriorated families, and are not feeble-minded or psychopathic" (1940:9-10). In contrast, the principle of differential association can explain the criminality of the affluent.

Thus, in many occupations, illegal practices are widely accepted as a way of doing business. White-collar workers, Sutherland notes, may "start their careers in good neighborhoods and good homes, [and] graduate from colleges with some idealism." At that point, however, they enter "particular business situations in which criminality is practically a folkway, and are inducted into that system of behavior just as into any other folkway" (Sutherland, 1940:11). Similar to slum youths and offenders who become professional thieves, therefore, their "association" with definitions favorable to violation of law eventually shapes their orientations and transforms them from white-collar workers into white-collar criminals. In effect, a criminal tradition has been transmitted.

The Chicago School's Criminology Legacy

The Chicago School has not escaped the critical eye of subsequent scholars. One limitation critics often note, for example, is that the Chicago criminologists emphasized the causal importance of the transmission of a "criminal culture," but offered much less detail on the precise origins of this culture. Similarly, although deploring the negative consequences of urban growth — such as crime and delinquency — the Chicago theorists tended to see the spatial distribution of groups in the city as a "natural" social process. This perspective diverted their attention from the role that power and class domination can play in creating and perpetuating slums and the enormous economic inequality that pervades urban areas.

Scholars have also questioned whether the Chicago School can account adequately for all forms of crime. The theory seems best able to explain involvement in stable criminal roles and in group-based delinquency, but is less persuasive in providing insights on the cause of "crimes of passion" or other impulsive offenses by people who have had little contact with deviant values. Sutherland's theory of differential association, moreover, has received special criticism. The formulation is plausible and perhaps correct, but can it be tested scientifically? Would it ever be possible to measure accurately whether, over the course of a lifetime, a person's association with criminal definitions outweighed his or her association with conventional definitions? (Empey, 1982; Pfohl, 1985; Vold and Bernard, 1986).

Despite these limitations, few scholars would dispute that the Chicago School has had a profound influence on criminology. On the broadest level, the Chicago criminologists leveled a powerful challenge — backed by a wealth of statistics — to explanations that saw crime as evidence of individual pathology. They captured the truth that where people grow up and with whom they associate cannot be overlooked in the search for the origins of crime.

The Chicago School also laid the groundwork for the development of two perspectives that remain vital to this day. On the one hand, as indicated, Shaw and McKay's premise that weakening social controls permit delinquency to take place was an early version of what has since become known as "control" or "social bond" theory (see Chapter 4). On the other hand, the Chicago criminologists' thesis that criminal behavior occurs as a consequence of cultural transmission or differential association gave rise to "cultural deviance" theory — a perspective which assumes that people become criminal by learning deviant values in the course of social interactions (Empey, 1982:187-211).

Cultural deviance theory has evolved along a number of paths, but we can identify four particularly influential versions. First, a number of criminologists have explored how "delinquent subcultures" arise in particular sectors of society (urban, lower-class areas). These subcultures are, in effect, relatively coherent sets of antisocial norms, values and expectations that, when transmitted or learned, motivate criminal behavior (Cloward and Ohlin, 1960; Cohen, 1955). We will return later in the chapter to this line of analysis.

Second, other researchers have developed a similar theme in arguing for the existence of "subcultures of violence." Wolfgang and Ferracuti (1982:314), for example, note that in areas in which such a subculture has taken hold (e.g., urban slums), people acquire "favorable attitudes toward . . . the use of violence" through a "process of differential learning, association, or identification." As a result, "the use of violence . . . is not necessarily viewed as illicit conduct, and the users do not have to deal with feelings of guilt about their aggression." In this regard, a raging theoretical and empirical debate is whether high rates of homicide in the south can be attributed to a regionally-based subculture of violence (Hawley, 1987).

Third, some criminologists have asserted that lower-class culture as a whole — not subcultures within lower-class areas — is responsible for generating much criminality in urban areas. Walter Miller (1979 [1958]) has offered perhaps the clearest and most controversial of these theories. According to Miller, urban gang delinquency is not a product of intergenerational poverty per se, but of a distinct lower-class culture whose "focal concerns" encourages not conformity but deviance. If the focal concerns of middle-class culture are achievement, delayed gratification, and hard work, then the lower-class counterparts are trouble, smartness, toughness, fate, and autonomy. As a result, middle-class youths are oriented toward good grades, college, and career, while lower-class youths are oriented toward physical prowess, freedom from any authority, and excitement on the street. Not surprisingly, Miller (1979 [1958]:166) contends, youths that adhere to such "cultural practices which comprise essential elements of the total life pattern of lower class culture automatically violate legal norms."

Finally, Ronald Akers and his associates have been instrumental in exploring the mechanisms through which criminal learning takes place (see, for example, Akers, 1977; Akers, Krohn, Lanza-Kaduce, and Radosevich, 1979; Burgess and Akers, 1966). The Chicago theorists, like Sutherland, emphasized that criminal values are learned through associations, but had little to say about how precisely this occurred. In his "social learning" theory, Akers addresses this issue. Borrowing from operant psychology, he proposes that social reinforcements — rewards and punishments — determine whether any behavior is repeated. Involvement in crime, therefore, depends on exposure to social reinforcements that reward this activity. The stronger and more persistent these reinforcements, the greater the likelihood that criminal behavior will occur and persist. As a result, crime rates will be highest in those groups characterized by associations which reinforce deviant rather than pro-social behavior (Pfohl, 1985:250-254).

The Consequences of Theory: Policy Implications

As we have noted, the Chicago criminologists rejected individualistic explanations in favor of elucidating crime's social roots. Consistent with this theoretical perspective, they offered the "first systematic challenge to the dominance of psychology and psychiatry in public and private programs for the prevention and treatment of juvenile delinquency" (Schlossman, Zellman, and Shavelson, 1984:2). The solution to youthful waywardness, they contended, was not in eradicating the pathologies that lie within individuals; rather the challenge was to eradicate the pathologies that lie within the very fabric of disorganized *communities*.

Beginning in the early 1930s, Clifford Shaw embarked on efforts to put his theory into practice, establishing the "Chicago Area Project" (CAP). Shaw's strategy was for CAP to serve as a catalyst for the creation of neighborhood committees in Chicago's disorganized slum areas. Committee leaders and the project's staff would be recruited not from the ranks of professional social workers but from the local community. The intention was to allow local residents the autonomy to organize against crime; unless the program developed from the "bottom up," Shaw felt, it would neither win the community's support nor have realistic prospects for successful implementation (Kobrin, 1959:25; Schlossman et al., 1984:8).

CAP took several approaches to delinquency prevention. First, a strong emphasis was placed on the creation of recreational programs that would attract youths into a pro-social environment. Second, efforts were made to have residents take pride in their community by improving the neighborhood's physical appearance. Third, CAP staff members would attempt to "mediate" on behalf of juveniles in trouble. This might involve discussions with school officials on how they might reduce a youth's truancy; or it might involve appealing to court officials to divert a youth into a CAP program. Fourth, CAP used staff indigenous to the area to provide "curbside counseling." In informal conversations as opposed to formal treatment sessions, these street-wise workers would attempt to persuade youths that education and a conventional lifestyle was in their best interest. "They served," observe Schlossman et al. (1984:15), "as both model and translator of conventional social values with which youths . . . had had little previous contact."

Was Shaw's project effective? Unfortunately, the lack of a careful evaluation using a randomized control group precludes a definitive answer. Even so, in 1984 Schlossman and his associates provided a "fifty year assessment of the Chicago Area Project." They concluded that the different kinds of evidence they amassed, "while hardly foolproof, justify a strong hypothesis that CAP has long been effective in reducing rates of reported juvenile delinquency" (1984:46; Kobrin, 1959:28). CAP reminds us, they added, "that despite never-ending hard times and political powerlessness, some lower-class, minority neighborhoods still retain a remarkable capacity for pride, civility, and the exercise of a modicum of self-governance" (1984:47).

While Shaw and McKay's social disorganization theory called for efforts to reorganize communities, the Chicago School's emphasis on cultural learning suggested that crime can be countered by treatment programs that attempt to reverse offenders' criminal learning. In general, the requirement is to place offenders in settings where they will receive pro-social reinforcement. This might involve, for example, placing youths in a program that uses positive peer counseling or in a residential facility that uses a "token economy" in which conformist behavior earns juveniles points that allow them to purchase privileges (e.g., home visits, ice cream, late curfew).

MERTON'S STRAIN THEORY

In 1938 Robert K. Merton published "Social Structure and Anomie." The original essay extended only 10 pages — other elaborations by Merton (1957, 1964, 1968:185-248) followed — but it succeeded in defining an approach that captured the imagination of criminologists. As we will see, Merton's paradigm became particularly influential in the 1960s, shaping both theory and policy in important ways. Even today, however, his theorizing occupies a prominent place in criminological writings (Bernard, 1984; Cullen, 1984; Messner, 1986).

Below we begin by reviewing Merton's main theoretical assertions. We follow this discussion by considering the context that shaped strain theory over the years, the criminological legacy of Merton's work, and the impact of the perspective on criminal justice policy.

America as a Criminogenic Society

The Chicago School believed that the roots of crime were embedded predominantly in one area of American society — city slums — and that people became criminal by learning deviant cultural values. Although Merton never rejected this formulation, he outlined a very different social process — one that involved conformity to *conventional* cultural values — that he felt produced high rates of crime and deviance.

Structurally-Induced Strain. America, in Merton's eyes, is an unusual society, not simply because the culture places an extraordinary emphasis on economic success but also because this goal is universal, held up for all to want and achieve. Poor people are not taught to be satisfied with their lot, but rather are instructed to pursue the "American dream"; through hard work, it is said, even the lowliest among us can rise from rags to riches.

This widespread aspiration for success, however, has an ironic and unanticipated consequence, for the "cardinal American virtue, 'ambition,'" Merton (1968:200) cautioned, ultimately "promotes a cardinal American vice, 'deviant behavior.'" But why should the desire for social mobility lead to deviance? The problem, Merton observed, is that the social structure limits access to the goal of success through legitimate means (e.g., college education, corporate employment, family connections). Members of the lower-class are particularly burdened because they start far behind in the race for success and must be exceptionally talented or fortunate to catch up. The disjunction between what the culture extols — universal striving for success — and what the social structure makes possible — limited legitimate opportunities — thus places large segments of the American population in the strain-engendering position of desiring a goal that they cannot reach through conventional means. This situation, Merton (1968:199) concluded, is not without important social consequences: It "produces intense pressure for deviation."

Typology of Adaptations. Merton (1968:194) proposed that different ways existed for people to resolve the strains generated from the inability to attain success. To conceptualize these possible responses, he developed his classic typology, which, as Table 3.1 shows, outlined five possible modes of adaptation.

Table 3.1 Merton's Typology of Modes of Individual Adaptation

Modes of Adaptation	Culture Goals	Institutionalized Means
I. Conformity	+	+
II. Innovation	+	−
III. Ritualism	−	+
IV. Retreatism	−	−
V. Rebellion	±	±

(+) signifies acceptance; (−) signifies rejection;

(±) signifies rejection of prevailing values and substitution of new values.

Merton realized that most people, even if they found their social ascent limited, did not deviate. Instead, the "modal response" was for people to conform, to continue to ascribe to the cultural success goal and to believe in the legitimacy of the conventional or "institutionalized" means through which success was to be attained. But for many others the strain of their situation proved intolerable. Since the means-goal disjunction was the source of their problem, a requisite for alleviating strain was either changing their cultural goal and/or withdrawing their allegiance to institutionalized means. In following either or both courses, however, they were deviating from norms prescribing what should be desired (success) or how this should be achieved (legitimate means like education or employment).

Thus Merton delineated four "deviant" modes of adaptation. Much criminal behavior, he felt, could be categorized as "innovation," because this adaptation encompasses those who continue to embrace as a worthy end pecuniary success but who turn to illegitimate means when they find blocked their legitimate prospects for economic gain. The behavior of the "Robber Barons," of white-collar criminals, and of scientists who report "discoveries" based on fraudulent research are examples of how the intense desire for success can produce innovation among the more affluent (Merton, 1957, 1968:195-198). Even so, this adaptation appears particularly prevalent in the lower strata. Faced with the "absence of realistic opportunities for advancement," the disadvantaged, Merton felt, are especially vulnerable to the "promises of power and high income from organized vice, rackets, and crime" (1968:199).

In contrast, "ritualists" maintain outward conformity to the norms governing institutionalized means. They mitigate their strain, however, by scaling down their aspirations to the point where these ends can be reached comfortably. Despite cultural mandates to pursue the goal of success, they are content to avoid taking risks and to live within the confines of their daily routines.

"Retreatists," however, make a more dramatic response. Strained by expectations of social ascent through a conventional lifestyle, they relinquish allegiance to both the cultural success goal and the norms prescribing acceptable ways of climbing the economic ladder. These are people who "are in society but not of it," and they escape society's requirements through various deviant means: alcoholism, drug addiction, psychosis, or vagrancy (Merton, 1968:207). Suicide, of course, is the ultimate retreat.

Finally, Merton described as "rebellious" citizens who not only reject but also wish to change the existing system. Alienated from prevailing ends and normative standards, they propose to substitute a new set of goals and means. In American society, an example of a rebel might be a socialist who argues for group rather than individual success and for norms mandating the distribution of wealth equally and according to need rather than unequally and according to the outcome of ruthless competition.

Anomie. Because much of Merton's analysis details the social sources of strains potent enough to generate high rates of nonconformity, scholars have often referred to his perspective as "strain theory" (Empey, 1982; Hirschi, 1969; Kornhauser, 1978; Vold and Bernard, 1986). We can recall, however, that Merton labeled his classic essay "Social Structure and *Anomie*." What role does "anomie" play in the genesis of crime?

Merton borrowed the notion of anomie — normlessness or deregulation, as it is usually defined — from Emile Durkheim, the French sociologist. In his 1897 classic work, *Suicide*, Durkheim (1951) used the concept to describe a social condition in which institutionalized norms lost their power to regulate human needs and action. He argued further that as Western society modernized, a great emphasis was placed on "achieving industrial prosperity" without a corresponding attention to restraining people's appetites for success. This development, he observed, had left the economic sphere in a "chronic state" of anomie. People were now free, if not encouraged, to seek seemingly limitless economic success. But disquieting consequences befell those who succumbed to these temptations. "Overweening ambition," warned Durkheim (1951:60), "always exceeds the results obtained, great as they may be, since there is no warning to pause here. Nothing gives satisfaction and all this agitation is uninterruptedly maintained without appeasement." For many, suicide posed the only means of escape from the pain of "being thrown back." We will return to Durkheim's theorizing in the next chapter.

Merton did not buy Durkheim's framework whole cloth, but he did borrow selectively from it (Cullen, 1984:76-77; Vold and Bernard, 1986:185-189). Most important, perhaps, he learned that institutionalized norms will weaken — anomie will take hold — in societies placing an intense value on economic success. When this occurs, the pursuit of success is no longer guided by normative standards of right and wrong; instead, "the sole significant question becomes: Which of the available procedures is most efficient in netting the culturally approved value?" (Merton, 1968:189, 211). The recent Wall Street insider-trading scandal seemingly provides one example of how the widespread preoccupation with amassing fortunes results in a breakdown of institutionalized norms — anomie sets in — and fosters the unbridled pursuit of pecuniary rewards.

We should also add that innovative conduct becomes especially prevalent as anomie intensifies. In contrast to ritualism (or con-

formity), this adaptation requires an ability to relinquish commitment to institutionalized means in favor of illegitimate means.
Fluctuations in levels of anomie, whether over time or within
certain sectors of society at any given time, can be expected to
determine not only overall rates of deviance but also rates of
particular kinds of deviance, including crime, the protypical innovative response.

Anomie and deviance, moreover, are mutually reinforcing. The
weakening of institutionalized norms initially allows a limited
number of people to violate socially approved standards. But such
deviance, once completed successfully and observed by others,
poses a concrete challenge to the norms' legitimacy. This process,
Merton (1968:234) noted, "enlarges the extent of anomie within
the system," which in turn heightens the chance that waywardness will become more pervasive.

The escalating use of marijuana perhaps illustrates this phenomenon. As norms prohibiting its use lost strength in the 1960s
— claims of "reefer madness" were ridiculed — increasing numbers of youths experimented with the substance, typically in social
situations. This widely-observed, if not flaunted, deviant behavior
undermined the legitimacy of institutionalized norms, even to the
point that in some locales police and courts refused to enforce
existing laws and recreational use was decriminalized. Anomie
thus became pervasive and restraints against "smoking pot" were
vitiated greatly — a development that made marijuana's use even
more pervasive.

Rejecting Individualism. In sum, Merton contended that the
very nature of American society generates considerable crime and
deviance. The disjunction between the cultural and social structures places many citizens, but particularly the disadvantaged, in
the position of desiring unreachable goals. Tremendous strains are
engendered that move many people to find deviant ways to resolve
this situation. The cultural emphasis on success, moreover, di-
minishes the power of institutional norms to regulate behavior. As
anomie becomes prevalent, people are free to pursue success goals
with whatever means are available, legitimate or illegitimate. In
this situation, innovation — an adaptation encompassing many
forms of crime — becomes possible, if not likely.

Like the Chicago theorists, Merton located the roots of crime
and deviance within the very fabric of American society. Again,

the Chicago School stressed the criminogenic role of the city and of conformity to a *criminal* culture, while Merton stressed the criminogenic role of conformity to the universal and *conventional* cultural goal of pecuniary success. This difference aside, however, both perspectives rejected the notion that crime's origins lay within individuals' minds or bodies.

Indeed, Merton was especially vociferous in his attack on the individualistic explanations that prevailed in the 1930s (Merton and Montagu, 1940). Most of these theories, he explained, were based on the fallacious premise that the primary impulse for evil lay within human nature. In contrast, Merton (1968:175) argued for a perspective that "considers socially deviant behavior just as much a product of social structure as conformist behavior," and which "conceives of the social structure as active, as producing fresh motivations which cannot be predicted on the basis of knowledge about man's native drives."

Strain Theory in Context

Robert K. Merton was 28 and teaching at Harvard University when "Social Structure and Anomie" was published in 1938; eventually he would become a professor at Columbia University (1941) and be elected as president of the American Sociological Association. His origins, however, were more modest. He was born in the slums of South Philadelphia, and attended college only by winning a scholarship to Temple University and then a graduate assistantship to Harvard University (Hunt, 1961; Persell, 1984).

In a very real sense, Merton's travels from city slum to elite institution meant that he had lived the "American Dream." We are limited to speculation, but this personal journey may have helped to focus Merton's attention on the prominent role in the national culture of social ascent. It seems reasonable as well to suggest that this social context shaped the theoretical emphasis he placed on the structural limitations to social mobility. As Stephen Pfohl (1985:211) notes, "most of Merton's slum neighbors did not fare so well. . . a lesson of slum life which Merton never forgot." He had also experienced the Depression era, and witnessed the consequence of large numbers of people deprived of the opportunity to reach what they had been taught to desire.

Regardless of how Merton came to formulate his paradigm, one point is clear: his essay on "Social Structure and Anomie" is perhaps the most cited article not only in criminology but in sociology as a whole (Pfohl, 1985:226). Even so, the essay did not receive widespread attention until nearly two decades after its 1938 publication (Pfohl, 1985:226; see also Cole, 1975). In part, the sudden interest in his work in the late 1950s and early 1960s was prompted by the appearance of two important books on juvenile gangs, which drew heavily from Merton's theorizing: Albert K. Cohen's *Delinquent Boys* (1955) and Richard A. Cloward and Lloyd E. Ohlin's *Delinquency and Opportunity* (1960). We can also point to the effects of Merton's (1957, 1959, 1964, 1968) own renewed interest in elaborating his earlier essay.

By themselves, however, these observations do not offer a complete explanation of why, as America turned into the 1960s, criminologists became so intensely fascinated by this particular way of thinking about crime, as opposed to some other set of ideas. The social context of the time, we believe, must also be considered.

As Charles Murray (1984:27) notes, prior to 1960 poverty was not viewed, in political circles at least, as a major social problem rooted in the very structure of American society. By the early part of the 1960s, however, a fundamental transformation in thinking had occurred. An increasing consensus had emerged, Murray (1984:29) argues, that poverty "was not the just deserts of people who didn't try hard enough. It was produced by conditions that had nothing to do with individual virtue and effort. *Poverty was not the fault of the individual but of the system*" (emphasis in original). The Civil Rights movement, moreover, provided a language for conceptualizing this issue: minorities and other disadvantaged citizens were being denied "equal opportunity."

This view of the world was embraced increasingly by government officials, journalists, and academics (Murray, 1984:42). Criminologists, too, were profoundly influenced by the legitimacy now given to the idea that large segments of the American population were denied access to the American dream. In this context, it becomes understandable why Merton's theory, and offshoots like the delinquency books by Cohen and by Cloward and Ohlin, suddenly gained attention. For at the core of Merton's paradigm was the lesson that America was a society in which all were expected to ascend economically, but whose very structure denied equal opportunity to attain this cherished goal. To criminologists of the 1960s, this premise rang true; it "made sense" that crime and deviance would be a consequence of a system that was to blame for holding back unfairly many of its citizens.

STATUS DISCONTENT AND DELINQUENCY

As indicated, the writings of Albert Cohen and of Richard Cloward and Lloyd Ohlin represented important extensions of Merton's deviance approach. Although these scholars offered different variants of strain theory, they shared common themes. First, they investigated how the theory could be applied to the study of juvenile gangs in urban areas. Second, they focused on the origins and effects of delinquent subcultural norms. And third, they drew not only from Merton's structural tradition but also from the Chicago School.

Delinquent Boys. While still an undergraduate at Harvard University, Albert K. Cohen enrolled in a senior course instructed by a young professor, Robert K. Merton. A year later, Cohen was off to Indiana University where he took a seminar run by Edwin H. Sutherland. As might be expected, this fortuitous encounter with two influential and persuasive scholars prompted Cohen to ponder how notions of cultural transmission and structurally-induced strain might be reconciled.

Sutherland had convinced Cohen that differential association with a criminal culture would lead youths into legal trouble. Yet Cohen also felt that this thesis of cultural transmission begged more fundamental questions. Where, Cohen wondered, did the criminal culture come from? Why did such subcultures have a specific social distribution, locating themselves in slum areas? Why did the subcultures have a particular normative content? And why did these values persist from generation to generation?

Returning to Harvard for his Ph.D., Cohen addressed these questions in his doctoral dissertation; a much revised version was published in 1955 carrying the title *Delinquent Boys: The Culture of the Gang.* He began by making several important observations. Delinquent gangs and the subcultural values they embrace are concentrated in urban slums. Moreover, the content of these subcultures is not simply supportive of crime but rather is "non-utilitarian, malicious and negativistic" (Cohen, 1955:25). Because slum youths learn and act on the basis of these values, they engage in delinquency that is contemptuous of authority and is irrational to conventional citizens; seemingly, the only guide for their conduct is that they do things for "the hell of it."

To account for these patterns, Cohen proposed that delinquent subcultures — like all subcultures — arise in response to the special problems people face. Following Merton's insights, he noted that lower-class youths are disadvantaged in their efforts to be successful and achieve status in conventional institutions. Schools, which embody middle-class values, present a particular obstacle; poor kids lack the early socialization and resources to compete successfully with their counterparts from more affluent families. Consequently, they are "denied status in the respectable society because they cannot meet the criteria of the respectable status system" (Cohen, 1955:121).

How can these status problems be solved? "The delinquent subculture," Cohen (1955:121) contended, "deals with these problems by providing criteria of status which these children can meet." In a process approximating a reaction formation, lower-class youths reject the middle-class goals and norms that they have been taught to desire but by which they are judged inadequate. In place of middle-class standards, they substitute a set of oppositional values; if conventional society values ambition, responsibility, rationality, courtesy, control of physical aggression, and respect for authority, these youths will place a premium on behavior that violates these principles. Accordingly, status will be accorded to compatriots who are truant, flout authority, fight, and vandalize property for "kicks" (Cohen, 1955:88-91, 133).

In short, Cohen suggested that the strains of class-based status discontent are conducive to the emergence of subcultural values supportive of delinquency. Lower-class youths, thrown together in high density urban neighborhoods and saddled with a common problem, find a common solution in embracing values that provide both the chance to gain status and the psychic satisfaction of rejecting respectable values that lie beyond their reach. Because American society continues to present each new generation of urban youths with status problems, a structural basis exists for the persistence of these delinquent norms and the gang organization

✻ middle class measuring rod

they nourish. Moreover, once in existence, the subculture assumes a reality of its own. As the Chicago theorists taught, this criminal culture can be transmitted to youths in the neighborhood. Even juveniles whose status discontent is insufficient in itself to motivate delinquency, Cohen (1955:148-151) cautioned, can be attracted by the lure of the gang and its offer of friendship, excitement, or protection (Cohen, 1955:148-151).

Delinquency and Opportunity. Like Cohen, Richard Cloward and Lloyd Ohlin's work brought together the traditions of the Chicago School and strain theory. And like Cohen, personal circumstance ostensibly played a role in making possible this attempt at a theoretical merger. Thus Ohlin had studied under Sutherland and later received his doctorate from the University of Chicago; Cloward, on the other hand, had been Merton's student at Columbia University. Eventually, they became colleagues on Columbia's social work faculty (Laub, 1983:204-213), and entered into a collaboration that bore the important fruit of "opportunity theory" (Cloward and Ohlin, 1960; see also Cloward, 1959).

From Merton, Cloward and Ohlin learned that the social structure generates pressures for deviance, pressures experienced most intensely in the lower class. Similar to Cohen's extension of Merton's work, they argued that slum youths face the problem of lacking the legitimate means — the opportunity — to be successful and earn status. In American society, where success in school and in career are valued and rewarded so greatly, this failure presents a special problem: the strain of status discontentment. "The disparity between what lower-class youths are led to want and what is actually available to them," as Cloward and Ohlin (1960:86) put it, "is the source of a major problem of adjustment." It causes "intense frustrations" and the "exploration of nonconformist alternatives may be the result."

But Cloward and Ohlin also drew an important lesson from the writings of the Chicago theorists. In reading works like the *The Professional Thief* and *The Jack-Roller* which elucidated how criminal roles are learned through cultural transmission, they were led to the conclusion that people are not free to become any kind of criminal or deviant they like. To become a doctor or lawyer, one must, of course, have access to the requisite legitimate means (education, financial resources); this logic, they reasoned, could be extended to the criminal world: to become a professional thief or jack-roller, one must have access to the requisite *illegitimate means* (contact with thieves, residence in a slum neighborhood). This lesson from the Chicago School helped to resolve a short-coming of Merton's paradigm. As discussed, Merton noted that strain could be adapted to through innovation, ritualism, re-treatism, or rebellion. He provided only rudimentary insights, however, on the conditions under which a person would choose one, rather than another, adaptation. The Chicago School, Cloward and Ohlin proposed, furnished an answer to this question: The selec-tion of adaptations is regulated by the availability throughout the social structure of illegitimate means. Thus affluent people may have access to the financial positions needed to embezzle or to embark on an insider-trading scheme; in contrast, though pre-cluded from white-collar crime, lower-class residents might have access to friends who would help them rob or teach them how to fence stolen goods.

Now Cloward and Ohlin believed that the concept of illegiti-mate means could illuminate why delinquent subcultures existed in slum areas and why they took a particular form. One relevant consideration was that lower-class youths experienced high levels of strain. But in itself this factor explains only why youths might be motivated to violate the law, not why subcultural responses of a particular type emerge. "To account for the development of pressures toward deviance," Cloward and Ohlin (1960:34) cau-tioned, "does not sufficiently explain why these pressures result in one deviant solution rather than another."

Accordingly, they proposed that delinquent subcultures could emerge and persist only in areas where enough youths were con-centrated to band together and to support one another's alienation from conventional values. They observed further, however, that the type of collective response the youths could make would be shaped intimately by the neighborhood in which they resided (1960:144-186). In organized slum areas, for example, "criminal subcultures" are possible because older offenders serve as role-models for a stable criminal life and train youths in the perfor-mance of illegal enterprises (e.g., through fencing stolen merchandise).

In more disorganized neighborhoods, on the other hand, access to such organized criminal apprenticeships is absent. Lacking the opportunity to embark on more lucrative, utilitarian illegal careers, youths turn to violence as a way of establishing "rep" or social status. Conditions are ripe, therefore, for the emergence of a "conflict" or fighting-oriented subculture.

Cloward and Ohlin also identified a third subcultural form: the "retreatist" or drug-using subculture. These groupings arise when sufficient numbers of youths exist who have been "double-failures": people who have failed to achieve status through either legitimate or illegitimate means. Thus these lower-class juveniles not only have been unsuccessful in conventional settings such as the school, but also "have failed to find a place for themselves in criminal or conflict subcultures." As a result, they look to "drugs as a solution" to their "status dilemma" (Cloward and Ohlin, 1960:183).

One final point warrants emphasis. While Cloward and Ohlin focused their substantive analysis on delinquent subcultures, they believed that their opportunity theory — a consolidation of the cultural transmission and strain traditions — offered a *general* framework for studying crime and deviance (Cloward, 1959; Cloward and Piven, 1979). Again, they were persuaded that Merton had identified a major source of pressures for deviance — denial of legitimate opportunity — but that strain theory was incomplete without a systematic explanation of why people solve their status problems in one way and not another. The issue of the selection of adaptations, they felt, could only be answered by focusing on how the illegitimate opportunity structure regulated access to different forms of crime/deviance for people located at different points in society (Cullen, 1984:39-51). Thus white-collar crime and mugging represent two possible "innovative" methods to acquire financial resources; even so, participation in one, rather than the other, of these offenses is determined not by strain but by social class differentials in the availability of illegitimate opportunities.

The Criminological Legacy of Strain Theory

As strain theory emerged in the early 1960s as the most prominent criminological explanation, it won considerable attention not only from adherents but also from opponents (Cole, 1975). The perspective's critics developed a variety of lines of attack (for summaries, see Empey, 1982:233-260; Pfohl, 1985:226-235; Vold and Bernard, 1986:197-201).

Some scholars, for example, questioned whether in a society as diverse as the United States, all citizens ascribed to the goal of pecuniary success. At the very least, possible variations in the degree to which different groups were socialized effectively into the American Dream would have to be investigated. Other scholars have disparaged strain theory for assuming that strain and deviance were more prevalent in the lower-classes. This class-biased assumption is said to ignore white-collar crime and to convey the impression that lawlessness is exclusively a lower-class problem (but see Merton, 1957; 1968:198). And still other, more radical, scholars have expressed concern over Merton's failure to offer a broader, more penetrating analysis (Taylor, Walton, and Young, 1973:101). In this view, Merton succeeded in identifying a contradiction central to American society — an open-class ideology and a restricted class structure — but stopped short of asking why this condition originated and persists unabated. The answer, as Pfohl (1985:234) and others argue, is that "the political-economic structure of capitalism must be seen as a basic source of the contradictions which produce high rates of deviance."

The attempts of Cohen and of Cloward and Ohlin to explain delinquent subcultures have also been criticized. Most frequently, commentators have questioned whether these theorists described accurately the content of subcultures. Cohen portrays delinquents as embracing "non-utilitarian, malicious, and negativistic" values, but some youths' criminality is consumption-oriented and ostensibly utilitarian. Similarly, Cloward and Ohlin delineate three distinct subcultural forms (criminal, conflict, retreatist), but delinquents appear to mix these activities. "Delinquent boys," LaMar Empey (1982:250) observes, "drink, steal, burglarize, damage property, smoke pot, or even experiment with heroin and pills, but rarely do they limit themselves to any single one of these activities" (see, for example, Short and Strodtbeck, 1965).

While these observations have merit, it is important to distinguish between the theorists' substantive analysis of subcultures (which may be in need of revision) and the general framework that they suggest for the study of crime. Cohen and Cloward and Ohlin not only identified potentially important sources of youthful disaffiliation from conventional norms, but also raised the critical theoretical question of why certain forms of crime (delinquent gangs, white-collar criminality) are differentially distributed throughout the social structure. Thus, if their description of juvenile subcultures did not prove fully satisfactory, their challenge to criminologists to explain the emergence, persistence, and differential selection of criminal adaptations remains valid.

Lastly, an empirical critique has been leveled against strain theory. Contrary to the perspective's predictions that frustrated ambitions push people outside the law, some researchers have reported that high aspirations are associated with conformity and low aspirations are associated with delinquent involvement (Hirschi, 1969; Kornhauser, 1978). Thomas Bernard's (1984) assessment of available research studies, however, shows that empirical data exist that clearly support strain theory (see also Cole, 1975). Moreover, studies that claim to falsify the perspective's premises often use questionable measures of key concepts, overlook supportive findings, and do not assess systematically all of the theory's components (Bernard, 1984; Messner, 1986). Bernard (1984:366) also notes that strain theory offers perhaps the most promising approach to understanding serious urban male delinquency. "The data on serious gang delinquency," he concludes, "virtually demand a strain type explanation."

Even so, it must be admitted that after dominating criminologists' attention in the 1960s, strain theory's popularity lessened. Some scholars were critical for purely intellectual reasons. But as we have cautioned, the popularity of criminological theories is also shaped, perhaps more profoundly, by changes in the social context that make previously cherished ideas seem odd and new ideas seem a matter of common sense. Particularly as we discuss the labeling and conflict perspectives (Chapters 5 and 6), we will see how events in the late 1960s and early 1970s caused many criminologists to shift their allegiance to theories that emphasized the role of the state and of power in defining what is crime and why people engage in it.

All this is not to imply, however, that strain theory was relegated to the criminological scrap heap; quite the contrary. Although it no longer captured the fascination of most criminologists, it remained an important perspective, a standard against which newer theories were compared. Moreover, in the past several years — perhaps as there has been a growing concern with the plight of the urban poor and homeless — a renewed interest in strain theory has cropped up (Agnew, 1985; Bernard, 1984; Cullen, 1984; Messner, 1986; Rosenfeld, 1986). The strength and influence of this interest remains to be determined.

THE CONSEQUENCES OF THEORY: POLICY IMPLICATIONS

If denial of opportunity generates criminogenic strains, then logic demands that the solution to crime lies in expanding legitimate opportunities. Most broadly, therefore, strain theory justifies programs that attempt to provide the disadvantaged with educational resources (e.g., Head Start), job training, and equal access to occupations. The perspective would also support efforts to introduce into prisons rehabilitation programs that allow offenders to earn educational degrees and to acquire marketable employment skills.

Apart from these general policy implications, it is noteworthy that strain theory has served as the basis for a variety of delinquency prevention programs (see Empey and Erickson, 1972; Empey and Lubeck, 1971), the most famous of which was Mobilization for Youth (Empey, 1982:240-245; Moynihan, 1969; Pfohl, 1985:222-226). "MFY," as the program was known, was based directly on Cloward and Ohlin's "opportunity theory." The two scholars, in fact, played an integral role in seeing their ideas put into practice.

In 1959 they had been asked by a coalition of settlement houses located in New York's Lower East Side community to develop a theoretical framework for a proposal to secure government funds to provide youths with social services (Laub, 1983:211). *Delinquency and Opportunity* was one by-product of this collaboration; the other product was a 617-page report carrying the title, *A Proposal for the Prevention and Control of Delinquency by Expanding Opportunities* (Empey, 1982:241).

In different social times this proposal might have found a home on a dusty shelf, but in the early 1960s it offered a blueprint for social engineering that made eminent sense. The Kennedy administration had recently taken office with hopes of creating a "New Frontier of equal opportunity" and ready to fulfill a longstanding family commitment to dealing with the problems of young Americans (Pfohl, 1985:224-225). In 1961, the administration created the President's Committee on Juvenile Delinquency and Youth Crime. David Hackett headed the committee.

In looking for promising strategies to address delinquency problems, Hackett learned of Cloward and Ohlin's work. As Stephen Pfohl (1985:224) notes, their opportunity theory "resonated well with the liberal domestic politics of John F. Kennedy," and particularly with the president's call for equal opportunity. Indeed, the fit between strain theory and the prevailing political context was so close that Lloyd Ohlin was invited to Washington, D.C. to assume a Health, Education, and Welfare (HEW) post and to assist in formulating delinquency policy. By May 1962, Mobilization for Youth (MFY) had received a grant of $12.5 million, with over half of that amount coming from the federal government. Richard Cloward, meanwhile, was chosen as MFY's director of research.

MFY drew heavily from Merton's strain theory, setting up programs that extended youths' educational and employment support. But this reform also drew insights from the Chicago School, particularly Shaw and McKay's admonition that community organization was a prerequisite for delinquency prevention. One philosophical difference, however, existed between MFY and Shaw's Chicago Area Project. While both programs were committed to community self-help, the leaders of MFY also felt the need to change the political structures that sustained inequities in opportunity. They agreed, for example, that the problem with employment was not simply that minorities lacked skills but that they were excluded from union apprenticeships; the problem of poor educational opportunities was not simply a matter of youths lacking books in the home but also of policies that assigned the newest and least talented teachers to schools in slum neighborhoods. What was needed to overcome such formidable barriers to opportunity, therefore, was not community organization but community *action* that attacked entrenched political interests. Accordingly, MFY promoted boycotts against schools, protests against welfare policies, rent strikes against "slum landlords," lawsuits to ensure poor people's rights, and voter registration.

Commentators have disputed the wisdom of moving from the more focused agenda of providing youths educational and employment training to a broader attempt to reform the opportunity structure by empowering slum residents (Moynihan, 1969). The

wonder why?

choice of strategy soon brought MFY into a political struggle with
city officials dismayed by threats of lawsuits and other efforts by
the poor to get their share of the pie. In the ensuing conflict, MFY
was subjected to FBI investigations on suspicions of misappropri-
ated funds and to claims by the *New York Daily News* that the staff
was infested with "Commies and Commie sympathizers." Although exonerated of these kinds of charges, the swirl of controversy led to the resignation of key MFY leaders, including
Cloward, and ultimately to the disappearance of much of the program (Liska, 1981:52). In Washington, meanwhile, the President's
Committee on Juvenile Delinquency and Youth Crime was allowed to wither away. "Influential members of Congress made it
clear," LaMar Empey (1982:243) notes, "that the mandate of the
President's Committee was to reduce delinquency, not to reform
urban society or to try out sociological theories on American
youths."

Thus attempts to reduce delinquency by changing fundamentally the nature of the opportunity structure met with much opposition. But should MFY be judged a failure? A less ambitious and
confrontational reform might have succeeded in gaining more
sustained political acceptance and support for programs. Two qualifications, however, must be added.

First, MFY must be credited for its attempt to attack the "root
causes" of crime that most criminal reforms leave untouched.
MFY's failure to avoid boisterous and powerful opposition says
less about the correctness of the approach taken and more about
the political interests that buttress America's structure of inequality. Second, while MFY's impact on delinquency has not been
established definitively (Liska, 1981:52), it did serve as a model for
similar community-action programs across the nation. Daniel
Moynihan (1969:123), a noted critic of the program, has nonetheless given MFY the credit it is due:

> MFY did lose in its battle with City Hall, but it set a pattern for the
> community action programs that were to spring up across the land
> at the very moment its own came under fire.... Preschool education,
> legal aid for the poor (not just to defend them, but to serve as
> plaintiffs), a theory of community organization, an emphasis on
> research and evaluation, and most especially the insistence on the
> involvement of the poor, all these were the legacy of Mobilization
> for Youth. It was no small achievement.

CONCLUSION

The Chicago School and Merton's strain theory represent early, yet bold and influential, efforts to show how the very fabric of American society — its slums, the contradictions between its cultural prescriptions and social structure — generates high rates of crime. They rejected as simplistic, if not as incorrect, previous theories that had sought to locate the causes of crime within individuals. Instead, they warned that the social organization of society constrains what people learn to become and what they might be pressured into doing. This is a lesson that cannot be casually overlooked, for it suggests, in a sense, that a society gets the crime it deserves.

The Chicago School and strain theory also illustrate the themes of this book. First, changes in the social context made each of these perspectives "make sense" to a good number of criminologists. For the Chicago School, the rapid growth and increasing diversity of urban America gave legitimacy to a theory that linked crime to these social transformations; for strain theory, the emergence of equal opportunity as a socio-political agenda provided an ideal context in which "opportunity theory" could win followers.

Second, the history of these perspectives shows how criminological theory can direct, or at least justify, criminal justice policy. The Chicago Area Project and Mobilization for Youth cannot be understood apart from the theories that provided the logic for their development and were convincing enough to prompt financial support. The writings of Shaw and McKay and of Cloward and Ohlin, therefore, clearly made a difference; ideas, as we have observed, have consequences.

4

Society as Insulation: Control Theory

The most important step in the solution to a problem, theoretical or otherwise, lies in asking the right questions about it. The proper formulation of the problem may often make the answer obvious. At the very least, asking the right question in the right way will contribute greatly to a solution. Asking the wrong question, or asking the right question in the wrong way, will result in no progress at all, although there may be an illusion of getting somewhere.

Unfortunately, the first step is also usually the most difficult. Not only does it require a thorough understanding of the nature of the situation with which one is faced, but it also demands the capacity to think about it in new and creative ways. Because we are not likely to ask questions about aspects of the situation which we take for granted, different criminologists have been led to see very different questions as the key to an understanding of crime and delinquency. What one takes for granted needs no explanation, but what one takes for granted depends upon assumptions, in this case assumptions about human nature and social order.

Most criminologists have taken conformity for granted as part of the natural order of things and have concentrated on trying to explain the "crime problem." As we have seen, they have found their explanations in spirits and demons, in theories tracing the nonconformity to individual factors such as biological abnormalities or personality defects, or in theories tracing the nonconformity to social factors such as social disorganization, subcultural traditions, or inequality of opportunity, all of these being factors presumed to operate so as to distort the natural order of conformity. But is conformity really the natural order of things? To what extent should it be taken for granted?

By the time a person is a certain age, he or she speaks a certain language shared by others, drives a car in general obedience to traffic regulations, avoids urination or defecation in public, and in most other ways "goes along." All this tends to be taken for granted, but the evidence indicates that it is not at all "natural" (Davis, 1948). In fact, great effort is expended by parents, teachers, and the individual involved in a concerted effort to produce these results. Viewed in this way, all this conformity is a striking thing much in need of explanation. That is the focus of *control theory*, which takes the position that because conformity cannot be taken for granted, *nonconformity such as crime and delinquency is to be expected when social controls are less than completely effective*.

In this sense, control theory is not so much a theory of deviance as a theory of conformity. It does not ask the question, "Why do people commit crimes and acts of delinquency?" It suggests that crime and delinquency are going to occur unless people conform to all the social demands placed on them and then asks, "Why do people conform?" From this perspective on human nature and social order, crime and delinquency can be expected unless the sociocultural controls are operating effectively to prevent such behavior.

Below we will review several of the more prominent examples of control theory as they have emerged within the general context of criminological theory. These will include Reiss's theory of personal and social controls, Nye's family-focused theory of social controls, Reckless's containment theory, the neutralization theory developed by Sykes and Matza as later modified by Matza's drift theory, and Hirschi's control theory with its focus on social bonds. First, however, we will examine some forerunners of contemporary control theory. As in the previous chapter, we will stress the significance of the work of Durkheim and the Chicago School. Both bodies of work remain rich sources of ideas about both human nature and social order. It is not surprising to find that they also contributed much to the reconsideration of the basic assumptions about the relationship between human nature and social order. This marked the development of control theory.

FORERUNNERS OF CONTROL THEORY

Durkheim's Anomie Theory

The origins of contemporary control theories of crime and delinquency are to be found in part in the work of French sociologist Emile Durkheim, in the same body of theory that inspired Merton's analysis of anomie as a source of crime (see Chapter 3). Durkheim's work was a product of the late nineteenth century, a period that had seen dramatic social change in the wake of the Industrial Revolution, and he described anomie not simply as "normlessness," but as the more or less complete collapse of social solidarity itself, the destruction of the fundamental bonds uniting individuals in a collective social order so that each person is forced to go it alone. Technological change had combined with the rise of capitalism, and the old world of agrarian society, where farmers and herdsmen lived simply in face-to-face relationships with interests in common, was rapidly giving way to a more complex, urban, technologically sophisticated social system. The sense of community was being eroded; the large, extended family consisting of many relatives working together was being torn apart and replaced with the new, "nuclear family" of parents alone with their children, and the pace of life was accelerating with an increasing division of labor separating different individuals into occupational specialties.

Describing London in 1844, Karl Marx's friend and collaborator Frederick Engels (Josephson and Josephson, 1962:32) painted the picture as follows:

> The restless and noisy activity of the crowded streets is highly distasteful, and is surely abhorrent to human nature itself. Hundreds of thousands of men and women drawn from all classes and ranks of society pack the streets of London. . . . Yet they rush past each other as if they had nothing in common. They are tacitly agreed on one thing only — that everyone should keep to the right of the pavement so as not to collide with the stream of people moving in the opposite direction. No one even thinks of sparing a glance for his neighbors in the streets. . . . We know well enough that this isolation of the individual — this narrow-minded egotism — is everywhere the fundamental principle of modern society.

As we shall see in Chapter 6, Marx and Engels saw this situation as a consequence of the underlying economic shifts that had generated capitalism. Writing in France later in the century, Durkheim disagreed. For him, the moral order was more fundamental than the economic order. The idea of social solidarity can almost be said to represent a religion to Durkheim. "Everything which is a source of solidarity is moral, everything which forces man to take account of other men is moral, everything which forces him to regulate his conduct through something other than the striving of his ego is moral, and morality is as solid as these ties are numerous and strong" (Durkheim, 1933:398).

The Importance of Integration and Regulation. In Durkheim's view, social solidarity was maintained by two distinct sets of social functions: those involving *integration* and those involving *regulation.* Integration was described as a state of cohesion amounting to a common "faith" sustained by collective belief and practices leading to strong social bonds and the subordination of self to a common cause (Durkheim, 1951:169). For Durkheim, collective activity was what gave purpose and meaning to life. When integrative functions failed, the "collective force of society" was weakened, "mutual moral support" was eroded, and there was a "relaxation of social bonds" leading to extreme individualism (Durkheim, 1951:209-214).

Where Durkheim saw *integration* as the sum of various social forces of *attraction* which drew people together, *regulation* was considered the sum of those forces of *constraint* which bound individuals to norms. Durkheim argued that the constraining regulative functions become more important in an urban society with a complex division of labor. Here different individuals may be attracted to a common goal and may be very willing to submit to the authority of the social system, but their efforts must be properly coordinated if society is to function smoothly. It is especially important that the regulative norms "deliver the goods," that they maintain their legitimacy by demonstrated effectiveness. Even if an individual wished to work with others toward a common social purpose, he or she might turn in a deviant direction if the norms regulating the common effort were perceived as unnecessary, overly burdensome, or otherwise questionable.

The Nature of "Man." Durkheim's viewpoint was deeply affected by his conception of human nature. According to his *homo duplex* conception, any person was a blend of two aspects. On the one side there was the social self, the aspect of self which looks to society and is a product of socialization and cultivation of human potentials — the "civilized" member of a community. On the other side there was the egoistic self, the primal self which is incomplete without society, and which is full of impulses knowing no natural limits. This conception of the primal aspect is somewhat similar to Freud's notion of the id. In Durkheim's view, conditions of social solidarity based on highly developed functions of social integration and social regulation allowed the more primal self to become fully humanized in a life shared with others on a moral common ground. One implication is that *unless* such social solidarity is developed and maintained, we may *expect* crime and delinquency.

The Influence of the Chicago School

As described in Chapter 3, the social upheaval which so concerned Durkheim in France was repeated even more dramatically in the United States a few decades later. During the early years of the twentieth century, and especially after World War I, the forces of technological change, increased industrialization combined with the rise of the large corporation, and rapid urbanization were accompanied by massive waves of immigration. Chapter 3 has already described the development of the Chicago School with its emphasis upon immigration and especially urbanization as the major forces of social change which were leading to crime through social disorganization. But the Chicago School mined a rich vein of ideas about human nature and the social order, ideas which led some criminological theorists not toward a search for criminogenic forces in society which might be pulling or pressuring people away from their normal conformity but toward control theories which refused to take conformity for granted as the natural order of things.

Like some of the criminological theories discussed earlier, these control theories were also influenced by the social disorganization perspective, some explicitly and some implicitly. Although the accent was somewhat different among the various control theorists, two related Chicago School themes remained central. The first had to do with the interpretations of the nature of "human nature." The second had to do with the nature of "community."

Conceptions of Human Nature. As to "human nature," the Chicago School developed the line of thought which explained the "self" as a blending of a primal self and a social self, but the focus was on showing just *how* the social self, so important to Durkheim, was formed. Although not at the University of Chicago himself, Charles H. Cooley can be considered part of "what came to be known as the Chicago School of Social Psychology" (Hinkle and Hinkle, 1954:30). Cooley's work influenced George Herbert Mead of the University of Chicago, and Mead carried forward this and other contributions. Both Cooley and Mead considered the common notion of *imitation* insufficient to explain social behavior and sought to understand the process by which something like the primal self became the social self.

Cooley pointed out that the human offspring is dependent on other human beings in the family setting for a prolonged period. The family was treated as an example of what Cooley called a "primary group" in which interaction is of an intimate, face-to-face character leading to a "we-feeling" or sense of belonging and identification with the group (Cooley, 1922). The child would not even develop a sense of "self" without the feedback provided by others serving as a mirror. According to Cooley's concept of the "looking-glass self," the child develops a concept of who he or she "really is" by imagining how he or she appears to others and how others interpret and evaluate what they perceive, and then by forming a sense of self based on that process (Cooley, 1902, 1909). Without interaction in primary groups, a person would not be fully human. For Cooley, "human nature" itself, defined as "those sentiments and impulses that are human in being superior to those of lower animals," was essentially the same throughout the world because the intense experience in primary groups was considered to be basically the same everywhere (Cooley, 1909:28).

Mead's social psychology was reminiscent of Durkheim's *homo duplex* in dividing the individual into an "I" and a "me." He did little to describe the "I" except to suggest that this represents a process of fundamental awareness which becomes focused in different ways leading to the development of the social self or "me." The focusing was said to occur though a process of "taking the role of the other" and seeing things from that perspective, with certain "significant others" being especially important and society representing a "generalized other" (Mead, 1934). It was through this process that socialization occurred.

If successful, such socialization was considered to lead to personally integrated social beings who would see the world not through the narrow and unstable perspective of the shifting "I" (to the extent that the "I" can be said to be capable of organized perception at all) but through a social "me" which included others' perspectives and interests as part of oneself. One implication was that *unsuccessful* socialization might lead to *personal disorganization*, to a "self" lacking in integration and consistency, or to a "self" that was internally integrated but not integrated into society — or both.

The Study of Community. The second related Chicago School theme, the study of "community," was reflected in the work of Park and Burgess and in the studies of the spatial distribution of "natural areas" and conflicting cultural traditions undertaken by Shaw and McKay as outlined in Chapter 3. There the stress was on the idea of *social disorganization.* In addition to this approach, much of the social psychological emphasis in the work of different members of the Chicago School had to do with the possibility of such social disorganization through the collapse of community as a consequence of increasing "social distance" among individuals who refused to get close to one another (Hinkle and Hinkle, 1954). Wirth (1938) described it as a problem of *segmentation* which separated people and made it impossible for them to relate to one another as total personalities. This theme emphasized the impersonality and anonymity of life in urban, industrialized societies, where people in the "community" did not know or care about one another and preferred it that way. The descriptions sounded like Durkheim's discussion of anomie or Engels's picture of London in 1844, only more so.

Beyond the concern with the apparent "decline of community" at a municipal or neighborhood level, some working within the tradition of the Chicago School focused attention on an even more ominous trend — the apparent decline in the "moral integration" of the basic primary groups themselves. Even the family, the most "primary" of all groups, seemed to be losing its influence over its members. If this proved true, it suggested not only social disorganization but also personal disorganization resulting from fundamental problems in the formation of the personal "self." It was out of this context of social transformation and sociological thought that control theory was to emerge in criminology.

VARIETIES OF CONTROL THEORY IN CONTEXT

The concept of "social disorganization" led different criminological theorists in different directions. As suggested in Chapter 3, ideas of social disorganization could be seen in terms of severe pressures which themselves *produce* crime and delinquency, as in the "strain theories," or in terms of a weakening of social controls which simply makes crime and delinquency more *possible*. The latter approach was taken by control theorists such as Reiss, Nye, Reckless, Sykes and Matza, and Hirschi. Each of these theorists, as we will see below, tended to take the position that crime and delinquency could be *expected* in conditions where controls were not effective.

Reiss's Theory of Personal and Social Controls

In the late 1940s Albert J. Reiss (1949) completed a Ph.D dissertation at the University of Chicago in which he attempted to develop an instrument for the prediction of juvenile delinquency. Two years later, he summarized part of his project in an article describing "Delinquency as the Failure of Personal and Social Controls" (Reiss, 1951). "Personal control" was defined as "the ability of the individual to refrain from meeting needs in ways which conflict with the norms and rules of the community" (Reiss, 1951:196). "Social control" was defined as "the ability of social groups or institutions to make norms or rules effective" (Reiss, 1951:196). According to Reiss (1951:196), "Delinquency results when there is a relative absence of internalized norms and rules governing behavior in conformity with the norms of the social system to which legal penalties are attached, a breakdown in previously established controls, and/or a relative absence of or conflict in social rules or techniques for enforcing such behavior in the social groups or institutions of which the person is a member." This approach was clearly influenced by the social disorganization tradition, but it had a control theory emphasis.

Reiss maintained that conformity might result either from the individual's *acceptance* of rules and roles or from mere *submission* to them. Such a distinction ran parallel to Durkheim's division of social solidarity forces into those representing *integration* and those representing *regulation*. Personal controls were said to include both "(a) mature ego ideals or non-delinquent social roles, i.e., internalized controls of social groups governing behavior in conformity with non-delinquent group expectations, and (b) appropriate and flexible rational controls over behavior which permits conscious guidance of action in accordance with non-delinquent group expectations" (Reiss, 1951:203). Considered from the "perspective of the person," social control was held to lie "in the acceptance of or submission to the authority of the institution and the reinforcement of existing personal controls by institutional controls" (Reiss, 1951:201). Considered "from the standpoint of the group," it was said to lie "in the nature and strength of the norms of the institutions and the effectiveness of the institutional rules in obtaining behavior in conformity with the norms" (Reiss, 1951:201).

In an obvious reference to Chicago School work in the tradition of Shaw and McKay, Reiss (1951:196-197) took pains to stress that "this formulation is not in contradiction with the formulations which view certain types of delinquency as a consequence of social control in the delinquent gang." He was not concerned with the way in which delinquency might be fostered through cultural transmission of norms which conflicted with those of the larger society but rather with underlying processes which seemed (1) to occur *prior* to any later processes such as conflicting cultural transmissions and (2) to be *necessary* before any such subsequent processes (whatever they might be) could ever take place. Being both antecedent and necessary, the processes involving loss of personal and social control might be considered more basic. As he himself put it, "The delinquent peer group is here viewed as a *functional consequence* of the failure of personal and social controls . . ." (Reiss, 1951:197; emphasis added).

It is important to remember that Reiss's goal was to develop a prediction instrument. As one reviewer pointed out at the time, Reiss was not seeking to explain what caused delinquency but to pin down those factors which had to occur before any such "causes" could be expected to produce their "effects." "The chief concern as a predictor was failure to submit to social controls, the 'why' of such action being less important" (Symons, 1951:208).

Following that tendency of the Chicago School tradition which stressed the *social psychological* dimension, Reiss (1951:198) began with the assumption that "primary groups are the basic institutions for the development of personal controls and the exercise of social control over the child." It followed that "delinquency and delinquent recidivism may be viewed as a consequence of the failure of primary groups to provide the child with appropriate non-delinquent roles and to exercise social control over the child so these roles are accepted or submitted to in accordance with needs" (Reiss, 1951:198). The key primary groups were identified as the family, the neighborhood, and the school.

Speaking of the family, for example, Reiss (1951:198-199) maintained that there is "social control over the child's behavior when the family milieu is structured so that the child *identifies* with family members . . . and *accepts* the norms." On the other hand, acceptance of or submission to such social control may decline if the family fails to "meet the needs of its members" and "provide for members' needs through the purchase of material goods and services" (Reiss, 1951:198). Control might also be lost if the family exercised either "over-control or under-control" of the child's behavior (Reiss, 1951:199).

Nye's Family-Focused Theory of Social Controls

One of the leading figures in the sociology of the family, F. Ivan Nye was a product of Michigan State University and very much under the influence of the Chicago School. In the late 1950s he set forth a more systematic version of control theory, making explicit the formulation of the problem as one of explaining conformity rather than nonconformity. According to Nye (1958:5), "It is our position, therefore, that in general behavior prescribed as delinquent or criminal need not be explained in any positive sense, since it usually results in quicker and easier achievement of goals than the normative behavior." Thus the problem for the theorist was not to find an explanation for delinquent or criminal behavior; rather it was to explain why delinquent and criminal behavior are not more common.

In this view, it was not necessary to find some "positive" factor(s) of a biological, psychological, or sociological nature which operates to "cause" crime and delinquency. The problem was to locate the social control factor(s) which inhibited such nonconformity, the implication being that when the factor(s) was operating ineffectively for some reason, crime and delinquency became a *possibility* available to an individual. Nye's theoretical and research focus was on adolescents, and he considered the family to be the most important agent of social control over them. As the major primary group representing society, the family could generate *direct control, internalized control, indirect control* and *control through alternative means of need satisfaction.* The same patterns of social control could be generated by other social institutions, although perhaps less powerfully.

These four modes of social control were also reminiscent of Durkheim's concepts of a combination of integration and regulation. Direct control was considered to be imposed on the individual by external forces such as parents, teachers, and the police through direct restraints accompanied by punishment for violation. Internalized control was considered to occur when the individual regulated his or her own behavior, even in the absence of direct, external regulation, through some process such as "conscience" or superego capable of restraining egoistic impulses. Indirect control had to do with the extent of affection and identification integrating the individual with authority figures in general and parents in particular. Such integration might serve to keep the person in line when regulation either through direct control or internalized self-control was minimal. Finally, a social system which made available various means of achieving satisfaction rather than demanding that everyone pursue exactly the same goal in exactly the same manner was held to exert social control by "delivering the goods" in such a variety of legitimate ways that the temptation to nonconformity was reduced.

Although these different modes of social control were held to operate somewhat independently, with one being more important in a particular situation and another in a different context, Nye pointed out that they were mutually reinforcing. The sense of identification with and affection for parents should, to use Reiss's terms, facilitate both an *acceptance* of and a *submission* to their direct controls. The same integration into the family unit should result in deeper internalization of parental expectations and regulations through an internal "conscience" which regulated behavior from within the individual. The fact that the family prepared the individual for the pursuit of alternative goals in life through a variety of means and that the larger society made this possible was a major force for the integration of the individual into the social order. Thus integration and regulation combined to reinforce one another and to reduce the likelihood of nonconforming behavior such as crime and delinquency.

Reckless's Containment Theory

Walter C. Reckless obtained his doctorate at the University of Chicago in the late 1920s, at the point of theoretical dominance for the Chicago School. He became especially interested in social psychology and in the social psychological aspects of criminology, asserting in the early 1940s that the central problem lay in explaining "differential responses" (Reckless, 1943:51). By this he meant that criminology ought to pursue a search for "self-factors" which would explain why some individuals succumbed to social pressures leading to crime and delinquency while others remained relatively law-abiding in the same circumstances. Partly as a result of his search for "self-factors" during the 1940s and 1950s, Reckless (1961) was able to present what he called his "containment theory" in some detail at the beginning of the 1960s.

The Social Psychology of the Self. Like Durkheim and the members of the Chicago School in general, Reckless argued that the great social transformation from life in fairly simple, integrated agrarian societies to life in complex, technologically sophisticated and highly industrialized urban environments placed a different set of pressures upon the individual and the social order. As he revised his theory during the 1960s, he became more explicit about the way in which the historical transformation represented in social psychological terms a "new pitch."

The new situation or "pitch" may be described as follows. In a fluid, mobile society which has emphasized freedom of action for its individuals, the person is able to soar like a balloon without the ballast of social relationships. He can readily aggrandize himself at the expense of others. His society does not easily contain him. He no longer fits into expected roles. . . . He plays his major themes in life without agreed-upon ground rules. (Reckless, 1967:21)

Turning specifically to an examination of "crime in the modern world," Reckless (1967:10-12), focused attention on the "individualization of the self."

As an entity in personal development, the self seems to have had a sort of natural history. It appears to be relatively unimportant in primitive, isolated societies in which individuals very seldom break away from the undifferentiated uniformity of kin, village, and tribe. When human society in the course of evolution becomes differentiated, develops an increasing division of labor, and presents alternate choices to its members, the selves of certain persons begin to individualize and take on separate and distinct identities, departing from the mass of the people. (Reckless, 1967:11)

Pushes and Pulls. As a control theorist, Reckless did not purport to offer a theory of crime causation. Indeed, he suggested that a variety of factors — including biophysical forces, psychological pressures, and social conditions such as poverty — might "push" a person toward crime or delinquency, while other factors — such as illegitimate opportunities — may "pull" one toward misbehavior. He recognized that the leading sociological theories in particular seemed to have effectively analyzed many of the central "pushes" and "pulls." One of his more graphic analogies compared the etiology of crime and delinquency to that of malaria, insisting that the sociological theories stressing social structural forces be complemented by social psychological concepts emphasizing differential response.

Sociological theories that do not account for a self factor to explain differential response are akin to explaining malaria on the basis of the lady mosquito, the swamp, or the lack of screens on houses. But everybody does not get malaria, even under conditions of extreme exposure. Some get a light touch. Some get a very severe attack. Some remain relatively immune. The resistance is within the person — his blood, his chemistry, his differential immunity. (Reckless, 1967:469)

Reckless's containment theory was meant to explain why *in spite of* the various criminogenic "pushes" and "pulls," *whatever they may be*, conformity remains the general state of affairs. He argued that to commit crime or delinquency requires the individual to break through a combination of outer containment and inner containment which together tend to insulate the person from both the "pushes" and "pulls." With rare exceptions, only when these powerful containing forces were weakened could deviance occur. And even then, it was not assured, because containment theory was considered a "risk theory," dealing in probabilities. Every weakening of containment was seen as tending to increase the odds for nonconformity by opening a breach in the armor provided by external social control and internal self-control.

Factors in Outer Containment. The listing of factors involved in outer containment differed somewhat in various statements of containment theory, as Reckless attempted to refine his theoretical position. He pointed out that the key factors binding the individual to the group might vary across different types of societies. Concentrating on "the external containment model for modern, urban, industrial, mobile society," he stressed (1) reasonable limits, (2) meaningful roles and activities, and (3) "several complementary variables such as reinforcement by groups and significant, supportive relationships, acceptance, the creation of a sense of belonging and identity" (Reckless, 1967:470-471). Durkheimian themes were clear here, although not spelled out in detail. Thus, for example, while the containing "limits" reflected effective regulation, the latter set of variables "can also be called incorporation or integration of the individual" (Reckless, 1967:471). Translated into Durkheimian terms, it is clear that the containing force of "meaningful roles and activities" involved a combination of regulation and integration.

> Groups, organizations, associations, bureaucracies, to operate, or stay in existence . . . must expect reasonable conformity. . . . If a group or organization can get its members to internalize their rules, it would be doing an excellent job of containing. If a group or organization can get its members to comply (although they have not internalized the regulations), they are doing an excellent job. If they can minimize the number of infractions or hold the violations to tolerable proportions (where members are effective, if not enthusiastic conformists), they are doing a fair job. (Reckless, 1967:470)

Factors in Inner Containment. For Reckless, however, the emphasis was on inner containment. In contemporary society, the individual who at one point might be operating in a context of powerful outer containment provided by regulating limits, meaningful roles, and a sense of integration into a particular family, organization, or community might in a short time be operating in another context with few regulations, meaningless activities, and a sense of alienation. Inner containment, on the other hand, would tend to control the individual to some extent no matter how the external environment changed. Reckless (1967) identified the key factors here as including *self-concept, goal orientation, frustration tolerance,* and *norm retention.*

The importance assigned to *self-concept* echoed Cooley's insistence on the significance of the "looking-glass self." As indicated in Chapter 3, members of the Chicago School such as Shaw and McKay focused attention on the manner in which certain "natural areas" of high delinquency tended to produce "bad boys." As a control theorist concerned with "differential response," Reckless asked the *opposite question*: Why were there still so many "good boys" in these "swamps" of high delinquency? In a series of studies focusing on this question, Reckless and his associates concluded that such boys were "insulated" by a "favorable self-concept" (Dinitz, Reckless, and Kay, 1958; Dinitz, Scarpitti, and Reckless, 1962; Reckless, 1967; Reckless and Dinitz, 1967; Reckless, Dinitz and Kay, 1957; Reckless, Dinitz, and Murray, 1956; Scarpitti et al., 1960). These studies suggested that an image of oneself as a law-abiding person of a sort not headed for trouble served to keep potential delinquents in relative conformity in spite of the "pushes" and "pulls" described above. The research suggested that parents were the most influential sources of favorable self-concepts, with teachers and other authority figures also having some influence.

Reckless (1967:476) maintained that inner containment was also greatly dependent upon *goal orientation*, defined as a sense of direction in life involving an orientation toward legitimate goals and an aspiration level "synchronized with approved and realistically obtainable goals." This approach ran directly opposite to the strain theory notion that social aspirations tended to become a major source of crime and delinquency because they were so frequently frustrated due to inadequate opportunity to achieve the goals in question. Instead, containment theory treated such goal orientation as providing a sense of direction which would keep the individual on the straight and narrow path of conformity. Such a perspective implied either the assumption that (1) opportunities were actually more widely available than was assumed by strain theory so that reasonable success goals were indeed "realistically obtainable," or the assumption that (2) realistic goal orientations would involve a scaling down of aspirations on the part of many individuals, or (3) both assumptions.

Considering *frustration tolerance* as a major factor in inner containment, containment theory accepted the possibility that the control of biophysical urges toward deviance may be very frustrating and that contemporary society may indeed generate considerable frustration as a result of such facts as that of differential opportunity. It did not argue against efforts to deal with the sources of crime and delinquency by movement toward greater equality of opportunity, but it suggested that (1) part of the differential response to familial, economic, political, and sexual frustrations can be accounted for by the fact that different individuals have developed different capacities for coping with frustration and that (2) contemporary individualism is generally characterized by low frustration tolerance and consequent lack of self-control. Thus Reckless (1967:20-21) maintained that the contemporary individual "develops a very low frustration tolerance to the ordinary upsets, failures, and disappointments in life," and that this may result in "the inability to exert self-control, to tolerate frustration, to recognize limits, to relate to others."

The fourth key component of inner containment, *norm retention*, referred to the "adherence to, commitment to, acceptance of, identification with, legitimation of, defense of values, norms, laws, codes, institutions, and customs" (Reckless, 1967:476). Where the emphasis on goal orientation stressed the integration of the individual through the containing power of direction toward legitimate ends, the emphasis on norm retention stressed the integration of the individual through identification with acceptable means. For containment theory the key problem here was not, however, norm retention but rather *norm erosion*, of understanding the processes by which this containing factor was sometimes eroded so as to allow for the possibility of crime and delinquency. Norm erosion was described as including "alienation from, emancipation from, withdrawal of legitimacy from, and neutralization of *formerly internalized* ethics, morals, laws, and values" (Reckless, 1967:476; emphasis added).

Summary. It is apparent that containment theory followed the Chicago School approach in a way which was very Dukheimian. It took an historical focus, seeing what was apparently an increase in crime and delinquency as a product of the modern world. Unlike strain theories, it did not stress economic inequality and argue that crime and delinquency must be dealt with primarily through a liberal political agenda stressing equality of opportunity. Like the Durkheimian tradition, it regarded the moral order as more fundamental than the economic order and concerned itself to a considerable extent with what it took to be the problem of the individual in a complex society who is increasingly cast adrift with boundless desires, little capacity to tolerate denial, and no real sense of direction or commitment to the traditional rules of social life.

Sykes and Matza: Neutralization and Drift Theory

As we have seen, control theorists such as Reckless considered many of the sociological theories of crime and delinquency to be overly deterministic. If these problems were caused by slums, criminal traditions, lack of economic opportunity, and the like, why was it that many if not most of those suffering from such pressures did not in fact become criminals or delinquent at all? In the late 1950s Gresham Sykes and David Matza had turned attention to a related issue. If the social pressures causing delinquency, for example, were so powerful, then why was it that even the worst of delinquents seemed to be fairly conventional people, actually conforming in so many other ways? And why was it that although they continued to live in areas of crime and delinquency and continued to be faced with lack of economic opportunity, most of them did *not* continue law-violating behavior beyond a certain age but rather settled down in law-abiding lives? Could it be that the delinquency which took up so small a part of their lives for so short a time was really some sort of aberration, a temporary, albeit occasionally dramatic, quirk rather than a basic characteristic?

Techniques of Neutralization. According to Sykes and Matza's

(1957) original statement, the delinquent had not really rejected the larger social order as suggested by notions such as that of delinquent subculture. In their view, such theories overemphasized the difference between "delinquents" and "nondelinquents." But how was it possible for them to violate the conventional morality if they had not in fact rejected it, if they remained essentially integrated into the society and generally respectful of its regulations? Sykes and Matza explained the possibility by arguing that part of the process through which one learned the conventional social norms consisted of the learning of excuses or "techniques of neutralization" by which those norms could be temporarily "neutralized," thus permitting violations *in certain cases* without the necessity of rejecting the norms themselves.

Specific "techniques of neutralization" were listed as: (1) denial of responsibility, (2) denial of injury, (3) denial of the victim, (4) condemnation of the condemners, and (5) appeal to higher loyalties. *Denial of responsibility* is exemplified by the excuse that, "A lot of the trouble I get into is not my fault." *Denial of injury* is exemplified by such excuses as, "They've got so much, they'll never miss it," while an excuse such as "I only steal from drunks ('queers,' 'rednecks,' 'outsiders,' etc.)" represents *denial of the victim. Condemnation of the condemners* amounts to an insistence that certain people have no right to condemn certain violations because, for example, "They're worse than we are," while "We have to do it to protect our turf" represents an excuse by *appeal to higher loyalties.* Sykes and Matza argued that it was the use of these "techniques of neutralization" which allowed delinquents to violate occasionally laws which they actually accepted and obeyed most of the time.

Drift Theory. This explanation of delinquency in terms of techniques of neutralization represented a control perspective in that their use was treated as neutralizing the existing social control, thereby *allowing the possibility* of delinquency. In fact, Ball (1966) has argued that the concept of "techniques of neutralization" is not sufficiently developed to constitute a theory in its own right and might be integrated into Reckless's more systematic containment theory by considering the various "techniques" as examples of the more general process of norm erosion posited by Reckless.

In any case, Matza (1964) himself developed the notion further in the middle 1960s, arguing that delinquents in general were no

more committed to their delinquency than to conventional enterprises, but that the delinquency was a matter of "drift" facilitated
by the existence of a "subterranean convergence" between their
own techniques of neutralization and certain ideologies of the
authorities who represented the official moral order. By this he
meant that the authorities themselves often excused violations by
blaming parents, citing provocation on the part of the victim, or
accepting explanations defining the infraction as involving self-
defense or "accident" in a way that reinforced the norm neutralization of the juveniles. In this double-edged way the controlling
power of conventional norms might either be weakened by all sorts
of qualifications built into them or eroded through time as attempts to apply them met with objections, excuses, and vacilla-
tions.

Still, neutralization merely makes delinquency *possible*. In
Matza's (1964:29) language, "Those who have been granted the
potentiality for freedom through the loosening of social controls
but who lack the position, capacity, or inclination to become agents
in their own behalf, I call drifters, and it is in this category that
I place the juvenile delinquent." Dealing with the argument
against control theory which holds that "Delinquency . . . cannot
be assumed to be a potentiality of human nature which automatically erupts when the lid is off " (Cohen and Short, 1958:30) but
must involve at least some triggering factors(s), he made a con-
cession which many other control theorists would not accept: He
agreed that because delinquency may involve unfamiliar and dangerous behaviors, something more than loss of control is necessary
to explain it. He held that the triggering factors consisted of a
combination of *preparation* and *desperation*.

For Matza, preparation involved a process by which the person
discovered that a given infraction could be pulled off by *someone*,
that the individual had the ability to do it *himself or herself*, and
that fear or *apprehension* could be managed. Even if a delinquent
infraction had become possible, it might not occur unless someone
learned that it was possible, felt confident that he or she could do
it, and was courageous or stupid enough to minimize the dangers.
Otherwise the possibility would fail to become a reality. As for the
element of desperation, Matza argued that the central force there
was a profound sense of fatalism, a feeling that the self was over-
whelmed, with a consequent need to violate rules of the system so

as to reassert individuality. Unlike Reckless, Matza did not criticize such a need for individuality as often amounting to a mis-
placed egoism.

The Context of the 1950s

When Reiss published his article treating delinquency as a
failure of personal and social controls at the beginning of the
1950s, the social disorganization themes of the Chicago School as
developed in the Roaring 20s were still in fashion, having been
reinforced by the experiences of the Great Depression, the coming
of World War II, and the rapid social change following the war. But
almost as if Americans were collectively exhausted by these upheavals and were determined to have peace and quiet, the 1950s
became a time of relative social conformity, at least on the surface.
Such television shows as "Lassie" or "Leave It to Beaver" are
almost caricatures of the era, with the (stereotypical) middle-class
American father coming home from the office to greet the happy
if slightly mischievous (stereotypical) children at their lemonade
stand before inquiring of his (stereotypical) wife (clad in her stereotypical housedress and apron), "What's for dinner, Honey?"
Conformity, conventionality, and complacency were the order of
the day.

Given this pervasive atmosphere, approaches such as Nye's
theory tracing delinquency to departures from the model of the
ideal family with all its conventional controls over the young
seemed almost like common sense. Social critics were more
alarmed by the atmosphere of stifling overconformity than by
concern over general social disorganization. By the close of the
1950s and even into the early 1960s, Americans were being criticized as a "nation of sheep" (Lederer, 1961), where the mother was
trapped at home in a set of stereotypes about women amounting
to a "feminine mystique" (Friedan, 1963) and the father went off
to work only to submit meekly as an "organization man" (Whyte,
1957). Despite the fascination with the apparent wildness of the
big-city gangs, the young in general were being criticized as a mass
of pop-culture conformists, and traditionally unruly college students were being castigated as so lacking in any willingness to
question things as to constitute a "Silent Generation" (Starr,

1985:238). Throughout the 1950s society as a whole seemed to be sleeping through the "American Dream."

Of course, not everyone was satisfied. As indicated in Chapter 3, there was concern in some quarters about continuing social inequality and differential opportunity, as evidenced by the renewal of interest in Merton's anomie theory. The general public was fascinated with and strangely alarmed by the apparently senseless behavior of highly publicized adolescent male, working class gangs in the large cities, exotic groups which in some strange way failed to fit into the "Dream." Cohen's delinquent subculture theory represented an effort to explain some of this, although Sykes and Matza maintained that delinquents were not as different as they might appear. By and large, opportunity theory fit the 1950s, stressing as it did the importance of everyone having access to full participation in the American Way of Life.

The tendency to stress the "strain theory" aspect of Merton's approach tells us a great deal about the preoccupations of the time. Although he himself used Durkheim's term and described the way in which the amorality coming with intense emphasis on economic success weakened social control through a de-emphasis on traditional normative standards of right and wrong, it was the idea of a discontinuity between success goals and the institutionalized means for their achievement that captured most of the attention. Many paid little attention to the powerful Durkheimian theme of moral erosion in their excitement over the theme which traced much of the nonconformity that did exist to a lack of access to legitimate opportunities to achieve those conventional economic aspirations so central to the "Dream."

Although the potentials for social change were seething under the surface of all this apparent tranquillity and were already beginning to be felt here and there, this general atmosphere still prevailed in large part when Reckless first set forth his containment theory at the beginning of the 1960s. The formulation had somewhat less impact than might have been expected from a major theoretical statement by one of the nation's leading criminologists. In some ways his containment theory seemed to reflect more of the social climate of the post-World War I years of the 1920s, when Reckless was a graduate student at the University of Chicago and concerns over "social disorganization" filled the air, than of the complacent 1950s. But the onslaught of the 1960s was to make control theory much more popular.

The Context of the 1960s. The massive social changes which took place in America of the 1960s, including the rising tide of protest over discrimination, the development of a youth counter-culture, and the reaction to the war in Vietnam, not only shook American society but also had a considerable impact on criminological theory. Although Martin Luther King's Southern Christian Leadership Conference (SCLC) had begun its work in the middle 1950s, the civil rights movement had not exploded into public consciousness until its rapid acceleration with the dramatic lunch counter sit-in by black students in Greensboro, North Carolina in 1960 (Zinn, 1964; Starr, 1985). The coming of the civil rights movement shattered much of the complacency of the 1950s, and its reliance on a nonviolent strategy of "civil disobedience" entailing the deliberate violation of segregation laws represented a direct repudiation of conventional social control in the name of a higher morality. But this was only the beginning.

The so-called "Beats," representing part of the avant garde literary world of the 1950s, had made a special point of defying conventionality by flaunting drug use, and the latter part of the decade had seen the birth of a strange new brand of rebellious music called "rock and roll." Even so, neither of these had shaken the Establishment. But between 1960 and 1966, the number of American students enrolling in college more than doubled, topping 7.3 million (Starr, 1985). Early in the 1960s, widely publicized student protests at such respectable and prestigious institutions as the University of California at Berkeley attacked the impersonality and complacency of the bureaucracies of higher education and demanded a place for individuality and greater freedom of expression. This developing counterculture tended to reject many of the conventional aspects of the "American Dream," including the characteristic overconformity, the model of the middle-class family, and the ruthless pursuit of material success. The search for an "authentic self" became a priority; "The perception of the banality of existence became the core of the youth revolt of the 1960s" (Aronowitz, 1973:331).

Changes such as these, as well as dramatic events such as the assassination of President Kennedy in 1963 and growing uneasiness over the slow escalation of military involvement in Southeast Asia, meant that Matza's theory positing "drift" associated

Civil rights, counterculture etc

with a decline in moral consensus and a combination of preparation and desperation could find a more receptive audience. And as the decade moved on, the continuing drama of the civil rights movement, the coming of militant feminism, the Vietnam protests, the appearance of the "hippies," the advocacy of psychedelic drug use on the part of respected Harvard professors, and a host of other dramatic social and cultural shifts seemed to many to signal the complete collapse of personal and social control.

By the middle of the 1960s the civil rights movement had taken on a different and more "radical" tone. The movement for black separatism, demanding that several states be set apart for blacks within the United States, had gained considerable strength. The "Black Muslim" movement had led many American blacks to reject Christianity as a "white man's religion," to change their names, and to embrace a variation of the Islamic faith. For many American blacks, much of the machinery of personal and social control seemed to be designed to ensure their continued social and emotional bondage.

As the escalation of American involvement in Vietnam accelerated under President Johnson, protests became more frequent and more violent. News media increasingly referred to the nation as being "torn apart" by the war. Social consensus appeared to have evaporated. The 1950s began to seem like an era in another and very different society.

As for the feminist movement of the 1960s, it represented in large part an attack on the revered institution of the conventional family as a deceptive front for the political, economic, and sexual oppression of women. The counterculture of "hippies" and others — which grew up among the new breed of college students and spread to include both students and nonstudents, youths and adults — seemed to mock the staid "buttoned-down" mentality of the 1950s as many "clean-cut," middle-class young men took to beards, sandals, beads, and shoulder-length hair, and previously demure young ladies adopted similar attire, minus the beards. Drugs, especially marijuana, seemed to be everywhere among them, and they were most united in their rejection of the middle-class preachments regarding conventional family life and dedication to the economic "rat race."

Hirschi's Control Theory

To many observers, the 1960s seemed to be characterized by loss of "self control" on the part of the individual and of "social control" on the part of organized religion, the family, educational institutions, the economic order and the political state. It sometimes appeared that everything was being called into question and that all the conventional institutions were crumbling. When at the close of the decade Travis Hirschi, himself working at Berkeley, set forth his own highly refined version of control theory, the times *were* ripe for acceptance of such a perspective if it could be formulated in appropriate theoretical terms.

Hirschi's Forerunners. Hirschi's theoretical position was expressed with special clarity through a critique of alternative perspectives, an exploration of the differences between his own formulation and those of his predecessors in the development of control theory, and an examination of his position in the light of empirical data. A review of his approach will provide not only a clear example of the way in which criminological theories reflect contexts of time and place, but also of the manner in which they are shaped by special considerations aside from the orientations of the particular theorists. Hirschi himself has shown an appreciation of this and unusual candor in admitting just how certain considerations affected the way in which he set forth his position. These included (1) the nature of the data available to him, and (2) the current unpopularity of one specific tradition through which he might have expressed his ideas — the social disorganization theme of the Chicago School.

Hirschi (Bartollas, 1985:190) has pointed out the significance of the *data factor* in a recent interview:

> Control theory as I stated it cannot really be understood unless one takes into account the fact that I was attached to a particular method of research. When I was working on the theory, I knew that my data were going to be survey data; therefore I knew that I was going to have mainly the perceptions, attitudes, and values of individuals as reported by them . . . Had I data on other people, or on the structure of the community, I would have had to state the theory *in a quite different way.* (emphasis added)

The problem with the *social disorganization* theme was that it had lost a great deal of its popularity as an explanation of social problems in general and crime in particular (Rubington and Weinberg, 1971). Like the older concept of "social pathology," it had come under intense criticism as a matter of vague generalities masking a lack of value-neutrality. As criminologist Marshall Clinard (1957:41) commented:

> There are a number of objections to this frame of reference. (1) Disorganization is too subjective and vague a concept for analyzing a general society . . . (2) Social disorganization implies the disruption of a previously existing condition of organization, a situation which generally cannot be established . . . (3) Social disorganization is usually thought of as something "bad," and what is "bad" is often the value-judgment of the observer and the members of his social class or other social groups . . . (4) The existence of forms of deviant behavior does not necessarily constitute a major threat to the central values of a society . . . (5) What seems like disorganization actually may often be highly organized systems of competing norms . . . (6) Finally, as several sociologists have suggested, it is possible that a variety of subcultures may contribute, through their diversity, to the unity or integration of a society rather weakening it by constituting a situation of social disorganization.

These and other criticisms of the concept of social disorganization were widely accepted in the 1960s, and Hirschi (Bartollas, 1985:190) has been equally candid in describing how he deliberately *avoided* linking his theory to the social disorganization tradition because of its unpopularity at the time:

> For example, I was aware at the time I wrote my theory that it was well within the social disorganization tradition. I knew that, but you have to remember the status of social disorganization as a concept in the middle 1960s when I was writing. I felt I was swimming against the current in stating a social control theory at the individual level. Had I tried to sell social disorganization at the same time, I would have been in deep trouble. So I shied away from that tradition. As a result, I did not give social disorganization its due. I went back to Durkheim and Hobbes and ignored an entire American tradition that was directly relevant to what I was saying. But I was aware of it and took comfort in it. I said the same things the social disorganization people had said, but since they had fallen into

disfavor I had to dissociate myself from them. Further, as Ruth Kornhauser so acutely points out, social disorganization theories had been associated with the cultural tradition. That was the tradition I was working hardest against; so in that sense, I have compromised my own position or I would have introduced a lot of debate I didn't want to get into had I dealt explicitly with social disorganization theory. Now, with people like Kornhauser on my side, and social disorganization back in vogue, I would emphasize my roots in this illustrious tradition.

So Hirschi was especially careful to avoid working explicitly out of the social disorganization tradition and to ground his position instead in the thought of other forerunners such as Durkheim and Hobbes. Concentrating upon a search for the essential variables providing control through *bonds to conventional society,* he developed his own position and presented a body of systematic research in support of it. This combination seemed to represent the epitome of tightly reasoned and empirically grounded control theory.

Hirschi's Sociological Perspective. The control theorists examined to this point tended to distinguish between control exerted from sources external to the individual and control exerted from within the individual. Indeed, Reckless had argued that the individual is so isolated in contemporary society, so free to move from one context of external control to another or even to escape from most of it, that internal control is the more basic factor in conformity. Hirschi's position was much more sociological in nature. The characteristics which other control theorists took to be aspects of the personality, he considered to be factors sustained by ongoing social relationships, which he termed *social bonds.*

Other control theorists gave great weight to the notion of *internalization*, the process by which social norms are taken so deeply into the self as to become a fundamental part of the personality structure. Citing Wrong's (1961) critique of this "oversocialized conception of man," Hirschi (1969:4) insisted instead that what seems to be deeply rooted internalization of social expectations is actually much too superficial to guarantee conformity. First, he rescued Durkheim from the "strain theorists." Pointing out that "because Merton traces his intellectual history to Durkheim, strain theories are often called 'anomie' the-

ories . . . ." he showed that "actually, Durkheim's theory is one of
the purest examples of control theory" (Hirschi, 1969:3). Next he
turned to the question posed by Hobbes, "Why do men obey the
rules of society?", observing that an assumption of internalization
was commonly used as a means of avoiding Hobbes's own conclusion, that conformity was based essentially on *fear*. Here there was
an echo of Reiss's distinction between conformity resulting from
acceptance of the rules and conformity based upon mere *submission*.

This willingness to acknowledge that conformity might be
based upon simple submission to the forces of social regulation
without internalized acceptance of the norms became fairly clear
in Hirschi's first citation of Durkheim as a control theorist. He
remarked that "both anomie and egoism are conditions of 'deregulation,' and the 'aberrant' behavior that follows is an automatic
consequence of such deregulation," without noting Durkheim's
complementary stress on *integration* as a factor in conformity
(Hirschi, 1969:3). Turning immediately to Hobbes, he put the matter with stark clarity as follows:

> Although the Hobbesian question is granted a central place in the
> history of sociological theory, few have accepted the Hobbesian
> answer . . . It is not so, the sociologist argued: There is more to
> conformity than fear. Man has an "attitude of respect" toward the
> rules of society; he "internalizes the norms." Since man has a
> conscience, he is not free simply to calculate the costs of illegal or
> deviant behavior. . .
>
> Having thus established that man is a moral animal who desires to
> obey the rules, the sociologist was then faced with the problem of
> explaining his deviance. (Hirschi, 1969:5)

For Hirschi, then, the problem of explaining deviance was a
false problem based on the mistaken assumption that people are
fundamentally moral as a result of having internalized norms
during socialization. He insisted, however, that it was an "over-
simplification" to say that "strain theory assumes a moral man
while control theory assumes an amoral man," because the latter
"merely assumes variation in morality: For some men, considerations of morality are important, for others they are not" (Hirschi,
1969:11). Unlike Matza, who felt it necessary to suggest forces of

preparation and desperation as a way of explaining why the mere loss of control might result in delinquency, Hirschi suggested no motivational factors and simply noted that loss of control sets the individual free to calculate the costs of crime. "Because his perspective allows him to free some men from moral sensitivities, the control theorist is likely to shift to a second line of social control — to the rational, calculational component in conformity and deviation" (Hirschi, 1969:11).

Social Control by Social Bonds. To explain conformity Hirschi stressed four control variables, each of which represented a major "social bond": *attachment, commitment, involvement,* and *belief.* These terms have been the source of some confusion, primarily because Hirschi employed them in a sociological sense rather than in the primarily psychological sense which had become commonplace in the age of the "individual" preoccupied with allegedly "internal states." He resisted the assumption that traced so much of human behavior to alleged internalization of attitudes and norms on the part of individuals.

By "attachment," for example, Hirschi did not mean the strength of an internal, emotional bond so subjective that it might grow even stronger in the absence of interaction, such as in the old adage, "Absence makes the heart grow fonder" (e.g., more "attached" to the distant other), but the very opposite. By "commitment" he did not mean some deep, internal dedication of self to others even to the extent of self-sacrifice, as when people speak of a loving mother being "committed" to her child or of two adults making a "genuine commitment" to one another, but the very opposite. By "involvement" he meant something quite different from the psychological notion of emotional entanglements, of being "bound up in one another" or emotionally "part of each other." And, finally, by "belief" he did not mean profound inner faith or even deep belief in someone or something, but a bond much less internalized. Perhaps human relationships had become more superficial, or perhaps individuals had never really internalized as deeply as had been assumed by some theorists.

Importance of the Family and School. Hirschi felt that the two conventional systems through which the adolescent could be expected to form the key bonds with society were the family and the school. "Attachment" was used to signify *continuing intimacy of interaction* as evidenced by the extent to which parents or teachers exerted supervision, the intimacy of communication with them, the extent to which the adolescent felt competent in and performed well in school settings, and the degree of concern felt for the opinions of parents and teachers. "Attachment" used in this sense is close, for example, to Sutherland's concept of differential association, except that it stresses the idea that the very bond formed by the attachment is more important than the specific content of the learning that may result. For Hirschi (1969:19) such an approach had the advantage of avoiding "the problem of explaining changes over time by locating the 'conscience' in the bond to others rather than making it part of the personality." The bond was considered to lie in the sociological nature of the ongoing association with conventional groups rather than in some subjective, psychological attachment independent of this ongoing association.

"Commitment" was defined not in terms of a surrender of self-interest but, on the contrary, as *the degree to which the individual's self-interest has been invested* in a given set of activities. For Hirschi (1969:20) this was the "rational component of conformity," essentially a matter of the rational calculation of potential gains and losses, so that the individual contemplating a deviant act "must consider the costs of this deviant behavior, the risk he runs of losing the investment he has made in conventional behavior." In this sense a youth who has invested much time and energy in conforming to the expectations of parents and teachers, working hard and perhaps graduating with honors, has a tighter bond with society because he or she has a powerful "stake in conformity" and much to lose by getting out of line. Of course, "in order for such a built-in system of regulation to be effective, actors in the system must perceive the connections between deviation and reward and must value the rewards society proposes to withhold as punishment for deviation" (Hirschi, 1969:162). Thus Hirschi (1969:162) went on to point out that "the stance taken toward aspirations here is virtually opposite to that taken in strain theories," because in control theory "such aspirations are viewed as constraints on delinquency." Where strain theory tended to see high aspirations as leading to frustration and consequent deviance, Hirschi, like Reckless, maintained that the opposite was true: legitimate aspirations gave a "stake in conformity" which tied one to the conventional social order, at least when the individual had invested in the pursuit of such goals instead of merely wishing for them.

As for "involvement" as a factor in social control, Hirschi (1969:21) stressed not the psychological theme of emotional entanglement but the sociological observation that "Many persons undoubtedly owe a life of virtue to a lack of opportunity to do otherwise." Acknowledging that the old thesis "Idle hands are the devil's workshop" and the common sense suggestion that delinquency could be prevented by keeping the young people busy and off the streets had so far found little support in research, he went on to examine the possibility that involvement defined in terms of sheer amount of time and energy devoted to a given set of activities might represent a key factor in social control. Aside from such findings as those relating time spent on homework to extent of delinquency, however, Hirschi's data failed to lend much support to the hypothesis that involvement, as he conceptualized it, represented a variable crucial to preventing wayward behavior.

Finally, Hirschi's use of the term "belief" was also much more sociological than psychological. He did not use the term to indicate deeply held convictions but to suggest *approbation* in the sense of *assent* to certain values and norms with some degree of approval. Used in this way, beliefs are not seen as profoundly internalized personal creeds but as impressions and opinions which are highly dependent upon constant social reinforcement. If the degree of approbation is slight, the "belief" becomes a matter of simple assent, of a willingness to submit and "go along," at least for the present. If the degree of approbation is greater, it may amount to a "belief" to which the individual gives eager approval and wholehearted cooperation. The point is that such beliefs were not taken to be "inner states" independent of circumstances but somewhat precarious moral positions much in need of social support based on the ongoing attachment to conventional social systems described above.

Hirschi (1969:24) was careful to point out that he was not accepting that approach to control theory in which "beliefs are treated as mere words that mean little or nothing if the other forms of control are missing." He was equally careful to reject the other extreme represented by Sykes and Matza's (1957) insistence that delinquents "believe" in the conventional morality to the extent that "techniques of neutralization" become necessary before violations can occur. He took the position that (1) individuals differ considerably in the depth and power of their "belief" and that (2) this variation is dependent upon the degree of attachment to systems representing the beliefs in question. As he put it, "The chain of causation is thus from attachment to parents, through concern for the approval of persons in positions of authority, to belief that the rules of society are binding on one's conduct" (Hirschi, 1969:200). In this view, it is not that people lack consciences, that they are in truth totally amoral beings who simply babble on about how much they think they "believe in" things. It is rather that "attachment to a system and belief in the moral validity of its rules are not independent"; what is called "belief" depends upon the strength of attachment and will decline with it (Hirschi, 1969:200).

> attachment ——> concern for approval ——> belief

CONCLUSION

With the exception of Reckless's containment theory, which was proposed to explain most forms of nonconformity (excluding that resulting from such factors as pathological brain damage on the one side or membership in a criminal tribe on the other), the other control theories examined above were developed specifically to explain juvenile delinquency. Thus it is hardly surprising that they tended to locate control influences primarily in the family and secondarily in the school. Nor is it surprising that Reckless tended to put much greater emphasis on "inner" or psychological factors such as self-concept and frustration tolerance, factors which might be more important in raising the odds of conformity on the part of an adult out of school and away from parental controls.

Similarities and Dissimilarities. There are certain similarities among these theories in addition to the fact that they all take the control perspective. Reckless's stress on *goal orientation* sounds very much like Hirschi's emphasis on *commitment.* Both consider legitimate aspirations to be a crucial factor in insulating a potential deviant from nonconformity. Reckless's concept of *norm erosion* as the obverse of *norm retention* is closely related to Sykes and Matza's concept of *techniques of neutralization* in such a way that the latter easily can be subsumed as one aspect of the former (Ball, 1966). Reiss's distinction between conformity as a consequence of *acceptance* and conformity as a consequence of *submission* is quite similar to Nye's distinction between *internalized control* and *di-*

rect control. All these theories bear the Durkheimian stamp and the mark of the Chicago School, but they vary somewhat in their interpretation of the forces of integration and regulation and in their attachment to an implicit or explicit social disorganization perspective.

Policy Implications. Unlike the Chicago School work which focused on delinquent neighborhoods, differential opportunity theory, or "labeling theory" to be examined in Chapter 5, control theory led to no new and startling policy implications. Instead, it tended to reinforce the sorts of prevention and intervention policies which had been around for decades and which had become a matter of "common sense" (Empey, 1982:268). Control theory itself seems to some to be the height of conventionality, but this is not entirely true. By stressing that personal control comes through social control, it located the burden of control in the social system rather than the individual. It emphasized prevention through the strengthening of conventional systems rather than through a policy of deterrence relying primarily on fear of getting caught. And it insisted that regulation of the individual must come through integration into the social order rather than through social isolation or punishment.

The control theories we examined may have less to say about the prevention and control of ordinary adult crime, professional crime, organized crime, or white-collar crime than about juvenile delinquency, but they do provide reinforcement for certain policies of delinquency prevention and control. With respect to prevention, they suggest programs to strengthen families, educational programs which facilitate maximum involvement in school activities and identification with the school, and the strengthening of conventional belief systems in such a way as to reduce the possibility of norm neutralization. With respect to reintegration, they suggest reestablishment of ties with conventional families and the strengthening of these families, involvement of youth in school activities, and some means of demonstrating the payoff of hard work toward conventional goals so as to draw the adolescent into a position of personal commitment where there is too much of a stake in conformity to lose by a return to delinquency.

Control theories are most impressive when applied to middle-class youth or to working-class youth from "good families." In control theory, the systems which are to accomplish the *regulation* of the individuals at risk for delinquency through their *integration* are systems defined in conventional, middle-class terms. But what if these systems themselves, or at least some of them, are problematic? Is the answer to delinquency simply to find ways to integrate youth more completely into them and to add to their power of regulation? As we will see in Chapters 5 and 6, some criminological theorists have argued that the major problems actually lie with the conventional systems themselves rather that with youths. The "labeling theorists" insist that the conventional systems tend to aggravate crime and delinquency by over-reacting to nonconformity, while the "conflict theorists" maintain that these systems are instruments of oppression.

Finally, even if one is convinced that conventional institutions such as the middle-class family model and the school do not create major problems through a tendency to label those who do not fit in well and that they are not instruments of social oppression, it does not follow that successful performance of their integration and regulation functions will solve crime or delinquency problems. Speaking of impoverished blacks, for example, Empey (1982:299) remarks that "it is not merely that underclass children are sometimes in conflict with their parents, or that their academic achievement is low, but that they are caught in an economic and political system in which they are superfluous." It is possible that (a) control theory offers no basic solutions at all or that (b) it offers certain solutions, but essentially within the confines of the present political and economic systems with all their flaws. If somehow the empirical data eventually proved the former possibility to be in fact the case, perhaps all criminologists would reject control theory. If the latter possibility were somehow proved to be the case, some would continue to criticize it vigorously as an incomplete explanation of crime.

5

The Irony of State Intervention: Labeling Theory

When people violate the law, we assume that the state's most prudent response is to make every effort to apprehend the culprits and to process them through the criminal justice system. Informing this assumption is the belief that state intervention reduces crime, whether by scaring offenders straight, by rehabilitating them, or by incapacitating them so they are no longer free to roam the streets victimizing citizens. Scholars embracing the labeling theory of crime, however, attack vigorously this line of reasoning. Rather than diminishing criminal involvement, they caution, state intervention — labeling and reacting to offenders as "criminals" and "ex-felons" — can have the unanticipated and ironic consequence of deepening the very behavior it was meant to halt.

Thus labeling theorists argue that the criminal justice system not only is limited in its capacity to restrain unlawful conduct, but also is a major factor in anchoring people in a criminal career. Pulling people into the system makes matters worse not better. This contention takes on importance when we consider the width of the net cast by criminal justice officials. On any given day, more than one American in every hundred is under some form of state control. The statistical count breaks down in this way: over 600,000 people in state and federal prisons; 300,000 in local jails; and 2 million offenders on either probation or parole supervision.

In this chapter, we examine why labeling theorists believe that state intervention is dangerously criminogenic, particularly in light of the faith current policymakers have in the power of prisons to solve the crime problem. We also consider why, in the 1960s and early 1970s, labeling theory — or, as it is also known, the "societal reaction" approach — grew rapidly in popularity and influenced markedly criminal justice policy. First, however, we will discuss how scholars in this school of thought rooted their work in a revisionist view of what crime is and of how its very nature is tied inextricably to the nature of societal reaction.

THE SOCIAL CONSTRUCTION OF CRIME

Before the advent of labeling theory, most criminologists were content to define crime as "behavior that violates criminal laws." This definition was useful in guiding inquiry and in setting rough boundaries for criminology as a field of study. Too often, however, the easy acceptance of this definition led criminologists to take for granted that they "knew" what crime was and could get on with the business of finding its causes either in offenders or in their environments. This reification of conceptual definitions blinded many scholars from seeing that as a socially constructed phenomenon, what is, or is not, "criminal" changes over time, across societies, and even from one situation to the next. Without this insight, scholars failed to explore the social circumstances that determine which behaviors are made criminal, why some people have the label of criminal applied to them, and what consequences exist for those bearing a criminal label.

Labeling theorists sought to correct this oversight. As a starting point, they urged criminologists to surrender the idea that behaviors are somehow inherently criminal or deviant. To be sure, behaviors — such as killing or raping another human being — are injurious by nature. Even so, what makes an act "criminal" is not the harm it incurs, but whether this label is conferred upon the act by the state. Thus it is the nature of the societal reaction and the reality it constructs, not the immutable nature of the act per se, which determines if a "crime" exists (Becker, 1963:9; Erickson, 1966:6). Stephen Pfohl's (1985:284) discussion of whether killing is "naturally deviant" illustrates nicely the essence of this position:

> Homicide is a way of categorizing the act of killing, such that taking another's life is viewed as totally reprehensible and devoid of any redeeming social justification. Some types of killing are categorized

as homicide. Others are not. What differs is not the behavior but the manner in which reactions to that behavior are socially organized. The behavior is essentially the same: killing a police officer or killing by a police officer; stabbing an old lady in the back or stabbing the unsuspecting wartime enemy; a black slave shooting a white master or a white master lynching a black slave; being run over by a drunken driver or slowly dying a painful cancer death caused by a polluting factory. Each is a type of killing. Some are labeled homicide. Others are excused, justified, or viewed, as in the case of dangerous industrial pollution, as environmental risks, necessary for the health of our economy, if not our bodies. The form and content of what is seen as homicide thus varies with social context and circumstance. This is hardly the characteristic of something which can be considered naturally or universally deviant.

Armed with this vision of crime as socially constructed, labeling theorists argued that criminologists could ill-afford to neglect the nature and effects of societal reaction, particularly when the state was the labeling agent. One important area they investigated was the origins of criminal labels or categories. Howard Becker (1963), for example, explored how the commissioner of the Treasury Department's Federal Bureau of Narcotics served as a "moral entrepreneur" who led a campaign to outlaw marijuana through the Marijuana Tax Act of 1937. In Becker's view, this campaign, marked by attempts to arouse the public by claims that smoking pot caused youths to lose control and commit senseless crimes, was undertaken to advance the Bureau's organizational interests. The Bureau's success in securing passage of the act, Becker (1963:145) concluded, resulted in "the creation of a new fragment of the moral constitution of society, its code of right and wrong" (see Galliher and Walker, 1977).

Numerous other scholars provided explanations of attempts to criminalize other forms of behavior. Thus Anthony Platt (1969) studied how, at the turn of the century, affluent women "invented delinquency" through their successful campaign to create a court exclusively for juveniles. With the establishment of this court, juveniles were treated as a separate class of offenders, and the state was granted the power to intervene not only when youths committed criminal acts but also when they showed signs of a profligate life-style — acts such as truancy or promiscuity, which became known as "status offenses." This movement, Platt ob-

"child savers"

served, was class-biased because it was directed primarily at "saving" lower-class youths, reaffirmed middle-class values, and left unaddressed the structural roots of poverty.

In a like vein, Stephen Pfohl (1977) investigated the "discovery of child-abuse," which prior to the 1960s had largely escaped criminal sanctioning. Pfohl showed how pediatric radiologists, who read x-rays in hospitals, were instrumental in bringing attention to the abuse of children. Their efforts, he claimed, were fueled by the incentive to demonstrate the importance of pediatric radiology and thereby to enhance the low prestige of this specialty in the medical community.

And Kathleen Tierney (1982) focused on the "creation of the wife beating problem." She revealed how wife battering did not emerge as a salient social issue deserving of criminal justice intervention until the mid-1970s, when feminist organizations and networks were sufficiently developed to make domestic violence socially visible, establish victim shelters, and earn the passage of new laws. Also critical to the battered women's movement was the media, which dramatized "wife beating" because "it mixed elements of violence and social relevance . . . [and] provided a focal point for serious media discussion of such issues as feminism, inequality, and family life in the United States — without requiring a sacrifice of the entertainment value, action, and urgency on which the media typically depend" (Tierney, 1982:213-214).

These and similar analyses showed, therefore, that what the state designated as criminal was not a constant, but the result of concrete efforts by men and women to construct a different reality, to transform how a particular kind of behavior was officially defined. Moreover, it was not simply the extent or harmfulness of the behavior that determined its criminalization; after all, drug use, juvenile waywardness, child abuse, and wife battering had long escaped state criminal intervention despite their pervasiveness and injurious effects. These behaviors were criminalized only when the social context was ripe for change and groups existed that were sufficiently motivated and powerful to bring about legal reform.

But what occurs once a form of behavior is defined as unlawful and a criminal label is created? To whom will this label be applied? The common answer to this question is that those who engage in the proscribed activity will be labeled as criminals. Labeling theorists, however, were again quick to point out that such thinking implicitly assumes that societal reaction can be taken for granted and treated as nonproblematic. It ignores not only that the innocent are occasionally falsely accused, but also that only some rule-breakers are actually arrested and processed through the criminal justice system (see Becker, 1963:20). A lawbreaker's behavior, therefore, is only one factor — and perhaps not the most important factor at that — in determining whether a criminal label is conferred.

A number of labeling theory studies illustrate this principle. In one experimental study conducted in Los Angeles, a racially-mixed college student sample, all of whom had perfect driving records in the past year, had "Black Panther" bumper stickers affixed to their car bumpers. Within hours of the experiment's start, they began to accumulate numerous tickets for traffic violations (e.g., for improper lane change), thus suggesting that police officers were "labeling" differentially on the basis of the bumper stickers (Hussanstamm, 1975). Other researchers, interested in police encounters with juveniles, observed that officers' decisions to arrest wayward youths were based less on what law was violated and more on the juveniles' "demeanor" — whether they were respectful and cooperative or surly and uncooperative (Piliavin and Briar, 1964).

And still another researcher, William Chambliss, examined one community's societal reaction to two groups of high school boys: a middle-class group he called "the Saints," and a working-class group known as the "Roughnecks." Although the two groups had a rate of delinquency that was "about equal," the "community, the school and the police react[ed] to the Saints as though they were good, upstanding, nondelinquent youths with bright futures but to the Roughnecks as though they were tough, young criminals who were headed for trouble" (Chambliss, 1984:126, 131). Why did this occur? In Chambliss's view, a major reason was the community's lower-class bias, which led police to define as "pranks" the Saints' behavior and to anticipate that the poorly dressed and poorly mannered Roughnecks were up to no good.

Through these and similar studies, labeling theorists revealed that the nature of state criminal intervention was not simply a matter of an objective response to illegal behavior but shaped intimately by a range of extra-legal contingencies (Cullen and

Cullen, 1978:15-19). Much attention was focused on how criminal justice decision-making was influenced by individual characteristics, such as race, class, and gender. In addition, however, researchers explored how rates of labeling vary according to the resources available to and political demands placed on police and other criminal justice organizations. This body of research also highlighted how "official" measures of the extent of crime — such as arrest statistics reported each year by the FBI — depend not only on how many offenses are committed but also on the arrest practices of police. Accordingly, official crime statistics may be inaccurate to the extent that they reflect a systematic bias in enforcement against certain groups (e.g., the urban poor) or fluctuations in the willingness of police to enforce certain laws (e.g., rape laws).

In sum, labeling theorists elucidated the importance of considering the origins of criminal labels and the circumstances that affected their application. But they did not confine their attention to these concerns. They proceeded to put forward the more controversial proposition that labeling and reacting to people as "criminals" comprised the major source of chronic involvement in illegal activity. State intervention, they claimed, created, rather than halted, crime. We consider this line of reasoning next.

LABELING AS CRIMINOGENIC:
CREATING CAREER CRIMINALS

Where should the search for the cause of crime begin? As we have seen, scholars have traditionally argued that the starting point for criminological inquiry should be either individual offenders themselves or the social environments in which they reside. Labeling theorists, however, argued that causal analysis should not commence with offenders and their environs but with the societal reaction that other people — including state officials — make to offenders. Again, their contention was based on the belief that labeling and treating lawbreakers as criminal have the unanticipated consequence of creating the very behavior they were meant to prevent.

Early Statements of Labeling Theory

The idea that criminal justice intervention can deepen criminality did not originate with the labeling theorists of the 1960s. A number of early criminologists, for example, noted that prisons — a severe form of societal reaction — were breeding grounds for crime. Jeremy Bentham, the classical school theorist, lamented that "an ordinary prison is a school in which wickedness is taught by surer means than can ever be employed for the inculcation of virtue. Weariness, revenge, and want preside over these academies of crime" (quoted in Hawkins, 1976:57). In 1911, Lombroso echoed this theme in his observation that "the degrading influences of prison life and contact with vulgar criminals . . . cause criminaloids who have committed their initial offenses with repugnance and hesitation, to develop later into habitual criminals" (Lombroso-Fererro, 1972:110-111). Willem Bonger (1969:118 [1916]), the Dutch Marxist scholar, noted similarly that in imprisoning "young people who have committed merely misdemeanors of minor importance . . . we are bringing up professional criminals." And Clifford Shaw (1930) felt compelled to title the chapter in the *Jack-Roller* on correctional institutions, "The House of Corruption."

While observations such as these anticipated the more developed views of later labeling theorists, Frank Tannenbaum (1938) was perhaps the earliest scholar to state in general terms the principle that state intervention is criminogenic because it "dramatizes evil." "Only some of the children [who break the law] are caught," he noted, "though all may be equally guilty." And this event is not without consequence. The youth is "singled out for specialized treatment" as the "arrest suddenly precipitates a series of institutions, attitudes, and experiences which other children do not share." Now the youth's world is changed fundamentally; people react differently and the youth starts to reconsider his or her identity. "He is made conscious of himself as a different human being than he was before his arrest," observed Tannenbaum. "He becomes classified as a thief, perhaps, and the entire world about him has suddenly become a different place for him and will remain different for the rest of his life" (1938:19). This is particularly true if the youth is placed in prison, for here incipient, "uncrystallized" criminal attitudes are "hardened" through the "education" older offenders provide (1938:66-81).

In the end, Tannenbaum cautioned, we would do well to weigh carefully taking the initial step of pulling a juvenile into the criminal justice system:

> The first dramatization of "evil" which separates the child out of his group for specialized treatment plays a greater role in making the criminal than perhaps any other experience. . . . He has been tagged. A new and hitherto nonexistent environment has been precipitated out of him. The process of making the criminal, therefore, is a process of tagging, defining, identifying, segregating, describing, emphasizing, making conscious and self-conscious; it becomes a way of stimulating, suggesting, emphasizing, and evoking the very traits that are complained of. . . . The person becomes the thing he is described as being. (1938:19-20)

In 1951, Edwin Lemert formalized further these insights when he distinguished two types of deviance: primary and secondary. "Primary deviance," he contended, arises from a variety of sociocultural and psychological sources. At this initial point, however, offenders often try to rationalize their behavior as a temporary aberration or see it as part of a socially acceptable role. They do not conceive of themselves as deviant or organize their life around this identity (1951:75).

In contrast, "secondary deviance" is precipitated by the responses of others to the initial proscribed conduct. As societal reaction intensifies progressively with each act of primary deviance, the offender becomes stigmatized through "name calling, labeling, or stereotyping" (1951:76-77). The original sources of waywardness lose their salience as others' reactions emerge as the overriding concern in the person's life and demand to be addressed. Most often, offenders solve this problem by accepting their "deviant status" and by organizing their "life and identity . . . around the facts of deviance." Accordingly, they become more, rather than less, embedded in nonconformity. As Lemert (1972:48) explained:

> Primary deviance is assumed to arise in a wide variety of social, cultural, and psychological contexts, and at best has only marginal implications for the psychic structure of the individual; it does not lead to symbolic reorganization at the level of self-regarding attitudes and social roles. Secondary deviation is deviant behavior, or

social roles based upon it, which becomes means of defense, attack, or adaptation to overt and covert problems created by the societal reaction to primary deviation. In effect, the original "causes" of the deviation recede and give way to the central importance of the disapproving, degredational, and isolating reactions of society.

Labeling as a Self-Fulfilling Prophecy

Though Tannenbaum and Lemert stated fairly explicitly the theme that societal reaction can induce waywardness, this view of labeling did not win wide intellectual attention and become an identifiable school of thought in the criminological community until the mid-to-late 1960s (Cole, 1975). As will be discussed below, the sudden, pervasive appeal of labeling theory can be traced largely to the social context in the 1960s that made it seem plausible that state intervention was the crime problem's cause and not its solution. Another circumstance, however, was also important in contributing to labeling theory's ascendancy: the existence of a group of scholars — Howard Becker (1963), Kai Erikson (1966), and John Kitsuse (1964) were perhaps the most influential among them — whose combined writings argued convincingly that societal reaction is integral to the creation of crime and deviance.

To show how societal reaction brings about more crime, these labeling theorists borrowed Robert K. Merton's (1968:475-490) concept of the "self-fulfilling prophecy." For Merton (1968:477), "the self-fulfilling prophecy is, in the beginning, a *false* definition of the situation evoking a new behavior which makes the originally false conception come *true*" (emphasis in original).

Consistent with this reasoning, labeling scholars argued that most offenders are falsely defined as "criminal." In making this claim, they did not mean to imply that offenders do not violate the law or that justice system officials have no basis for intervening in people's lives. Instead, the falseness in definition is tied to the fact that criminal labels, once conferred, do not simply provide a social judgment of offenders' behavior but also publicly degrade their moral character (Garfinkel, 1956). That is, being arrested and processed through the justice system means that citizens not only define the offenders' lawbreaking *conduct* as "bad" but also assume that the offenders as *people* are criminal and, as a consequence, are the "kind" that soon again would be in trouble. Yet, as Lemert's (1951) work suggests, such predictions about personal character and future behavior are likely to be incorrect. Much "primary deviance" — including initial experiments in crime and delinquency — is not rooted fundamentally in character or in lifestyle, and thus is likely to be transitory, not stable (see Scheff, 1966).

In short, theorists observed that the meaning of the label "criminal" in our society leads citizens to make assumptions about offenders that are wrong or only partially accurate. These assumptions, moreover, are consequential because they shape how people react to offenders. Equipped with false definitions or "stereotypes" of criminals, citizens treat all offenders as though they were of poor character and likely to recidivate. On one level, these reactions are prudent, if not rational; after all, it seems safer not to chance having one's child associate with the neighborhood's "juvenile delinquent" and not to employ a "convicted thief" to handle one's cash register. Yet, on another level, these reactions have the power to set in motion processes that evoke the very behavior that was anticipated, that transform an offender into the very kind of criminal that was feared.

But how is the prophecy fulfilled? How are incipient criminals, who might well have gone straight if left to their own devices, turned into chronic offenders? Again, the conferring of a criminal label singles a person out for special treatment. The offender becomes, in Becker's (1963:34) words, "one who is different from the rest of us, who cannot or will not act as a moral human being and therefore might break other important rules." As a result, being a "criminal" becomes the person's "master status" or controlling public identification (Becker, 1963:33-34; see also Hughes, 1945). In social encounters, citizens do not consider the offender's social status as a spouse, as a parent, or perhaps as a worker, but instead focus first and foremost on the fact they are interacting with a "criminal."

Admittedly, this public scrutiny might scare or shame some offenders into conformity. But for other offenders, the constant accentuation of their criminal status and the accompanying social rebuke has the unanticipated consequence of undermining the conforming influences in their lives and of pushing them into a criminal career. Thus, in the face of repeated designation as a criminal, offenders are likely to forfeit their self-concept as a conformist or "normal" person, and internalize increasingly their public definition as a deviant. As this identity change takes place, the offender's self-concept loses its power to encourage conformity: The pressure to act consistently with one's self-concept now demands breaking the law.

Similarly, people who are stigmatized as criminal are often cut off from previous prosocial relationships. As their reputation as a reprobate spreads, phone calls are not returned, invitations to social engagements are not extended, friends suddenly no longer can find time to meet, and intimate relationships terminate. One solution to being a social pariah is to bind together with those of a like status. Accordingly, conditions are conducive for offenders wearing a criminal label to differentially associate with other lawbreakers, thus forming criminal subcultural groupings. Such associations are likely to reinforce further antisocial values and to provide a ready supply of partners in crime.

The abrogation of ties to conventional society, labeling theorists warned, is most probable when state intervention involves institutionalization. Imprisonment entails the loss of existing employment and strains family relations to the point that they may not survive. It also mandates that offenders reside in a social setting where contact with other, more hardened criminals is enforced. Education in crime, as Tannenbaum (1938) and other early criminologists noted, is the likely result.

Finally, saddling offenders with an official criminal label — particularly when they have spent time in jail and carry the status of "ex-convict" — limits their employment opportunities. Through their sentences, offenders may "pay back" society for their illegal behavior, but they find it far more difficult to shake their definition as a person of bad character who may fall by the wayside at any time. Employers, therefore, see them as poor risks and hesitate to hire them or to place them in positions of trust. Most often, offenders are relegated to low-paying, dreary jobs with few prospects for advancement. In this context, crime emerges as a more profitable option and a lure that only the irrational choose to resist.

In sum, labeling theorists asserted that the false definition of offenders as permanently criminal and destined for a life of crime fulfills this very prophecy by evoking societal reactions that make conformity difficult and criminality necessary, if not attractive. The labeling process thus is a powerful criminogenic force that stabilizes participation in illegal roles and turns those marginally involved in crime into chronic or career offenders. It is an especially dangerous source of crime, moreover, because its effects are unanticipated and rarely observed. Indeed, the common response to escalating crime rates is not to minimize societal reaction but to arrest and imprison more people. From a labeling perspective, such "get tough" policies will ultimately prove self-defeating, for they will succeed only in subjecting increasing numbers of offenders to a self-fulfilling process that makes probable a life in crime.

Assessing Labeling Theory

Few criminologists would dispute that labeling theory succeeded in bringing attention to the issue of societal reaction or that this distinctive focus won the perspective many adherents. Even so, labeling theory's central propositions have not escaped considerable critical analysis (Gove, 1975, 1980). As we will see, this assessment suggests the need to temper some of the perspective's boldest claims, but also indicates that it would be unwise to discount the insights set forth in the labeling tradition.

One line of criticism came from conflict or radical criminologists. Though they agreed that crime was socially constructed and labels differentially applied, they did not believe that labeling theorists went far enough in their analysis. Radical scholars argued that the origins and application of criminal labels were influenced fundamentally by inequities rooted in the very structure of capitalism. As the next chapter shows in greater detail, the radicals insisted that differences in power determined that the behaviors of the poor, but not those of the rich, would be criminalized. Labeling theorists understood that political interest and social disadvantage influenced societal reaction but, again, they did not make explicit the connection of the criminal justice system to the underlying economic order. As Taylor, Walton, and Young (1973:168-169) observed, they failed "to lay bare the structured inequalities in power and interest which underpin processes whereby laws are created and enforced," and thus they stopped short of exploring "the way in which deviancy and criminality are shaped by society's larger structure of power and institutions."

A very different critique was leveled by criminologists of a traditional positivist bent, who maintained that labeling theory's major tenets wilted when subjected to empirical test. These critics contended — correctly, we believe — that the perspective's popularity had little to do with its empirical adequacy, but rather with its voicing a provocative message that meshed with the social times (Hagan, 1973; Hirschi, 1975:181). After all, in asserting that state intervention deepened criminality, none of the early labeling theorists had presented "hard data" supporting this thesis.

These positivist or empirically-oriented criminologists brought data to bear on what were considered labeling theory's two principal propositions. First, they assessed the premise that "extralegal" factors, such as an offender's race, class, and gender, are more important in regulating criminal justice labeling than "legal" factors, such as the seriousness of the illegality or the offender's past record. Contrary to the expectations of the labeling theorists, research studies found repeatedly that the seriousness of the crime, not the offender's social background, was the largest determinant of labeling by police and court officials (Sampson, 1986:876). Extra-legal variables, the critics concluded, exert only a weak effect on labeling (Gove, 1980:264; Hirschi, 1975:191-195; Tittle, 1975b:163-170).

Recent research by Robert Sampson (1986), however, forces a reconsideration of the critics' sweeping rejection of the idea that official reactions are influenced by a variety of contingencies. In perhaps the most systematic test to date, Sampson (1986) uncovered an "ecological bias" in police control of juveniles. Even when he took into account the seriousness of lawbreaking behavior, police were found to be more likely to make arrests in poor as opposed to more affluent neighborhoods. One possible explanation for this ecological pattern is that police resources are concentrated more heavily in lower-class areas, where it is assumed that anyone encountered is likely to have a character sufficiently disreputable to warrant close surveillance (Sampson, 1986:877). In any case, Sampson has provided convincing evidence of an extra-legal circumstance that causes differential selection into the criminal justice system.

Labeling theory's second major proposition is that state intervention through the justice system causes stable or career crim-

inality. Phrased in these terms, however, the proposition is
difficult to sustain. As critics point out, many offenders become
deeply involved in crime *before* coming to the attention of criminal
justice officials (Mankoff, 1971). Chronic delinquency, for example,
seems far more tied to the criminogenic effects of spending years
growing up in a slum neighborhood than to being arrested and
hauled into juvenile court as a teenager. Similarly, we know that
offenders become extensively involved in such illegalities as corporate crime, political corruption, wife battering, and sexual abuse
without ever being subjected to criminal sanctioning.

Tests of labeling's causal effects have yielded mixed results
(Bazemore, 1985; Klein, 1986; Morash, 1982; Palamara, Cullen,
and Gersten, 1986; Shannon, 1982; Thomas and Bishop, 1984).
One interpretation of this finding is that criminal justice labeling
has "no effects" (Hirschi, 1975:198). If this view is accurate, it
means that state intervention neither deepens criminality as the
labeling theorists have claimed nor deters criminality as advocates of punishment have asserted (Thomas and Bishop, 1984).
Alternatively, it suggests, as traditional criminologists have argued, that the sources of why people experiment with crime, become chronic offenders, or recidivate after incarceration are to be
found not in the operation of the criminal justice system but in the
social forces that impinge upon offenders in their everyday lives.

Another interpretation is possible of the studies' mixed results.
It may well be that labeling's overall effect remains unclear because researchers have yet to disentangle the conditions under
which contact with the criminal justice system increases or di-
minishes commitment to crime (Palamara et al., 1986:91; Tittle,
1975b:408). At present, research has addressed in only a rudimentary way how vulnerability to criminal labels might vary by
factors such as individual socio-demographic characteristics, stage
in a criminal career, family strength, or neighborhood context.
Until these empirical issues are settled, general statements about
"labeling effects" remain premature.

In sum, critics have provided a necessary corrective to bold
claims that extra-legal variables dominate the discretionary
decision-making of criminal justice officials and that societal reaction is the major source of career criminality. Even so, it would
be misguided to make the opposite error of assuming that labeling
theory "points to processes that exist but their overall impact is

small" (Gove, 1980:268) and "appears off the mark on almost every aspect of delinquency it is asked to predict or explain" (Hirschi, 1975:198). As research by Sampson (1986) and others (Link, Cullen, Frank, and Wozniak, 1987) cautions, societal reaction is a complex process and its effects have yet to be understood fully or established empirically.

LABELING THEORY IN CONTEXT

A central theme informing this book has been that changes in society expose people to new experiences, which in turn prompt them to think differently about many issues, including crime. The 1960s was just such a period when social change gripped America and caused citizens and criminologists alike to take stock of their previous assumptions about criminal behavior (Sykes, 1974). We have seen in Chapter 4, for example, that the tumultuous context of the 1960s sensitized some scholars to the importance of controls in constraining human conduct; in Chapter 6, we will see how the decade's events radicalized other scholars and led them to assert that crime and criminal justice were shaped intimately by the conflict and inequities inherent in capitalism. More relevant to our present concerns, we can recall that the 1960s also proved fertile ground for the growth of labeling theory (Cole, 1975).

Why did many criminologists suddenly embrace the notion that state intervention through the criminal justice system was the principal cause of the crime problem? In the absence of strong empirical evidence, why did labeling propositions — voiced earlier by Tannenbaum (1938) and Lemert (1951) — suddenly "strike a chord" and seem "sensible" to so many scholars?

The key to answering these questions, we believe, lies in understanding how the prevailing context led many people to lose trust or confidence in the government. In the early 1960s, optimism ran high. As noted in Chapter 3, the Kennedy administration instilled the expectation that a "New Frontier of equal opportunity" was within reach; a "Great Society" was possible that would eliminate poverty and its associated ills, like crime. Moreover, this agenda reaffirmed the Progressives' belief that the government should play a central role through social programs in effecting this change. The state could be trusted to do good.

But as the 1960s unfolded, this optimism declined, eventually turning to despair as the bold promises made at the decade's start went unfulfilled (Bayer, 1981; Empey, 1979). Thus the Civil Rights Movement laid bare not only the existence of pernicious patterns of racism, sexism, and class inequality, but also revealed the inability, if not the unwillingness, of government officials to address these long-standing injustices. Vietnam raised other concerns. Although the use of American troops was justified as necessary to protect democracy, this policy lost its moral value as many citizens perceived the U.S. as merely propping up a corrupt regime. More disquieting, however, was the government's response to political protest. Americans witnessed not only demonstrators being chased and beaten by police, but also students being gunned down at Kent State. The Attica riot, in which troopers storming the prison fatally wounded 29 inmates and 10 guards being held hostage, confirmed the state's proclivity to abuse its power in the suppression of insurgency. The state's moral bankruptcy seemed complete with the disclosure of the Watergate scandal, which showed that corruption not simply penetrated to but rather pervaded the government's highest echelons (Cullen and Gilbert, 1982:104-107).

In short, the state faced what commentators have called a "legitimacy crisis" (Friedrichs, 1979) or a "confidence gap" (Lipset and Schneider, 1983): Citizens no longer trusted the motives or competence of government officials. Such feelings spread and intensified as the 1960s advanced and turned into the 1970s, and they created a context ripe for harvesting the ideas of labeling theorists who blamed the state for the crime problem. Due to their social experiences, it now "made sense" to many criminologists, policymakers, and members of the public that government officials would label the disadvantaged more than the advantaged, and would operate prisons — like Attica — that drove offenders deeper into crime. Accordingly, labeling theory won wide support and offered a stiff challenge to traditional theories of crime. The stage was set, moreover, for a reexamination of existing crime control policies.

THE CONSEQUENCES OF THEORY: POLICY IMPLICATIONS

Labeling theory, LaMar Empey (1982:409) observes, "had a profound impact on social policy." As the ranks of the perspective's proponents swelled, an increasingly loud warning was sounded that pulling offenders into the criminal justice system only contributed to the crime problem. The prescription for policy change was eminently logical and straightforward: if state intervention causes crime, then take steps to limit it (Schur, 1973).

But how might this be accomplished? As Empey (1982:409) notes, labeling theorists embraced four policies — each coincidentally beginning with the letter "D" — which promised to reduce the intrusion of the state into offenders' lives: decriminalization, diversion, due process, and deinstitutionalization. These four reforms were implemented to different degrees and with uneven consequences. Even so, the agenda identified by labeling theory remains to this day an important vision of the direction criminal justice policy should take.

Decriminalization

Labeling theorists insisted that the "overreach of the criminal law" constituted a critical public policy problem (Morris and Hawkins, 1970:2; Schur, 1965; Schur and Bedeau, 1974). Thus the criminal justice system has traditionally been used to control not only threats to life and property, but also a range of "victimless crimes" (e.g., public drunkenness, drug use, gambling, pornography) as well as juvenile "status offenses" (e.g., truancy, promiscuity). The morality of these behaviors might be open to debate, theorists admitted, but using the criminal law as a means of control is an "unwarranted extension [that] is expensive, ineffective, and criminogenic" (Morris and Hawkins, 1970:2).

Edwin Schur (1965; with Bedeau, 1974), for example, argued that the criminalization of victimless deviance — such as drug use — creates crime in various ways. First, the mere existence of the laws turns those who participate in the behavior into candidates for arrest and criminal justice processing. Second, it often drives them to commit related offenses, such as when drug addicts rob to support their habits. Third, by prohibiting the legal acquisition of desired goods and services, criminalization creates a lucrative illicit market, whose operation fuels the coffers of organized crime. And fourth, the existence of such illicit exchanges fosters strong incentives for the corruption of law enforcement officials, who are enticed through pay-offs to "look the other way."

Accordingly, labeling theorists argued for the prudent use of "decriminalization": the removal of many forms of conduct from the scope of the criminal law. This policy might involve outright legalization or treating the act much like a traffic violation (such as speeding) where penalties are limited to minor fines. In any case, the goal was to limit the law's reach and thus to reduce the extent to which people were labeled and treated as criminals.

The policy of decriminalization evoked much debate and encouraged some significant legal changes. Thus abortion was legalized by U.S. Supreme Court decision; possession of small amounts of marijuana frequently was reduced to a minor violation; the criminal status of pornographic material was left to communities to decide; forms of gambling — such as state-run lotteries and casinos — were legalized; and status offenses were made the concern of social welfare agencies. These changes, however, did not occur across all states, and other forms of behavior remained illegal. Especially noteworthy, the most controversial of the labeling theorists' policy proposals — the call to decriminalize all forms of drug use — fell on deaf ears. Indeed, as we have seen in recent years, an enormous campaign has been launched to stop the flow of drugs and to place those participating in this illicit market behind bars (Inciardi, 1986).

Diversion

Given that laws exist and offenders come to the attention of law enforcement officials, how should the criminal justice system respond? Labeling theorists had a ready answer: "diversion." For juveniles, as Empey (1982:410) indicates, this policy might entail taking youths from the province of the juvenile court and placing them under the auspices of "youth service bureaus, welfare agencies, or special schools." For adults, it might involve release to a privately-run mental health agency, community substance-abuse program, or government sponsored job training class. Diversion might also involve the substitution of a less severe intervention, such as when offenders are "diverted" from prison and are placed instead in the community under "intensive probation supervision" or under "home incarceration" (Ball, Huff, and Lilly, 1988; Binder and Geis, 1984; Latessa, 1987).

Diversion programs became widespread in the past two decades, a development that can be traced at least in part to the persuasive writings of labeling theorists (Klein, 1979:146). The current inmate crowding problem, moreover, is furnishing fresh incentives for jurisdictions to establish diversion programs that will help empty their prisons and jails. Diversion's popularity, however, has given labeling theorists little cause for celebration.

Originally conceived as an alternative to involvement in the criminal justice system or to incarceration, diversion programs have most often functioned as an "add on" to the system. That is, participants in programs have not been those who would have stayed in the system or gone to jail, but rather those who previously would have been released, fined, or perhaps given a suspended sentence. Ironically, the very policy suggested by labeling theorists to lessen state intervention has had the effect of increasing that intervention: diversion has "widened the net" of state control by creating a "system with an even greater reach" (Klein, 1979:184; see also Frazier and Cochran, 1986; Binder and Geis, 1984).   "net widening"

Due Process

Labeling theorists were also quick to join the mounting "due process" movement, which sought to extend to offenders legal protections (e.g. right to an attorney, right not to be searched illegally). As Empey (1982:410) points out, though labeling theory did not prompt the concern for offender rights, the perspective and the concern for due process had a common source: "both were part of the growing distrust of governmental and other institutions in the 1960s."

Labeling scholars' call for expanding due process was tied up with their critique of the "rehabilitative ideal." As noted in Chapters 2 and 3, reforms in the Progressive era had provided criminal justice officials with enormous discretion to effect the "individualized treatment" of offenders. Such discretionary powers were unbridled in the juvenile court, in which the state was trusted to "save children" by acting as a "kindly parent" (Platt, 1969; Rothman, 1978, 1980). Labeling theorists, however, accused state officials of abusing this trust. "Individualized treatment," they claimed, was merely a euphemism for judicial decisions that discriminated against the powerless and for parole board decisions that denied release to inmates who dared to resist the coercive control of correctional officials.

The solution to this situation was clear. "Individualized justice," Edwin Schur (1973:169) urged, "must give way to a *return to the rule of law*" (emphasis in original). The worst abuses must be curbed by an extension of constitutional protections, particularly to juveniles who had been left blindly in the hands of the state. Labeling theorists, moreover, embraced what amounted to the principles of the classical school: Punishments should be prescribed by law and sentences should be determinate. Accordingly, discretionary abuse would be eliminated: Judges would be forced to sentence according to written codes, not to whim, and determinate sentences with set release dates would replace parole decision-making.

Labeling theorists hoped that these policies would result in shorter and more equitable sentences and thus reduce the extent and worst effects of state intervention. This blind faith in the "rule of law," however, has proven a mixed blessing. On the one hand, due process has provided offenders with needed protections against state abuse of discretion. On the other hand, it remains unclear whether the corresponding attack on rehabilitation has succeeded in creating a system that is less committed to interventionist policies and more committed to humanistic ideals (Cullen and Gilbert, 1982). As we will see in the final chapter, recent trends in criminal justice policy do not furnish reason for optimism on this point.

Deinstitutionalization

Finally, labeling theorists took special pains to detail the criminogenic effects of incarceration and to advocate vigorously the policy of lessening prison populations through "deinstitutional-ization." The time had come, they insisted, for a moratorium on prison construction and for the move to a system that corrected its wayward members in the community.

This proposal received a stunning test in 1972 when Jerome Miller, commissioner of Massachusetts's Department of Youth Services, took the bold action of closing the state's major juvenile facilities and of placing youths in community programs (Empey, 1982:487). Only a small number of youths remained in secure detention (Klein, 1979:187). Significantly, a subsequent evalua-tion revealed that recidivism rates were only slightly higher after the institutions were emptied. More instructive, the researchers found that in those sections of the state where the reform was pursued enthusiastically through the creation of "a large number of diverse program options, so that the special needs of each youth could be more nearly met," the recidivism rate was *lower* than before Miller's deinstitutionalization policy was implemented. The researchers termed these results "dramatic" (Miller and Ohlin, 1985:70; see also *Corrections Magazine*, 1975).

One might have expected that these empirical results would have caused policymakers in other states to consider the wisdom of making a community rather than an institutional response to crime. But as we have noted, policy decisions are based less on research and more on what "seems sensible" and thus politically feasible. In the past decade, the tenor of American society changed, and new ways of thinking about crime emerged (see Wilson, 1975). Not surprisingly, policies have reflected this change in thinking, as we have abandoned the idea of deinstitutionalization and cho-sen instead to incarcerate offenders in unprecedented numbers.

CONCLUSION

Labeling theory's distinctive focus on societal reaction suc-ceeded in sensitizing criminologists to the important insights that the "criminal" nature of behavior is socially constructed by the response to it and that a variety of factors can shape who comes to bear a criminal label. The perspective also forced consideration of the possibility that state intervention can have the ironic, unanticipated consequence of causing the very conduct — lawlessness — it is meant to suppress. Empirical research has yet to confirm convincingly this causal thesis, but neither has it shown that criminal labeling does not play a contributing role in stabilizing certain kinds of offenders in criminal careers. In any case, labeling theory provides an important reminder that the effects of criminal justice intervention are complex and may contradict what "common sense" would dictate. This warning assumes significance, when we consider policymakers' current assurances that the panacea for the crime problem can be found in widening the reach of the criminal law and in the enormous expansion of prison populations.

6

Social Power and the Construction of Crime: Conflict Theory

As shown in Chapter 5, theories purporting to explain crime by locating its sources in biological, psychological, or social factors associated with the offender have tended to ignore the way in which "crime" is produced and aggravated by the *reaction* to real or imagined attributes or behavior of those who are being labeled "offenders." Labeling theory tried to correct this oversight, going into great detail in an effort to explain the labeling process and its consequences. But, as the previous chapter also indicates, some criminological theorists did not feel that labeling theory went far enough. The labeling theorists showed some appreciation for the way in which political interests and political power affected social reaction, but they did little to explore these deeper issues.

What determines whether a label will stick? What determines the extent to which those labeled are punished? The nature of the labeling may depend upon differences between those labeled and those doing the labeling. Whether labels can be made to stick and the extent to which those labeled can be punished may depend essentially on who has power. Theories which focus attention upon struggles between individuals and/or groups in terms of power differentials fall into the general category of *conflict theory.*

Some conflict theories try to search for the sources of the apparent conflicts. Some seek to elucidate the basic principles by which conflict evolves. Others try to develop a theoretical foundation for eliminating the conflict. Some try to do all this and more.

In this chapter we will examine some of the leading criminological conflict theories, beginning with conflict theory in general as found in the pioneering work of Marx and Engels and in the later work of Simmel. Next we will examine Bonger's attempt to develop a Marxist theory of crime, Sutherland's and Sellin's focus upon the relationship between culture conflict and crime, and Vold's effort to build a criminological conflict theory on the tradition exemplified by Simmel. Because contemporary American criminological conflict theory, like other criminological control theories, drew much of its inspiration from the turmoil of the 1960s, it will be necessary to reexamine the 1960s from another point of view before proceeding to a consideration of such influential conflict theories as those of Turk, Chambliss, and Quinney. Finally, we will consider some of the consequences within criminology as well as the policy implications of conflict theory.

FORERUNNERS OF CONFLICT THEORY

Marx and Engels: Capitalism and Crime

As indicated in Chapter 4, Karl Marx and Friedrick Engels were already expressing concern over the apparent decline in social solidarity by the middle of the 1800s, preceding Durkheim by several decades. For Marx and Engels as well as for Durkheim, crime was to some extent a symptom of this decline and would diminish (although Durkheim made it clear that it would never disappear) if social solidarity could be regained. Where they differed was in their analysis of the source of the erosion of solidarity and their prescription for its restoration.

Durkheim saw the situation as a *moral* problem and argued that the social solidarity of the future would depend upon an effective combination of controls through modes of social integration and social regulation which could operate in tune with the new division of labor that had been created by industrialization. Marx and Engels saw the problem in *economic* terms, denounced the new division of labor as the unjust exploitation of one social class by another, and insisted that social solidarity could be regained only with the overthrow of capitalism itself. They proposed revolution followed by a period of socialism. Because in their view the political state existed essentially as a mechanism for the perpetuation of capitalism, it was deemed historically inevitable that the state would then "wither away," leaving a society based on the true brotherhood and sisterhood of communism (Marx and Engels, 1848).

Marx himself had very little to say about crime. Those criminological theorists who cite him as a major forerunner tend to extrapolate from his general approach, to cite his collaborator Engels's more directly relevant writings on the assumption that Marx agreed, or to do both by citing Marx in general with a specific quotation from Engels to nail down the point. Certainly Marx and Engels stressed differences in *interests* and in *power* much more than did Durkheim. For them, conflict was inherent in the nature of social arrangements under capitalism, for it was capitalism which generated the vast differences in interests and capitalism which gave the few at the top so much power over the many at the bottom. Above all, their theoretical approach was action-oriented; they were less concerned with the pure understanding of social problems than with changing things for what they considered the better.

Although the work of Marx and Engels was extremely complex, certain basic propositions stand out (Turner, 1978). First, there was the proposition that conflict of interests between different groups will be increased by inequality in the distribution of scarce resources (food, clothing, shelter, etc.). A second proposition was that those receiving less of the needed resources would question the legitimacy of the arrangement as they became aware of the nature of the "raw deal" they were getting. The third proposition was that these groups would then be more likely to organize and to bring the conflict out in the open, after which there would be polarization and violence leading to the redistribution of the scarce resources in such a way that they would be shared by everyone. Capitalism was considered to be at the root of the conflict because it was taken to be the source of the unjust inequality. In this view, greater integration and regulation would simply tend to perpetuate an unjust economic system. The way to solve the problem of collapsing social solidarity was not to find some new sources of faith in the social order or some more effective means of regulating its members but to destroy capitalism and build toward the one just form of social solidarity — communism.

Simmel: Forms of Conflict

Like Marx, George Simmel was a German intellectual with a deep interest in social theory. On the other hand, Simmel was a contemporary of Durkheim, doing his theoretical work a few decades later than Marx and concerning himself with a search for precise intellectual understanding of abstract laws governing human interaction rather than with changing the world. Simmel was an exponent of "sociological formalism" (Martindale, 1960:233). He was concerned not so much with the changing *content* of social life as with its recurring *forms* or patterns. Speaking of Simmel, Wolff (1964:xviii) has remarked that his approach represented a "preponderance of the logical over the normative." His interest was not in particular conflicts but in conflict in general, and he was less concerned with normative questions such as the "justice" of a particular outcome than with the abstract logic of conflict itself.

While Simmel was deeply interested in conflict as a form common in social life, he was not as preoccupied with it as was Marx, seeing it as a normal part of life and as one form of interaction among others, some of which were operating in different and even opposite directions in an integrated social system (Turner, 1978). Conflict was regarded not as a problem necessarily calling for solutions or even leading to change but rather as a typical aspect of social order which often actually contributed to that order. Of equal importance is that while Marx focused on the *causes* of conflict and sought to find means for their elimination, Simmel focused on the *consequences* of conflict, with little interest in its sources and great interest in the complex, formal patterns through which it developed.

Bonger: Capitalism and Crime

Early in the twentieth century, the conflict perspective of Marx and Engels was applied specifically to criminological theory by the Dutch criminologist Willem Bonger (1969 [1916]). As we will see later, the turbulence of the 1960s brought renewed interest in Marxist theory and in the work of Bonger. In the introduction to an abridged edition of Bonger's major work brought out near the end of the 1960s, the American criminologist and conflict theorist

Austin T. Turk (1969b: 3) spoke of him appreciatively as a man who "combined a passion to alleviate human misery with an equal passion for scientific research." Like Marx and Engels, and unlike Freud and Durkheim, Bonger felt that the human being was innately social. If so, crime would have to be traced to an unfavorable environment which distorted human nature. Bonger held that just such an unfavorable environment had been generated by the rise of capitalism.

Under capitalism, said Bonger, there had arisen a sharp division between the rulers and the ruled which did not originate in innate differences between them but in the economic system itself. In such an unfavorable environment, where people were pitted against each other in the economic struggle, where the individual was encouraged to seek pleasure by any means possible without regard for others, and where the search required money, human nature was distorted into an intense "egoism" which made people more capable of committing crimes against one another. Thus, like the control theorists as far back as Durkheim, Bonger traced crime in part to individual egoism. Unlike them, however, he took the Marxist position that the decline of social integration and the rise of extremely disruptive individualism could be traced to capitalism. Such egoism could never be reduced by social controls which bound the individual more closely to society, for society under capitalism was itself the very *source* of the egoism.

Bonger traced much crime to the poverty generated by capitalism, both directly because crime among the subordinate class was sometimes necessary for survival, and indirectly because the sense of injustice in a world where many had almost nothing while a few had everything was held to demoralize the individual and stifle the social instincts. At the same time, however, he recognized that the more powerful "bourgeoisie" also committed crimes. He traced this to (1) the opportunities which came with power and (2) the decline of morality which came with capitalism. Crime was seen as a product of an economic system which fostered a greedy, egoistic, "Look out for Number 1" mentality while at the same time making the rich richer and the poor poorer.

Long before the labeling theorists, Bonger stressed that while it was certainly true that "crime" fell into the category of "immoral actions," definitions of morality varied. Indeed, he went further, insisting that the source of the prevailing definitions and of their variations could be found in the interests of the powerful. In Bonger's view, behaviors were defined as crimes when they significantly threatened the interests of the powerful and "hardly any act is punished if it does not injure the interests of the dominant class" (Turk, 1969b:9). Thus he took note of the statistics showing a lower crime rate among the bourgeoisie and traced this to the fact that the legal system "tends to legalize the egoistic actions of the bourgeoisie and to penalize those of the proletariat" (Turk, 1969b:10). Given Bonger's theory of the causes of crime, his conclusion that the abolition of capitalism and the redistribution of wealth and power would restore a favorable environment and almost entirely eliminate crime followed as a matter of political logic.

Sutherland and Sellin: Culture Conflict and Crime

In criminological theory, Edwin H. Sutherland is best known for his differential association theory discussed in Chapter 3. As indicated in Chapter 3, the concept of differential association was built upon the concept of "differential social organization," which was itself an attempt to move away from the value judgments entailed in describing situations organized differently as representing "social disorganization." The concept of differential social organization represented one type of conflict perspective; inherent in the notion was the assumption that society did not rest on complete consensus but was made up of different segments with conflicting cultural patterns. Individual criminal activity could be explained by assuming that a person whose associations were dominated by relationships with those in a less law-abiding segment of society would tend to learn criminal techniques and develop criminal orientations.

Sutherland had already begun systematic research into the crimes of the wealthy and powerful by the middle 1920s. During the 1930s he pioneered the study of "white-collar criminality," publishing a groundbreaking article at the beginning of the 1940s (Sutherland, 1940) and a widely cited book on the subject by the end of the decade (Sutherland, 1949). In these works he called attention to the fact that powerful economic interests, such as the huge corporations, which had arisen in the twentieth century represented a segment of society whose organization and policy made them "habitual criminals," while their wealth and political power protected them from prosecution in the criminal courts. As pointed out in Chapter 3, he explained the participation of *individuals* in the white-collar crimes of these corporations in terms of their *differential association* by way of immersion in the criminal patterns of the business.

During the Depression of the 1930s, another criminologist, Thorsten Sellin, best known today for his studies of capital punishment and his efforts at developing crime indices, argued, like Sutherland, for a broader definition of "crime" and a less conventional approach to criminological theory. Sellin (1938) stressed the problem of "culture conflict" as a source of crime, maintaining that different groups learned different "conduct norms" and that the conduct norms of one group might clash with those of another. As for which conduct norms would become a part of the criminal law, Sellin (1938:3) held that "the conduct which the state denotes as criminal is, of course, that deemed injurious to society, or in the last analysis, to those who wield the political power within that society and therefore control the legislative, judicial, and executive functions which are the external manifestations of authority."

Vold: Conflict and Crime

Near the close of the 1950s, George B. Vold (1958) set forth the most extensive and detailed treatment of criminological theory from a conflict perspective yet seen in criminology. Citing Simmel, he agreed that conflict should not be regarded as abnormal but rather as a fundamental social form characteristic of social life in general. He argued that "as social interaction processes grind their way through varying kinds of uneasy adjustment to a more or less stable equilibrium of *balanced forces in opposition*, the resulting condition of relative stability is what is usually called social order or social organization" (Vold, 1958:204; emphasis added). In this perspective, social order was not presumed to rest entirely upon consensus but in part upon the stability resulting from a balance of power among the various conflicting forces which comprise society. The conflict between groups was analyzed in Simmelian terms as potentially making a *positive contribution* to the strengthening of the different groups, because participation in the struggle resulted in group *esprit de corps* and in-group solidarity. According to this analysis, it was perfectly normal for groups in a complex society to come into conflict as their interests clashed and "politics, as it flourishes in a democracy, is primarily a matter of finding practical compromises between antagonistic groups in the community at large" (Vold, 1958: 208).

As to the nature of legal compromises, Vold (1958:209) cited Sutherland's work from the 1920s, noting that "those who produce legislative majorities win control over the police power and dominate the policies that decide who is likely to be involved in violation of the law." He considered politics the art of compromise and insisted that "the principle of compromise from positions of strength operates at every stage of this conflict process" (Vold, 1958:209). His own theoretical interest in the *forms* rather than the *content* of such conflict may be seen in his comparison of the delinquent gangs' patterns to those formed by conscientious objectors in time of war. Both were analyzed as identical patterns or social forms in which group ideology existed in conflict with established authority. Like Simmel, Vold was concerned with the similarity of the forms of conflict rather than with normative distinctions such as the nature of the morality involved.

Vold pointed out that much crime was of an obviously political nature. He included crimes resulting from protest movements aimed at political reform, noting that "a successful revolution makes criminals out of the government officials previously in power, and an unsuccessful revolution makes its leaders into traitors subject to immediate execution" (Vold, 1958:214). His formal analysis avoided the "normative" and stuck to the "logical." Regardless of who was "right" and who was "wrong," those who lost were the "criminals." In this sense, their (formal) "crime" consisted of losing.

Vold also gave attention to crimes involving conflicts between union and management and between different unions themselves. In a statement portending what was to come in the civil rights movement in the United States of the 1960s and elsewhere in the world in the 1980s, he pointed out that "numerous kinds of crimes result from the clashes incidental to attempts to change, or to upset the caste system of racial segregation in various parts of the world, notably in the United States and in the Union of South Africa"

(Vold, 1958:217). He undertook an intensive analysis of organized crime and white-collar crime as examples of groups organizing themselves in the pursuit of their interests, examining the strategies and tactics employed in the conflict.

THEORY IN CONTEXT: THE TURMOIL OF THE 1960s

Although the various forerunners of conflict theory discussed above had anticipated much of what was to follow, it was not until the social upheavals of the 1960s that criminological conflict theory came into its own. The 1960s represented a major turning point for criminology. As we have already seen, it was within the context of those times that both control theory and labeling theory developed from theoretical seeds planted earlier. The same was true for conflict theory. Where control theory reacted by stressing the tenuous nature of complex society under conditions of rapid social change and insisted that crime and delinquency tended to spread with any significant weakening of forces containing the individual, conflict theory highlighted the newly revealed patterns of social division and questioned the legitimacy of the motives, strategies, and tactics of those in power. Where labeling theory exposed the way in which crime was a social construction of moral entrepreneurs and others in a position to influence the definitions developed by the political state and sometimes pointed to class-bias in the labeling process, conflict theory was much more explicit about the connection between the criminal justice system and the underlying economic order, sometimes condemning the state itself.

Seeking to explain the rise of criminological conflict theory (there termed "critical theory") during the 1960s, Sykes (1974) has pointed to three factors of special importance. First, there was the impact of the Vietnam war on American society. Second, there was the growth of the counterculture. Finally, there was the rising political protest over discrimination, particularly racial discrimination, and the use of the police power of the state to suppress political dissent, associated issues which had been smoldering and threatening to break into the open since World War II.

As the war in Vietnam escalated, doubts deepened not only

about the wisdom of governmental policy but also about the fundamental motives and credibility of those in power. Reasons given for the escalating involvement seemed to many to be rather far-fetched, and doubts were increased by discoveries of "disinformation" — a bureaucratic term for governmental lies. Protest marches spread. Armed troops fired on and killed apparently peaceful protesters on college campuses and elsewhere. The "conscientious objectors" about whom Vold had written so coolly were everywhere, voluntarily choosing to become "criminals" by leaving for Canada or burning their draft cards in heated public protests.

As indicated in Chapter 4, the developing counterculture represented in large part a repudiation of middle-class standards. Countercultural behavior dramatized a fundamental conflict in values. Millions were now engaging in a variety of activities which they considered harmless but which the legal system regarded as criminal offenses — such so-called "victimless crimes" as fornication, vagrancy, and illegal drug use. The latter had in fact become not only a way to "get high" but a symbolic political protest.

As Chapter 4 has emphasized, along with the impact of the Vietnam war and the growth of the counterculture came the rise of social movements aimed at eliminating discrimination and demanding an end to the suppression of political dissent. The feminist movement spoke more and more militantly in terms of the political, economic, and sexual oppression of women. The homosexual community became more politicized, organizing to resist labeling and discrimination. Underlying social conflict came more and more into the open as the civil rights movement seemed to make it clear that blacks were not going to gain social equality without civil disobedience, that the only way to deal with the unjust laws enforcing segregation was to violate them en masse, for the protesters to become "criminals" and spend some time in jail as the price for their beliefs.

At the same time, a society which had tolerated the McCarthyism of the 1950s was upset to learn that some of its most revered symbols of law and order, such as the FBI, had become involved in the dissemination of internal "disinformation" aimed at destroying political opposition and had fallen into the use of illegal tactics in dealing with citizens seeking to express legitimate grievances. It often appeared that the agents of the political state, whether Southern sheriffs threatening black school-children with police dogs or Congressmen harassing as "radicals" or "communists" those who seriously questioned the political order, were really "moral criminals" disguised as "legally constituted authority." The impression of society as comprised of groups in conflict, with the legal system tending to brand as criminal significant threats to the interests of the powerful, became more and more prevalent, providing fertile ground for the development of conflict theory.

VARIETIES OF CONFLICT THEORY

The new criminological conflict theory went much further than criminologists had taken it before, appealing to Marx and Bonger as well as to Simmel. As Gibbons and Garabedian (1974) have pointed out in their own examination of the conflict theory movement (there termed "radical criminology"), "Sutherland certainly did not characterize the seventy corporations that he studied as 'exploiters of the people'; instead, he stopped far short of that sort of condemnation." Similarly, Sellin may have noted that the law is defined and applied in the interests of dominant groups, but he did not denounce them in the manner of Marx. As for Vold's analysis of the state of affairs, what had seemed like a bold outline of the conflict perspective in the late 1950s now struck some as in need of much more elaboration and others as far too abstract, "academic," and aloof from the injustices that so angered them.

Sykes (1974) has listed four major factors behind the shift. First, there was now a profound skepticism toward any theory which traced crime to something about the individual, including not only the biological and psychological theories but sociological theories referring to inadequate socialization and the like. Second, there was a marked shift from the assumption that the inadequacies of the criminal justice system were to be traced to incompetent or corrupt individuals or minor organizational flaws to the conclusion that these problems were inherent in the system, either because it was fundamentally out-of-control or because it had been so designed by powerful interests. Third, the older assumptions that (1) the criminal law represented the collective will of the people and that (2) the job of the criminologist was to do theoretical analysis and empirical research and not to deal in normative issues of "right" and "wrong" were increasingly rejected as fallacies which made it impossible to ask the basic questions. Finally, as discussed in Chapter 5, it had not only become clear that "official" crime rate figures did not reflect the amount of criminal behavior actually present in society but also that what they did reflect was more often the labeling behavior of the authorities.

During the 1960s several criminologists, influenced by a blending of labeling theory with political theory, began to develop their own brand of criminological conflict theory. It is fair to characterize their work as part of a theoretical movement. Here we will concentrate upon the efforts of three of the leading conflict theorists — Turk, Chambliss, and Quinney. As we will see, they were not working in isolation but rather in close contact within a particular sociohistorical context. Each of them presented the outlines of their own approach in articles written during the 1960s, and each published a book-length volume in 1969. Their differences were to depend to a considerable extent upon influences from the various theoretical forerunners discussed above.

Turk: The Criminalization Process

Completing his graduate work at the beginning of the 1960s, Austin T. Turk had come to be increasingly interested in the culture conflict perspective of criminologists such as Sellin and in the emerging labeling theory. As with any theorist, his perspective was influenced by his life experiences. Turk (1987:3) himself has put it this way:

> Growing up as a working class boy in a small segregated Georgia town, I learned early that life is neither easy nor just for most folks; that irrationality and contradiction are very much part (maybe the biggest part) of social reality; that access to resources and opportunities have no necessary association with ability or character; that the meaning of justice in theory is debatable, and of justice in practice manipulable; and that whatever degree of freedom, equality, brotherhood, or security exist in a society are hard-won and tenuous.

By the end of the 1960s, Turk (1969a) had presented a complete statement of his own brand of conflict theory in *Criminality and the Legal Order*, quoting at length from Sutherland in the Introduction and citing the more recent efforts of Vold and Dahrendorf. It was this effort to build on Dahrendorf's perspective, along with his Simmelian-Voldian approach which treated conflict not as some abnormality but as a fundamental social form, that distinguished Turk's theoretical contribution. For Turk, recognition of social conflict as a basic fact of life represented simple realism rather than any particular tendency toward cynicism.

Although also a conflict theorist, Dahrendorf (1958, 1968) disagreed with Marx on the question of inequality. Instead of tracing inequality back to an unjust economic system, Dahrendorf located the source in *power* differences, more specifically in differences in *authority*, or power which had been accepted as legitimate. Unlike Marx, who had argued for the abolition of inequality, Dahrendorf took the position that because cultural norms always exist and have to depend upon sanctions for their enforcement, some people *must* have more power than others so as to make the sanctions stick. In Dahrendorf's view, it was not the economic inequality resulting from capitalism which produced social inequality; rather inequality was an inescapable fact because the basic units of society *necessarily* involved dominance-subjection relationships. Thus the idea of eliminating inequality was treated as a utopian dream.

Turk seems to have been persuaded of the essential relativity of "crime" in much the same way as the labeling theorists. For him the theoretical problem of explaining "crime" lay not in explaining varieties of behavior, for these may or may not be crimes depending on time and place. Instead, the problem lay in explaining "criminalization," the process of "assignment of criminal status to individuals" (Turk, 1969a:xi), which results in the production of "criminality" (Turk, 1969a:1). Dahrendorf's influence was clear in Turk's definition of the study of "criminality" as "the study of relations between the statuses and roles of legal *authorities* . . . and those *subjects* — acceptors or resisters but not makers of such law creating, interpreting and enforcing decisions" (emphasis in the original).

Such an approach was deemed necessary if the criminologist was to explain such "facts" as variations in crime rates or to

develop better methods of dealing with "criminals." Turk stressed
that assignment of criminal status to an individual may have less
connection with the behavior of that person than with his or her
relationship to the authorities. "Indeed, criminal status may be
ascribed to persons because of real or fancied *attributes*, because
of what they *are* rather than what they *do*, and justified by reference to real or imagined or fabricated behavior" (Turk, 1969a:9-
10; emphasis in the original). From this point of view, even if the
criminologist could eventually succeed in explaining the *behavior*
of criminals, such an achievement would not help in accounting for
their *criminality*, which had more to do with the behavior of the
authorities in control of the criminalization process.

Central to the concept of *authority* is its accepted legitimacy;
authority differs from raw power because it is regarded as legitimate power, the use of which is accepted by those subject to it. Any
theorist concerned with the relationship between subjects and
authorities must investigate the basis for such acceptance. Like
some of the control theorists, Turk rejected the argument that
acceptance of authority must be the result of internalization. He
maintained that acceptance could be explained as a consequence
of people learning the *roles* assigned to the *statuses* they occupied
and simply acquiescing and "going along" as a matter of routine.
Some have the status of authorities; others play the part of subjects. "The legality of norms is defined solely by the words and
behavior of authorities," to which subjects will tend to defer (Turk,
1969a:51).

Like Simmel and Vold, Turk was concerned with the logical
consequences of the fact that some people had authority over
others, not with the sources of this authority or whether it was just
or unjust according to some normative conception of justice. In fact,
logical consistency might be expected to force anyone who was
convinced that concepts such as "crime" were a matter of "labeling" relative to time and place to a similar position with respect
to concepts such as "justice." In any case, Turk focused upon the
logical consequences of authority relationships, holding that "how
authorities come to be authorities is irrelevant" to such an analysis.

Because of his argument that the assignment of the criminal
status would have to be justified by the authorities "by reference
to real or imagined or fabricated behavior" which was held to

represent a violation of legal norms, Turk found it important to make a formal distinction between two types of legal norms — cultural norms and social norms. The first he defined as those set forth in symbolic terms such as words, as norms dealing with *what is expected*. The second he identified as those found in patterns of actual behavior, in terms of *what is being done* rather than what is being said. Turk pointed out that the cultural norms and the social norms in a given situation might or might not correspond.

According to Turk (1969a:53), a satisfactory theory accounting for the assignment of criminal status would include "a statement of the conditions under which cultural and social differences between authorities and subjects will probably result in conflict, the conditions under which criminalization will probably occur in the course of conflict, and the conditions under which the degree of deprivation associated with becoming a criminal will probably be greater or lesser." Like Simmel, he proceeded to examine the nature of these conditions through a series of formal, logical propositions.

Thus, Turk argued that given that cultural and social norms may not agree, the existence of a difference between authorities and subjects in their evaluation of a particular attribute, such as past membership in a radical political organization, or a particular act, such as marijuana use, logically implies four situational possibilities. Each logical possibility carries a different conflict potential. The conflict probability would be highest, for example, in the "high-high" situation in which there was (1) high congruence between the cultural norms preached by the authorities and their actual behavior patterns, and (2) similarly high congruence between the cultural evaluation of a particular attribute or act and the actual possession of that attribute or commission of that act on the part of the subjects. If both sides not only *hold* different standards but also *act in accordance* with them, there is no room for compromise. In a situation in which the authorities not only say "Smoking marijuana is wrong" but also act to stop it, for example, *and* marijuana users not only say "Pot is Okay" but also insist on using it in spite of the normative clash, the conflict potential would be logically greatest.

On the other hand, Turk's logic suggested that the conflict potential would be *lowest* in situations where there was neither agreement between authorities' stated cultural norms and their actual behavioral norms nor between the cultural norms and the social norms of subjects. In such situations, the preachments would clash, but since neither side practices what it preaches in any case, the probability of conflict would be low. Why should they fight over words when neither side lives by them anyhow?

A third logical possibility was described as one in which authorities' talk and behavior was highly congruent, while there was little if any agreement between the words and actions of subjects. Such a situation would fall somewhere in the middle in terms of Turk's formal logic of conflict potential, but with a somewhat higher conflict potential than that logically inherent in the fourth and final possibility. The latter situation was described as one in which the attribute or act as described in the announced cultural norm happened to be in close agreement among subjects while the cultural norm preached by the authorities actually had little relationship to their behavior. According to Turk, the third possibility would entail somewhat more conflict potential than would the fourth, because the authorities would be less likely to tolerate norms different from their own when their cultural norms were reinforced by their social norms.

According to Turk's analysis, the logic of the relationships between cultural and social norms is complicated by additional formal propositions. Under the assumption that an individual who has group support is going to be more resistant to efforts to change him or her, he concluded that the probability of conflict with authorities grows with the extent to which those having the illegal attributes or engaging in the illegal activities are *organized*. Under the assumption that the more sophisticated norm-resisters would be better at avoiding open conflict through clever tactical maneuvers (e.g., pretending to submit while secretly continuing as before), he concluded that the probability of conflict increases as the authorities confront norm-resisters who are less *sophisticated*. The logical possibilities resulting from combination of the two variables of organization and sophistication were set forth as follows: (1) organized and unsophisticated, (2) unorganized and unsophisticated, (3) organized and sophisticated, and (4) unorganized and sophisticated. Conflict odds were attached to each combination.

Proceeding through formal analysis of the four formally distinct possibilities, Turk reached certain conclusions. First, he concluded that conflict between authorities and subjects is most probable where the latter are *highly organized and relatively unsophisticated* (e.g., delinquent gangs). He then concluded that the odds of such conflict declined to the extent that the subjects involved were *unorganized and unsophisticated* (e.g., skid row transients) and still further to the extent that they were *organized and sophisticated* (e.g., syndicate criminals). It followed logically that the lowest probability of conflict would be associated with a situation in which the norm-resisting subjects are *unorganized and sophisticated* (e.g., professional con-artists). These formal deductions may or may not match empirical reality, but they have a certain logical consistency, and Turk encouraged research designed to assess their actual empirical validity.

As for the authorities themselves, Turk pointed out that they must be *organized* or by definition they would not be the authorities but some sort of illegitimate mob. He concluded that the probability of conflict between these authorities and subjects resisting their norms would be greatest where the authorities were *least sophisticated* in the use of power. Interestingly enough, his logic carried him to the same conclusion as that reached by the control theorist Hirschi at the same time — that the probability of conflict was affected by the "nature of the bonds between authorities and subjects" (Turk, 1969a:61). He concluded that "where subjects are strongly identified with the authorities and generally agree in moral evaluations, an announced norm may be accepted in a 'Father knows best' spirit" (Turk, 1969a:61). But where Hirschi stressed these "bonds" as central, Turk devoted much less attention to them, considering society to be less a matter of Durkheimian bonds and more a matter of constant Simmelian conflict working itself out over time. We must remember, of course, that Hirschi was focusing theoretical attention on juvenile delinquency, while Turk was devoting considerable attention to organized crime, political crime, and white-collar crime in general. Accordingly, the relative stress on "bonds" as compared to "conflict potentials" is hardly surprising.

For Turk, an analysis of conflict probabilities was only a first step. The key question was: "Once conflict has begun, what are the conditions affecting the probability that members of the opposition will become criminals . . . that they will be subjected to less or more severe deprivation?" (Turk, 1969a:64). Part of the answer was traced to the same factors outlined above, which would continue to affect probabilities throughout the criminalization process. Turk concluded, however, that additional variables tended to come into play with actual criminalization.

First, he admitted that while the crucial norms defining the conflict were those of the higher authorities, the major factor in the probability of criminalization was likely to be the extent to which the official, legal norms agreed with both the cultural norms and the social norms *of those specifically charged with enforcing the legal norms*, especially the police, but also prosecutors, judges, and the like. Because of the importance of police discretion and decisions on-the-spot, he concluded that the extent to which the police agreed with the legal norms they were expected to enforce would have a major effect on the odds of arrest and criminalization. Prosecutors, judges, juries, and others were expected to affect the probabilities somewhat, but ultimately it would be the police as the front-line enforcers who would determine the extent to which norm resisters would actually be defined as criminal.

In Turk's analysis, the *relative power of enforcers and resisters* became still another variable affecting the odds of criminalization. He proposed that the greater the power difference in favor of norm enforcers over resisters, the greater would be the probability of criminalization. He asserted that the reluctance of the enforcers to move against very powerful resisters would keep the criminality of the very powerful low regardless of their behavior. He added the qualification, however, that some of the disapproved behavior of the least powerful might also be ignored if they seemed to pose no threat and "weren't worth the bother."

The final set of variables to which Turk assigned special significance in determining the odds of criminalization had to do with the *realism of conflict moves*. While in part a matter of the sophistication mentioned above, success in avoiding criminalization or producing criminalization was also regarded as dependent upon factors beyond the use of knowledge of others' behavior patterns in manipulating them. Any move by *resisters* was considered to be unrealistic if it: (1) increased the *visibility* of the offensive attribute or behavior, thus increasing the risk that the authorities would be forced to act; (2) increased the *offensiveness* of the attribute or behavior (e.g., by emphasizing it, calling attention to additional offensive attributes, or violating an even more significant norm of the authorities); (3) increased *consensus* among the various levels of enforcers (e.g., by moving from simple opposition to a particular norm or set of norms to a wholesale attack upon the system with emphasis on stereotyping of enforcers as brutal, ignorant, and corrupt); or (4) increased the *power difference* in favor of the enforcers (e.g., by upsetting the public in such a way that enforcers would be able to get significantly increased resources such as budget increases).

In Turk's analysis, any move by the *authorities* was likely to be unrealistic if it: (1) *shifted the basis of their legitimacy away from consensus* toward the "norm of deference" or obligation to obey despite disagreement, which would be likely in the case of "power plays"; (2) represented a *departure from standard legal procedures*, especially if the shifts were unofficial, sudden, or sharp; (3) *generalized from a particular offensive attribute* so that additional attributes of the opposition also became grounds for criminalization (e.g., if "roundups" of similar types were used in lieu of a systematic search for a particular offender); (4) *increased the size and power of the opposition* (e.g., by creating martyrs among them so that they gain sympathy and other resources from other segments of society); or (5) *decreased consensus* among the various levels of enforcers.

Turk went much further than this in pointing out additional factors which may be expected to alter the nature and outcome of social conflict. He attempted to provide a logical integration of his propositions so as to demonstrate how various combinations affect conflict probabilities differently, and went into great detail in describing possible indicators which might be used to operationalize his propositions so as to facilitate research. Thus, he dealt with the means by which legal norms could be classified in practice, with the question of the best measures of key concepts such as normative-legal conflict, the significance of legal norms, relative power, and realism in conflict moves, and with other issues which would have to be solved if his theory were to be tested by data.

Chambliss: Crime, Power, and Legal Process

Finishing his own graduate work in the same year (1962) as had Turk, William J. Chambliss (1964:67) had become interested in the development of criminal law, specifically in "sociologically relevant analyses of the relationship between particular laws and the social setting in which these laws emerge, are interpreted, and take form." Chambliss (1987:5-6) too has been candid about the relationship between his theoretical perspective and his life experiences.

> After I graduated from UCLA I hitchhiked across the country again to see my father. It was 1955 and in short order I was drafted into the army and sent to Korea with the Counter Intelligence Corps (CIC). I learned a lot about crime during that period. American and Korean soldiers raped, stole, assaulted, intimidated and generally terrorized the Koreans. Because they had the power, nothing was done about it . . . . How could crime be understood from the paradigms I learned in psychology and sociology?

Chambliss completed his graduate work at Indiana University before going on to teach at the University of Washington and then to postdoctoral studies at the University of Wisconsin. It is worth noting (1) that both Turk and Richard Quinney, the third of the contemporary criminological conflict theorists to be examined in this chapter, completed their graduate work at the University of Wisconsin in the same year that Chambliss was completing his at Indiana, and (2) that Turk himself joined the faculty at Indiana after completion of his graduate work at Wisconsin. The ties between these institutions were very close, and there was considerable mutual influence.

> Our lives are far more dependent on chance occurrences than we ever want to acknowledge. A year after I arrived at Washington the University hired Pierre van den Berghe, who was extremely knowledgeable about Marxism. I organized a faculty seminar on the sociology of law with Pierre, a philosopher, and two anthropologists . . . . About this time the Russell Sage Foundation decided to support the resurrection of the sociology of law. I was awarded a fellowship to study law at the University of Wisconsin. (Chambliss, 1987:3,7)

Like Turk, Chambliss was impressed by the relativity of "crime" and the way in which the criminal label seemed to be the product of social conflict. But where Turk's work was influenced by a formal, Simmelian approach, Chambliss was at first inspired less by the older, European tradition of conflict theory than by the American tradition of *legal realism*, the pioneering work of the American legal scholar Jerome Hall, and by the results of his own empirical research. Chambliss had undertaken a study of the development of vagrancy law in England, concluding that these laws could be traced to vested interests. "There is little question that these statutes were designed for one express purpose: to force laborers . . . to accept employment at a low wage in order to insure the landowner an adequate supply of labor at a price he could afford to pay" (Chambliss, 1964:69).

In the same year that Turk published *Criminality and the Legal Order*, Chambliss (1969) published *Crime and the Legal Process*, an edited volume consisting of actual empirical research studies of the legal system, tying them together with his own theoretical framework. This was soon followed by a more elaborate presentation, *Law, Order, and Power* (1971), in collaboration with Robert T. Seidman, a professor of law at the University of Wisconsin. In the earlier statement, Chambliss (1969:8) simply identified his position as representing an "interest-group" perspective rather than a "value-expression" perspective, a distinction which he compared to that to be seen in "the debate in social science theory between the 'conflict' and 'functional' theorists." His approach was very much influenced by the American school of *legal realism*, which concerned itself with the distinction between the "law in the books" and the "law in action." It insisted that the study of abstract legal theory must be complemented by the study of the law as it works itself out in actual practice. It is interesting to note that while the first of these had been the focus of the classical school discussed in Chapter 2, the new attention to the "law in action" represented the influence of positivism in legal studies. Chambliss hoped to develop a theory of the "law in action," a theory based on empirical research.

Early in the second volume, Chambliss and Seidman (1971:31) sounded an almost Durkheimian theme, asserting that the "first variable in our theoretical model is the relative complexity of the society." They went on, however, to insist that (1) the complexity, which comes with technological development and necessitates more complicated, differentiated, and sophisticated social roles actually operates to (2) put people *at odds with one another*, thus (3) requiring *formal institutions* designed to sanction what some consider norm violations. This argument was reminiscent of Dahrendorf's, with the major difference being that formal, sanctioning institutions were not regarded as inherently necessary to society but as a contemporary necessity resulting from increasing social complexity. Their conflict perspective led them to a theory of legal development almost exactly opposite to that expounded in Durkheim's (1964) control theory approach, which maintained that increased societal complexity tended to lead society from an emphasis on "repressive" law to a stress on "restitutive" law. Instead, Chambliss and Seidman (1971:32) argued that, "We may formulate, therefore, the following proposition: the lower the level of complexity of a society, the more emphasis will be placed in the dispute-settling process upon reconciliation; the more complex the society, the more emphasis will be placed on rule-enforcement."

Chambliss and Seidman had begun by arguing that increasing *social complexity* itself tended to call for sanctioning institutions designed to keep order among the conflicting interests. Going further, they maintained that this sanctioning process would become even more pronounced to the degree that the social complexity became a matter of *social stratification*, with some groups having more wealth and power than others: "The more economically stratified a society becomes, the more it becomes necessary for the dominant groups in the society to enforce through coercion the norms of conduct which guarantee their supremacy" (Chambliss and Seidman, 1971:33). Here was something of a Marxian theme, although Chambliss and Seidman stopped short of a clearcut Marxian position that traced the most serious problems of social stratification to polarization produced by capitalism.

Chambliss and Seidman also stressed the significance of the fact that the developing sanctions tended to be enforced through bureaucratic organizations. In their view, the basis of the sanctioning would be organized in the interests of the "dominant groups," but the actual application of the sanctions tended to come through bureaucracies which had their own interests. In this sense, the "law in action" might be expected to reflect a combination of the interests of the powerful and the interests of the bureaucratic organizations created to enforce the rules.

Because the essence of Chambliss's theory was aimed at explaining the law in action in contemporary, complex, industrial societies, we can concentrate upon the second and third variables in the theory of the "law in action" — *social stratification* and *bureaucracy.* In *Crime and the Legal Process* Chambliss (1969:10-11) stressed that, "The single most important characteristic of contemporary Anglo-American society influential in shaping the legal order has been the emerging domination of the middle classes," along with "the attempt by the middle class to impose their own standards and their own view of proper behavior on people whose values differ." In this view, the middle class was coming to represent the conventional morality, but Chambliss emphasized that behind the "values" lay self-interest.

In *Law, Order, and Power,* Chambliss and Seidman (1971:473-474) set forth five fundamental propositions with respect to the relationship between social stratification and the law, beginning with the proposition that (1) *the conditions of one's life affected one's values and norms.* They then asserted that (2) *complex societies were composed of groups with widely different life conditions,* and that (3) *complex societies were therefore composed of highly disparate and conflicting sets of norms.* As for the relationship between these conflicting norms and the law itself, they maintained that (4) *the probability of a given group's having its particular normative system embodied in law was not distributed equally but was closely related to the political and economic position of that group.* These propositions taken together led them to the final proposition that (5) *the higher a group's political or economic position, the greater was the probability that its views would be reflected in the laws.*

 Most of Chambliss and Seidman's theoretical explanation for the law in action was focused on the argument that, although the law represents the values and interests of the more powerful elements in the stratification system of complex societies, it is specifically *created* and *enforced* by bureaucratic organizations with their own agendas. In *Crime and the Legal Process* Chambliss (1969:84) insisted that "the most salient characteristic of organizational behavior is that the ongoing policies and activities are those designed to maximize rewards and minimize strains for the organization." Furthermore, "This general principle is reflected in the fact that in the administration of the criminal law *those persons are arrested, tried, and sentenced who can offer the fewest rewards for nonenforcement of the laws and who can be processed without creating any undue strain* for the organizations which comprise the legal system" (Chambliss, 1969:84-85; emphasis in the original). In Chambliss's view, the criminal justice bureaucracies tended to treat those of lower social-class position more harshly for the same offenses committed by middle-class and upper-class people because (1) they had little to offer in return for lenience and (2) they were in no position to fight the system. Meanwhile, he insisted, these bureaucracies tended to ignore or deal leniently with the same offenses when committed by those higher in the stratification hierarchy.

The process by which the goals of bureaucratic efficiency and avoidance of trouble displace the official goal of impartial law enforcement has been termed *goal displacement* or goal substitution. According to Chambliss, a bureaucratic organization might be expected to take the easy way out, the path of least resistance, especially in contexts where (1) the members have little motivation to resist the easy way out, (2) they have a great deal of discretion in how they will actually behave, and (3) adherence to the official goals is not enforced. "It will maximize rewards and minimize strains for the organization to process those who are politically weak and powerless, and to refrain from processing those who are politically powerful" (Chambliss and Seidman, 1971:269). Thus, "The failure of the legal system to exploit the potential source of offenses that is offered by middle- and upper-class violators . . . derives instead from the very rational choice on the part of the legal system to pursue those violators that the community will reward them for pursuing and to ignore those violators who have the capability of causing trouble for the agencies" (Chambliss, 1969:88).

Speaking of the police, Chambliss and Seidman (1971:391) presented evidence leading to the conclusion that as a bureaucracy, "they act illegally, breaching the norms of due process at every point: in committing brutality, in their searches and seizures, in arrests and interrogation." This illegality takes place not because the police are evil, but because (1) they are not committed to due process in the first place, (2) they have enormous discretion, and (3) there is little enforcement of due process norms by the public or other agencies of the criminal justice system. As for prosecution following an arrest, Chambliss and Seidman (1971:412) concluded that, "How favorable a 'bargain' one can strike with the prosecutor in the pretrial confrontations is a direct function of how politically and economically powerful the defendant is." The alleged safeguards provided by the right to trial by jury were taken to be largely a matter of myth because of the "built-in hazards of the jury trial . . . which exert the greatest pressure on accused persons to plead guilty," leading the powerless to surrender the so-called "right" in nine cases out of ten (Chambliss and Seidman, 1971:444). Finally, Chambliss and Seidman (1971:468-469) attempted to establish the validity of the proposition that "the tendency and necessity to bureaucratize is far and away the single most important variable in determining the actual day to day functioning of the legal system" by demonstrating how even in sentencing "institutionalized patterns of discrimination against the poor are inevitable."

For several years prior to Chambliss's original presentation of his theoretical framework, he had been involved in a study of the relationship between professional crime and the legal system in a large American city. His experiences while conducting this study clearly influenced his thinking, especially with respect to the impact of bureaucracy on the legal system. Pointing out that while at first glance "it would appear that the professional criminal (be he a thief, gambler, prostitute, or hustler) would have little to offer the law enforcement agencies," he noted that there appeared in practice to be a situation of "symbiosis" or mutual dependence there (Chambliss, 1969:89). He argued that because law enforcement agencies in fact depend upon the professional criminal for inside information which makes their job easier, they tend to cooperate with these offenders rather than enforcing the law against them. In the later elaboration Chambliss and Seidman went into much more detail with respect to the "symbiosis" involving organized crime, presenting evidence in support of the proposition that, "From the standpoint of the sociology of legal systems, the most important aspect of the widespread presence of organized crime . . . is that such organizations are impossible without the cooperation of the legal system" (Chambliss and Seidman, 1971:489).

Chambliss used this argument to explain some characteristics of the Anglo-American legal system which seem somewhat illogical. As he pointed out, "Ironically, most of the criminal-legal effort is devoted to processing and sanctioning those persons *least* likely to be deterred by legal sanctions" (Chambliss, 1969:370; emphasis in the original). He cited the use of harsh punishments against drug addicts and capital punishment against murderers as examples of severe sanctioning in exactly those cases where it has little deterrent effect. In contrast, he cited the reluctance to impose stiff sanctions against white-collar criminals and professional criminals as examples of allowing precisely those criminals who do tend to be deterred by sanctions to escape them. According to his argument, such a policy went directly against the formal logic of deterrence, but fit perfectly the bureaucratic logic of demonstrating "effectiveness" by harsh treatment of the powerless while avoiding the organizational strains that would follow from taking on the powerful.

As for Durkheim's control theory argument that law contributed to social solidarity, Chambliss (1969:373) concluded that "the imposition of legal sanctions is likely to increase community solidarity only when the emergent morality also serves other interests of persons in positions of power in the community." While admitting that law might *occasionally* contribute to social solidarity, he stressed instead the manner in which the law in action *splintered the community* by labeling and excluding certain of its (powerless) members and the way in which policies such as the death penalty "may play an extremely important role in the general attitude toward the legitimacy of the use of extreme violence to settle disputes" (Chambliss, 1969:376). In Chambliss's view, the creation and enforcement of law grew out of social conflict and then tended to *add to and reinforce that conflict.*

By the middle 1970s, however, political events in general and developments in social theory in particular seem to have combined to produce a significant shift in Chambliss's perspective. The social changes of the 1960s, which had influenced both Turk and Chambliss, had at the same time led a number of important social theorists to return to the Marxist tradition that had laid dormant during the war years of the 1940s and the McCarthyism of the 1950s. These Marxist theorists traced the problem of racial discrimination and the involvement in Vietnam directly to the economic interests of capitalists, and they argued that the countercultural response to the "American Dream" was politically naive and would be crushed unless its adherents developed a revolutionary, socialist mentality. As we will see in greater detail below, the end of the 1960s saw the emergence of a political "backlash," which threatened not only to block the prospects for reform that were implicit in Chambliss's critique of the law in action but also to "turn the clock back" so as to restore the social and political climate of the 1950s. Chambliss apparently concluded that the problems lay deeper than he had suspected, that the Marxists had come closer to the truth, and that his own analysis must be turned in a Marxist direction.

Chambliss's (1975) shift was reflected in nine specific propositions. With respect to the *content and operation of criminal law*, he now asserted that, (1) "acts are defined as criminal because it is in the interests of the ruling class to so define them," that (2) "members of the ruling class will be able to violate the laws with impunity while members of the subject class will be punished," and that (3) "as capitalist societies industrialize and the gap between the bourgeoisie and the proletariat widens, penal law will expand in an effort to coerce the proletariat into submission" (Chambliss, 1975:152). As for the *consequences of crime for society*, he maintained that, (1) "crime reduces surplus labor by creating employment not only for the criminals but for law enforcers, welfare workers, professors of criminology, and a horde of people who live off the fact that crime exists," that (2) "crime diverts the lower classes' attention from the exploitation they experience and directs it toward other members of their own class rather than toward the capitalist class or the economic system," and that (3) "crime is a reality which exists only as it is created by those in the society whose interests are served by its presence" (Chambliss, 1975:152-153).

Summarizing his position and its implications, Chambliss (1975:153) argued that (1) "criminal and noncriminal behavior stem from people acting rationally in ways that are compatible with their class position . . . a reaction to the life conditions of a person's social class," that (2) "crime varies from society to society depending on the political and economic structures of society," and that (3) "socialist countries should have much lower rates of crime because the less intense class struggle should reduce the forces leading to and the functions of crime." The similarity to Bonger's position was clear, and the use of terms such as "bourgeoisie," "proletariat," "exploitation," and "class struggle" stressed the shift to a more Marxist formulation focusing on capitalism as the problem and socialism as a way of dealing with it.

Quinney: Social Reality, Capitalism, and Crime

As pointed out above, the third of the criminological conflict theorists to be examined in this chapter, Richard Quinney, also completed graduate work in 1962, entering criminology along with Turk and Chambliss at a time when the ferment of the 1960s was already producing a markedly different social atmosphere. Quinney was to become not only the most prolific of the criminological conflict theorists, but also the most controversial, revising his theoretical perspective time after time. Beginning with a position similar in many ways to that of Turk and Chambliss, he was to alter it almost immediately, only to develop a Marxist perspective at about the same time as did Chambliss and then to move in still another direction. Quinney has explained these theoretical turns as follows:

> I have moved through the various epistemologies and ontologies in the social sciences. After applying one, I have found that another is necessary for incorporating what was excluded from the former, and so on. Also, I have tried to keep my work informed by the latest developments in the philosophy of science. In addition, I have always been a part of the progressive movements of the time. My work is thus an integral part of the social and intellectual changes that are taking place in the larger society, outside of criminology and sociology. One other fact has affected my work in recent years: the search for meaning in my life and in the world. (Bartollas, 1985:230)

In the same year that saw publication of Turk's (1969) *Criminality and Legal Order* and Chambliss's (1969) *Crime and the Legal Process*, Quinney (1969) set forth his own position in the Introduction to an edited volume on the sociology of law called *Crime and Justice in Society*. At this point, Quinney's perspective was similar to that of Turk in some ways and to that of Chambliss in others. Like Chambliss, he focused on the sociology of conflicting "interests." He preferred, however, to begin with the *sociological jurisprudence* of Roscoe Pound (1942) rather than with the "so-called legal realists," arguing that it was Pound who had first made the "call for the study of 'law in action' as distinguished from the study of 'law in the books' (Quinney, 1969:22-23). But unlike Pound, who had seen law as operating for the good of society as a whole, Quinney (1969:29), like Turk, and also citing Dahrendorf, took a position "based on the coercion model of society as opposed to the integrative."

Quinney (1969:26) defined law as "the creation and interpretation of specialized rules in a politically organized society." He then asserted that "Politically organized society is based on an interest structure," that this structure "is characterized by unequal distribution of power and by conflict," and that "law is formulated and administered within the interest structure" (Quinney, 1969:27-29). Referring to the "politicality of law," Quinney (1969:27) argued that "whenever a law is created or interpreted, the values of some are necessarily assured and the values of others are either ignored or negated." In this view, law was to be seen as part of the interest structure of society, with changes in the law reflecting changes in the interest structure and as changing with changes in that structure.

One year later, Quinney (1970a, 1970b) published *The Problem of Crime* and *The Social Reality of Crime*, two volumes in which he presented somewhat different versions of criminological conflict theory. Like both Turk and Chambliss, Quinney was impressed by the relativity of "crime." In *The Problem of Crime* he began by taking the position, like Turk's, that crime must be considered in relative terms as a "legal status that is assigned to behaviors and persons by authorized others in society" with the criminal defined as "a person who is assigned the status of criminal on the basis of the official judgment that his conduct constitutes a crime" (Quinney, 1970a:6-7). Like both Turk and Chambliss, he also argued that social differentiation and social change tended to produce complex societies with different and often conflicting conduct norms prevailing in different segments. His critique of criminal justice statistics was quite similar to those of Turk and Chambliss. He asserted that "the crucial question is why societies and their agencies report, manufacture, or produce the volume of crime they do" (Quinney, 1970a), and his analysis of American society as a criminogenic social system drew from the traditions described in earlier chapters — except for the accent on the "politicality of crime" (Quinney, 1970a:180). By the "politicality of crime" Quinney (1970:180) meant that "the actions of the criminally defined are not so much the result of inadequate socialization and personality problems as they are conscientious actions taken against something . . . the only appropriate means for expressing certain thoughts and feelings — and the only possibilities for bringing about social changes."

In his discussion of philosophical principles underlying his approach, however, Quinney diverged considerably from Turk and Chambliss. This distinct difference was to set him apart. Quinney (1970a:134) pointed out that a number of criminologists had expressed concern over the positivistic conception of "cause," outlined deeper issues beneath this philosophical debate, and concluded that, "Under the impact of the philosophical implications of modern physics, most physical scientists have abandoned the idea that science is a *copy of reality*" (emphasis in the original). This amounted to a total rejection of positivism. Drawing upon the European tradition of *philosophical idealism*, he took the position that "Accordingly, to state the extreme, there is no reality beyond man's conception of it: *reality is a state of mind*" and argued that, "There is no reason to believe in the objective existence of anything" (Quinney, 1970a:136-138; emphasis in the original). As Quinney saw it, the problem was not to understand some "reality" that stood apart from the observer but rather to formulate ideas which were helpful in terms of one's purposes.

To criminologists untrained in philosophy, this may sound highly implausible or even ridiculous. Nevertheless, philosophical idealism (the theory that the "world" is a product of "mind") has a long and distinguished history going back to Plato and beyond. It holds that what we take to be the objective world outside us is an image produced by our senses and the thoughts which interpret what they seem to reflect. Thus, for example, the "world" would be different for another creature with different "senses" and a different "mind," and no creature's "world" is any more "real" than that of another. Labeling theory itself had represented a modest move in this direction, throwing light on "crime" as a matter of perception and definition. Quinney was going a step further, following the lead of the "social constructionists" in pointing out that "social reality" in general, as well as deviance or crime in particular, is a matter of changing perceptions and interpretations.

Many variations on some form of philosophical idealism were "blowing in the wind" in the 1960s, from the political commitment to achieving major social change through moral persuasion and nonviolence which Martin Luther King had learned from Gandhi to the "far-out" activities of the so-called countercultural "Yippies," who may be taken as an example of the extremes to which this approach can be taken. In some ways the 1960s seemed to be a time when it appeared possible to *change things* by *redefining them* through the development of a *new consciousness*. The more extreme version of such "consciousness politics" aimed at "blowing peoples' minds" is captured in the following summary:

> To blow peoples minds was to confront them with a situation that could shatter their cultural assumptions and, perhaps, liberate them from ruling-class images . . . . Without question, the master mindblowers in the New Left were a scruffy band of self-described "anti-intellectual action freaks" who called themselves the Youth International Party (YIP).
>
> Lacking any theory or organization and with a narrow social base, the Yippies concentrated on tactics. They used dramatic irony to reveal absurd contradictions in a social order whose legitimacy depended on the appearance of rationality.
>
> The Yippies' first major prank was to shower dollar bills from the visitors gallery onto the floor of the New York Stock Exchange.
>
> The Yippies appeared naked in church; invaded university classrooms, where they stripped to the waist and French kissed; dressed as Keystone Kops and staged a mock raid on the State University of New York Stony Brook campus to arrest all the whiskey drinkers; planted trees in the center of city streets; dumped soot and smokebombs in Con Edison's lobby; and called a press conference to demonstrate a drug called "lace," which when squirted at the police, made them take their clothes off and make love (Starr, 1985:267-270).

Quinney was no Yippy, but he was clearly influenced by the pervasive sense of the way in which the taken-for-granted aspects of social life were really a matter of collective definitions with which people went along largely without thinking. His position was laid out in greater detail in *The Social Reality of Crime* (Quinney, 1970b). There Quinney developed an analysis of the "social reality" of crime, drawing from Schutz (1962), Berger and Luckmann (1966) and others. Whatever physical reality may be, these theorists had argued that *social reality* consisted of the "meaningful world of everyday life" which was tied together by the fact that "human behavior is *intentional*, has *meaning* for the actors, is *goal-oriented*, and takes place with an *awareness* of the consequences" in such a way that the individuals share a collective reality made up of shared meanings and understandings (Quinney, 1970b:14; emphasis in the original). For Quinney the theoretical problem lay in the exploration and explanation of the *phenomenological processes* by which this collective meaning is developed and sustained.

The theory set forth in *The Social Reality of Crime* consisted of six propositions, beginning with a general definition of crime in which it is to be regarded as "a definition of human conduct that is created by authorized agents in a politically organized society," followed by the proposition that, "criminal definitions describe behaviors that conflict with the interests of segments of society that have the power to shape public policy" (Quinney, 1970b:15-16). Here Quinney indicated his indebtedness to both Vold and Turk; thus he observed that the probability of powerful segments of society formulating criminal definitions becomes greater with an increase in the conflict of interests between the segments of a society, and he insisted that the history of law reflected changes in the interest structure of society.

Quinney's (1970b:18) third proposition focused on the "law in action," asserting that "criminal definitions are *applied* by the segments of society that have the power to shape the enforcement and administration of criminal law" (emphasis added). He argued that "the probability that criminal definitions will be applied is influenced by such community and organizational factors as (1) community expectations of law enforcement and administration, (2) the visibility and public reporting of offenses, and (3) the occupational organization, ideology, and actions of the legal agents to whom authority to enforce criminal law is delegated" (Quinney, 1970b:19-20). In a fourth proposition dealing with the sources of the behavior resulting in the criminal label, he asserted that, "Behavior patterns are structured in segmentally organized society in relation to criminal definitions, and within this context persons engage in actions that have relative probabilities of being defined as criminal" (Quinney, 1970b:20). Taking the position that it is not the quality of the behavior but the action taken against it that makes it criminal, Quinney (1970b:21) went on to say that, "Persons in the segments of society whose behavior patterns are not represented in formulating and applying criminal definitions are more likely to act in ways that will be defined as criminal than those in the segments that formulate and apply criminal definitions."

Quinney (1970b:22) argued further that the definitions of crime developed by certain social segments had to be successfully diffused within the overall society before the generally accepted "social reality" could be altered: "Conceptions of crime are constructed and diffused in the segments of society by various means of communication." His final proposition summarized the entire theoretical framework: "The social reality of crime is constructed by the formulation and application of criminal definitions, the development of behavior patterns related to criminal definitions, and the construction of criminal conceptions" (Quinney, 1970b:23).

Four years later, however, Quinney (1974a, 1974b) published *Critique of the Legal Order: Crime Control in Capitalist Society* and *Criminal Justice in America: A Critical Understanding*, two volumes which reflected a significant shift to a Marxist approach. He now criticized not only positivism but also the sort of social constructionism and phenomenology that he had used so effectively four years earlier, charging that, "Positivists have regarded law as a natural phenomena; social constructionists have regarded it relativistically, as one of man's conveniences; and even the phenomenologists, though examining underlying assumptions, have done little to provide or promote an alternative existence" (Quinney, 1974a:15). Like Marx, he seems to have concluded that the point was not simply to understand social life as a collective construction but to change it, going on to say that, "With a sense of the more authentic life than may be possible for us, I am suggesting that a critical philosophy for understanding the social order should be based on a development of Marxist thought for our age" (Quinney, 1974a:15).

This shift in thinking was influenced by his reading of the work of the Frankfurt School of German social theorists, including Marcuse (1960, 1964, 1972)) and Habermas (1970, 1971), recent American work in the revived Marxist tradition mentioned above (Baran and Sweezy, 1966; Milibrand, 1969; Edwards, Reich and Weisskopf, 1972), and by his own interpretation of the "backlash," particularly the "War on Crime" as it had developed in the Johnson and Nixon administrations. Just when Chambliss and Quinney were calling for further change, the backlash appeared, exemplified initially by the "crackdown" on crime in the Johnson administration and then by the election of Richard Nixon, a political figure who had been twice rejected by the voters in the early and middle 1960s only to be elected President by the end of the decade. While criminologists such as Chambliss and Quinney were crying for *more* reform, the voters were electing a President who promised just the opposite.

It is also apparent that Quinney himself felt, much like many people around him, that the foundations of American life had to be changed if people were to regain a more "authentic existence." Quinney's six Marxist propositions read as follows:

> (1) American society is based on an *advanced capitalist economy*; (2) The state is organized to serve the interests *of the dominant economic class*, the capitalist ruling class; (3) Criminal law is an instrument of the state and ruling class to *maintain and perpetuate the existing social and economic order*; (4) Crime control in capitalist society is accomplished through a variety of institutions and agencies *established and administered by a governmental elite*, representing ruling class interests, for the purpose of establishing domestic order; (5) The contradictions of advanced capitalism — the disjunction between existence and essence — require *that the subordinate classes remain oppressed by whatever means necessary*, especially through the coercion and violence of the legal system; and (6) Only with the collapse of capitalist society and the creation of a new society, *based on socialist principles*, will there be a solution to the crime problem. (Quinney, 1974a:16; emphasis added)

This line of argument followed Engels in asserting that the institution of the political state arises only at a point in the development of society when private property appears and then becomes concentrated in the hands of a few, and that the law is "the ultimate means by which the state secures the interests of the ruling class" (Quinney, 1974a:98). Developing the argument contained in *The Social Reality of Crime* in a Marxist direction, Quinney (1974a:137) maintained that the clever manipulations of the ruling class were obscured by an ideology serving to justify the system and that, "Manipulating the minds of the people is capitalism's most subtle means of control." He stressed that the sort of socialism advocated was not that of a centralized state bureaucracy such as existed in the Soviet Union and some East European societies but rather a "democratic socialism" based on equality and giving everyone a chance to participate in control over his or her own life (Quinney, 1974a:188).

Quinney's thought continued to evolve in reaction to criticisms leveled at Marxist criminology and newer contributions to Marxist theory. Three years later he published *Class, State, and Crime* (Quinney, 1977), a volume in which he criticized recent theories of justice, arguing that they were all rooted in an implicit acceptance of the current economic order. He now laid great stress on the Marxist argument that capitalism generates a *surplus population* made up of unemployed laborers. The general problem of the capitalist state was seen as providing support for the growth of capitalism while trying to manage the resulting problems by such mechanisms as the welfare state and the criminal justice system. According to Quinney, some members of the surplus population are not coopted by such mechanisms as the welfare system, especially in view of the fact that capitalism finds it difficult to fund this mechanism adequately. They may adapt to their plight by turning to crime. "Nearly all crimes among the working class in capitalist society," he held, "are actually a means of *survival*, an attempt to exist in a society where survival is not assured by other, collective means" (Quinney, 1977:58).

At the same time, he moved from a position which seemed to suggest that the state was in the hands of a powerful and all-seeing elite to one emphasizing a "dialectical" concept of social class. Thus he asserted that, "A theory which posits an opposition between an elite (or a 'ruling class') and the 'masses' (or the 'people') fails to provide an adequate understanding of the forces of capitalist society" (Quinney, 1977:64). His new emphasis was closer to a structural Marxism which saw political outcomes as "natural"

results of the dynamics of the economic system than to an instrumental Marxism which saw political strings being pulled by a
small elite looking out for itself. Crime was considered in Engels's
terms as a "primitive form of insurrection, a response to deprivation and oppression," but one which "in itself is not a satisfactory form of politics" (Quinney, 1977:98-99). Although there were
still signs of the older conception of the "politicality of crime,"
crime was now clearly considered an unsatisfactory form of politics: it was not a sufficiently rational response to oppression unless
it succeeded in developing a revolutionary consciousness so that it
represented an *informed rebellion* against capitalist conditions.

Class, State and Crime also presented a typology of crime,
including *crimes of domination* and *crimes of accommodation and
resistance*. Crimes of domination were said to include *crimes of
control* (e.g., police brutality), *crimes of the government* (e.g.,
Watergate-style offenses) and *crimes of economic domination* (e.g.,
white-collar crime and organized crime). Crimes of accommodation
and resistance were said to include *predatory crimes* (e.g., theft)
and *personal crimes* (e.g., homicide), which were provoked by the
conditions of capitalism, and *crimes of resistance* (e.g., terrorism)
which involved the political struggle against the state.

Throughout Quinney's theoretical turns there was a constant
tension between the realms of the "subjective" and the "objective." Where *The Social Reality of Crime* had taken a subjec-
tively oriented, phenomenological, or "constructionist" view of the
world, *Critique of Legal Order* had thrown him into a Marxist
tradition of strict *materialism*, a tradition which not only explicitly rejected philosophical idealism but which regarded it as the
enemy. This tension broke through in the second edition of *Class,
State and Crime* (Quinney, 1980), which is heavily theological in
content. Indeed, it is interesting that current textbooks tend to
remain content with an examination of Quinney's "social reality"
period and his later Marxism without mention of this later development, almost as if it is either embarrassing or irrelevant. It
was certainly not irrelevant to Quinney, whose thought tended
thereafter to deal less with criminology per se and more with
existential philosophy and theology.

In the preface to the second edition of *Class, State, and Crime*,
Quinney (1980:ix) argued that, "Ultimately, the answer to the
human predicament is a salvation achieved through the overcom-

ing and healing of the disparity between existence and essence."
While continuing to advocate a socialist solution to the crime
problem, he increasingly emphasized the *religious* nature of the
goal, going so far as to reject Marxist materialism in favor of the
theology of Tillich: "The contemporary capitalist world is caught
in what Tillich, going beyond Marx's materialistic analysis of
capitalism, calls a *sacred void*, the human predicament on both a
spiritual and a sociopolitical level" (Quinney, 1980:3). The deeper
problem was described as follows: "Among the vacuous characteristics of present civilization are a mode of production that en-
slaves workers, an analytic rationalism that saps the vital forces
of life and transforms all things (including human beings) into
objects of calculation and control, a loss of feeling for the trans-
lucence of nature and the sense of history, a demotion of our world
to a mere environment, a secularized humanism that cuts us off
from our creative sources, a demonic quality to our political state,
and a hopelessness about the future" (Quinney, 1980:3). Returning
to the theme of justice and citing the Biblical prophets, he asserted
that, "Justice is more than a normative idea; it is charged with the
transcendent power of the infinite and the eternal, with the essence of divine revelation" (Quinney, 1980:30-31). What was necessary, he now argued, was a "prophetic understanding" of reality
(Quinney, 1980:40).

Much of the second edition of *Class, State, and Crime* was
devoted to discussions of the religious implications of socialism.
"The rise of political consciousness in the late stage of capitalism,"
Quinney (1980:112) asserted, "is increasingly accompanied by a
consciousness about matters of ultimate concern." He held that
Marx had erred in considering religion merely the "opium of the
people," and that, "A social criticism that does not consider the
sacred meaning of our existence systematically excludes the full
potential and essence of our being" (Quinney, 1980:199). "Prophetic criticism," he held, "takes place with an awareness of divine involvement in history." Quinney (1980:204) drew heavily
from theological writings such as Tillich's work on religious socialism, seeing the effort in this direction as one in which "we hope
to recover our wholeness, to heal our estrangement from the source
of our being." "The socialist struggle in our age," he concluded, "is
a search for God at the same time that it is a struggle for justice
in human society" (Quinney, 1980:204).

Conflict Theory and the Causes of Crime

During the 1960s, many criminologists had turned away from the search for the "causes" of crime. As we have seen, control theory focused upon the sources of *conformity*, under the assumption that crime and delinquency should be expected when there was a decline in the holding power of the conformity influences. Labeling theory treated crime as a matter of definition, with the source of the definition being the labelers. The early work of the conflict theorists Turk, Chambliss, and Quinney explored the criminalization process with a focus upon factors which might explain *the behavior of the authorities* rather than that of the offenders.

Still, criminological conflict theory did have something to say about the causes of offenders' behavior. We have already seen some examples. Turk had referred to cultural and social norms; Chambliss had considered crime as a rational reaction to exploitation; and Quinney had discussed the "politicality of crime" as involving the use of the only available and appropriate means to express certain thoughts and bring about certain changes. The question of causality, however, became more important in the criminological conflict theory which began to appear with the shift in the social climate at the end of the 1960s and the beginning of the 1970s. While mentioning possible sources of offenders' behavior from time to time, the earlier conflict theorists had concentrated on the way in which the traditional search for "causes" of criminal and delinquent behavior had deflected attention away from the fact that "crime" was the result of the criminalization of certain behavior by the powerful. Having made the point so powerfully, criminological conflict theory then turned more attention to the sources of the *behavior* which was being criminalized.

Early in the 1970s, for example, Gordon (1971) offered a Marxist economic analysis which traced a great deal of crime to the underlying economic structure of American society. He attempted to show how many crimes represented a rational response to the fact that the economic position of many people was kept in constant danger by the very nature of capitalism. By the middle of the decade, Spitzer (1976) had set forth the argument that capitalism generated both a *surplus population* which consisted essentially of economic outcasts and a series of *internal contradictions* in the institutions developed to maintain capitalist domination. He maintained that members of the surplus population were chronically unemployed outsiders who sometimes turned to deviant behavior including crime, and that additional deviance resulted from the tensions in such institutions as schools, which are said to serve youth but really serve the ruling class.

Focusing upon the sources of delinquency, Greenberg (1977), for example, argued that theft was one response to a situation in which adolescents in capitalistic society were put under heavy pressure to spend considerable money in a consumption-oriented youth culture even as the economic system was eliminating their employment opportunities. This lack of employment opportunities was said to produce considerable anxiety about prospects for achieving secure adult status, just at a time when institutions such as the school were taking away any sense of independence and subjecting the young people warehoused there to a variety of humiliating experiences. Greenberg maintained that such circumstances tended to produce a deep resentment and fear of failure which precipitated violent behavior, itself a reflection of a demand for respect.

Early in the 1980s, Colvin and Pauly (1983) attempted to combine control theory with a Marxist approach to social class issues. In their view, capitalist society tended to exert a pattern of "coercive control" over the lower classes, threatening those at or near the bottom with loss of jobs or of any economic assistance unless they conformed completely to the expectations of the powerful. Colvin and Pauly maintained that this pressure produced an "alienative involvement" on the part of those under such oppression, breaking what Hirschi might term their "bonds to society" and increasing the likelihood of criminal activity.

A number of other conflict theorists have also attempted to say something about the *causes* of criminal and delinquent *behavior*, but the focus has remained on the notion of crime as an outcome of definitions imposed as part of the consequences of conflict among various segments of society. Seen this way, the central theoretical problem is still to understand the nature of social conflict. Some of the more recent developments in criminological conflict theory will be examined in Chapter 7.

CONSEQUENCES OF CONFLICT THEORY

Criminological conflict theory has had notable consequences in terms of subsequent theorizing and rethinking within mainstream criminology but has had relatively little direct impact upon social policy. As indicated earlier, and as we will see in greater detail in the following chapter, the period of social turmoil that gave rise to contemporary criminological conflict theory was followed by a period of exhaustion and a social backlash of conservatism — as if people were trying to pretend that the 1960s had not happened and were determined to recapture the sense of tranquillity of the complacent 1950s. Some of the conflict perspective could be integrated into contemporary criminological theory and applied to social policy, but much was rejected. What was accepted and what was rejected depended primarily upon whether the formulations called for further social reform in the tradition of some of the earlier theories or demanded social revolution.

Turk's conflict approach had been highly formalized and had treated conflict patterns as essentially inevitable, so it was not to be expected that his theoretical perspective would lead to specific alterations in social policy. It did, however, have considerable impact not only within criminology but also within the more general field of "deviant behavior" studies. The concept of "criminal" as a *status* assigned by the authorities as a result of a process working itself out through conflict probabilities was especially appealing to those with a formal, sociological orientation who were interested in the conflict perspective but were put off by the ideological fervor of many Marxists.

As for the conflict perspective presented by Chambliss in *Crime and the Legal Process* and elaborated in the later work with Seidman, it is worth noting that a number of the policy implications inherent in that approach had already been addressed by the U.S. Supreme Court under Chief Justice Earl Warren. Indeed, the Warren Court was in its own way as much a part of the turbulent 1960s as was the civil rights movement, the counterculture, and the Vietnam protests. Years before Chambliss began his work, the Warren Court had shown considerable appreciation for the legal realists' distinction between the "law in the books" and the "law in action." It had extended the legal rights of convicted offenders as well as suspects and private citizens, so as to provide them with additional protections in their struggles with the bureaucratic agendas of the police, courts, and corrections. Chambliss himself was well aware of this, and he actually dedicated his first book to Chief Justice Warren. It is ironic that it appeared at the time of President Nixon's appointment of the conservative Warren Burger to replace the retiring Earl Warren which took the Court back into a posture which gave much *less* attention to the way in which the "law in action" might differ from the "law in the books."

Chambliss's use of the tradition of legal realism has been of considerable influence within criminology and, like Turk's work, has also been influential within the field of "deviant behavior" studies. Quinney's early work had essentially the same theoretical implications as Turk's, but any interpretation of its policy implications depends upon one's interpretation of philosophical idealism. As noted above, Quinney later decided that his earlier phenomenological, "constructionist" approach tended to impede efforts to change things. Nevertheless, the earlier position seems to have had more impact upon both criminological thought and "deviant behavior" studies than his later Marxist or theological approaches. The concept of crime as a result of the "social construction of reality" is broader still than labeling theory, and the general perspective has become extremely influential in the larger field of "social problems" theory (Ball and Lilly, 1982).

As long as the conflict theories went only one step further than the theories tracing crime to criminogenic elements in society as discussed in Chapter 3 or the labeling theories pointing to the relativity of crime as discussed in Chapter 5, they tended to strengthen the case for policies of social reform suggested by those perspectives. In fact, they gave the appearance of greater political realism. They recognized that the inequalities stressed by the opportunity theories and the stigmatizing processes emphasized by the labeling theories had a great deal to do with the perceived interests of the powerful and they suggested how the powerful and the bureaucracies representing them might be held more accountable. Thus, for example, some of the radicals took an active part in community campaigns to curb police brutality, raise bail for poor defendants, abolish the death penalty, stop the repression of political dissidents, and provide support for prisoners (Greenberg, 1981). Some pushed for policies allowing for greater social diversity without criminalization of those who were "different" and for

more informal, community-based policies of conflict accommodation such as arbitration, informal dispute settlement, and conflict
resolution through negotiation outside the mechanisms of the
political state (Mathiesen, 1974; Pepinsky, 1976; Quinney, 1974a).

But when they called for the abolition of capitalism, the radical
criminologists produced mostly charges of either misunderstanding Marxism (which indicated that they were not to be taken
seriously) or of understanding it too well (which indicated that
they were dangerous revolutionaries of the sort Senator McCarthy
had warned America against in the 1950s). This was in general the
fate of the later work of both Chambliss and Quinney.

Even if society had been ready for further dramatic social
change in the late 1970s, the problem of policy impact would have
probably remained, simply because of the inability or unwillingness of Marxist conflict theorists to provide blueprints for policy.
The tendency of Marxists was to condemn capitalism and insist
that individuals equipped with a revolutionary consciousness
would be able to work their way through policy changes as they
came. They generally held, for example, that it was too early to try
to spell out exactly what law and criminal justice (if such continued
to exist) would look like under democratic socialism. While some
were willing to predict, for example, that prisons would probably
still be needed, although for many fewer prisoners in a very different setting, others were less inclined to offer blueprints for the
future. Although this stance can be understood in terms of the
Marxist focus upon principles of "dialectical logic," it made no
sense to contemporary policy makers (and many criminological
theorists) who knew and trusted only the "instrumental logic" of
ends-means calculation which insists that the policy makers spell
out precisely what they expect to find at the end of the political
journey before undertaking it in the first place (Ball, 1978, 1979).

Although conflict theory had little direct impact upon social
policy, it has had a great deal of impact within criminology itself.
It lead to considerable rethinking as to the nature of law, with most
textbooks taking a more critical stand than was the case at the
beginning of the 1960s. More recent criminological conflict theorists working in the Marxist tradition have moved toward structural Marxism and away from the instrumental Marxism which
seemed so close to the notion of a conspiracy of dominance by a tiny
elite at the top. This instrumental Marxism had tended to portray

the capitalist elite as an omniscient few who knew everything and always pulled the strings at exactly the right moment to see that their interests were served. Structuralism locates the basis of social control factors such as law in class relations generally rather than asserting that it was entirely within the total, conscious control of the capitalists at all times. Structural Marxism bears a resemblance to the formalism of Simmel, Vold, and Turk because it maintains that social conflict is a matter of the inherent social dynamics of a particular system. It differs by taking a more historically relative position, maintaining that the key to understanding these dynamics lies not in formal logic which deals with social systems *in the abstract* but in a "dialectical logic" which is rooted in an understanding of the structural features of capitalism *in particular.*

At the same time that the Marxist conflict theories were attacking capitalism, they had criticized conventional criminology. This criticism had consequences, even if only in making it more difficult to be complacent about the field. These criticisms included charges that conventional criminology was itself a part of the capitalist system and tended to support it, thereby contributing to the crime problem rather than to its understanding or its solution. The more radical conflict theorists insisted that conventional criminology had tended to accept the law as given, concentrating on the behavior of the "offender" and searching for some pathological source of this behavior in biological, psychological or social factors. They maintained that this very search tended to exaggerate the notion that the criminal was in some important way "different from the rest of us" when in fact the problem lay in the creation and enforcement of the laws that produced the criminals. Some demanded that crimes also be considered from the perspective of the criminal, using the writings of prisoners as part of an attempt to escape a narrow, class-biased point of view.

Some of the radical criminologists leveled heavy criticisms at the efforts of conventional criminology to maintain a value-free, "scientific" posture which refused to get involved in political debate or political action, insisting that scientific criminology confine itself to the "facts." This position went back to the development of the positivistic approach discussed in Chapter 2. By refusing to take a moral stand, the critics of positivism charged, conventional criminology was implicitly accepting the moral ideology provided by the powerful and forced on the powerless. When mainstream criminologists responded that they were not simply accepting the ideology of the powerful at all but were in fact operating on the basis of broad social consensus, the radicals argued that this public consensus was a misleading mirage based on the power of the elite to shape public opinion (Michalowski and Bohlander, 1976; Quinney, 1970; Reiman, 1979). As such, it seemed to them to represent a "manufactured consensus" (Greenberg, 1981:9). Indeed, conventional criminologists seemed to some of them to "reproduce the hegemony of the existing relations of property, race, and sexual privilege," either so as "to regain prestige, to build research empires, or because they truly believe in the ideas of those in positions of power" (Krisberg and Austin, 1978:119).

Even the reforms urged by conventional criminology, the radical theorists had insisted, were simply minor tinkering which tended to support the further survival of a corrupt social system by making it appear that the powerful do care and that progress is being made toward economic and political "justice." Meanwhile, they added, conventional criminology was providing the knowledge necessary to detect and control those seen as threats to the powerful. Thus, for example, Platt (1969) had argued that the original establishment of the juvenile court was not a means of helping youth but rather a technique by which upper-class, Republican, Protestant women extended control over the children of the Catholic and Jewish immigrants. In a similar vein, the concept of rehabilitation was criticized as a tool of political oppression which justified prolonged and invasive tinkering with the minds and bodies of prisoners under the guise of assisting them (Smith and Fried, 1974; Wright, 1973).

One does not have to accept radical conflict theory to realize that it is easy to be taken in by the assumptions of the times. Indeed, this volume itself represents an effort to show how thinking about crime is shaped intimately by the nature of social context. Complacency has no place in criminology, and conflict theory, especially of the radical variety, is anything but complacent. Whatever its defects, criminological conflict theory has certainly succeeded in providing for a broadened reorientation and an increased sensitivity to issues previously overlooked or treated only in passing (Thomas and Hepburn, 1983).

7

Conservative Criminology: Revitalizing Individualistic Theory

The objectives of this concluding chapter are those outlined in Chapter 1 and sought throughout the book. We will examine the context, content, and policy implications of criminological theory in America with a focus on developments during the 1980s. As the chapter unfolds it will become clear that some of the theoretical paths that had emerged in previous periods continued to develop into the 1980s, but that the emphasis shifted once again in accordance with the context of the times. Our central theme centers upon the way in which the conservatism of the 1980s formed a context contributing to the revitalization of those perspectives which locate the sources of crime in the individual. It is as if criminological theory had come full circle, with a return to the classical school depiction of crime as the result of individual actors exercising rational choice or the positivistic portrayal of crime as the result of organic anomalies or psychological defects.

We have deliberately focused much of the substantive material on the America of the 1980s because of sources readily available in the mass media. It is difficult to analyze the 1980s from a point too close to the time to allow for historical perspective, and a more balanced analysis must await the work of scholars to come. Our hope here is both to capture something of the "flavor" of the 1980s and to encourage the reader to ponder the images portrayed in the mass media of the period as something more than "just news," something amounting to the construction of a collective sense of social reality.

CONTEXT: THE AMERICA OF THE 1980s

So as to make our analysis more manageable, we will concentrate upon developments in the United States. As indicated in Chapter 6, the turmoil of the 1960s was succeeded by a political "backlash" leading to the election of Richard Nixon to the Presidency. Nixon was elected in part because of promises to "get tough" on crime and because he indicated that he would extricate the United States from the quagmire of Vietnam by way of a "secret plan." He made "perfectly clear" his extreme distaste for the dress and drugs of the "counterculture," and his election signaled the return to power of those who had little enthusiasm and limited tolerance for the civil rights and feminist movements of the time. Within a few years the United States was subjected to the episodes associated with Watergate and to the first resignation of a President.

Behind the scenes, however, certain economic and political tensions had been building for decades. Indeed, these institutionalized contradictions had been very important to the sense of peace and prosperity of the 1950s and the radical shifts of the 1960s, and they were to play a major role in the events of the 1970s and 1980s.

The Economic Decline of the United States

By the close of the second world war in 1945, the United States' share of world manufacturing was nearly 50 percent, a proportion so great that never before or since has it been attained by a single nation. The United States came out of the war so strong economically that Henry Luce, one of the nation's newspaper publishers, proclaimed that it was the beginning of the "American Century." Indeed, such a prediction was reasonable at the time; in 1945, for example, the United States owned two-thirds of the world's gold reserves and all of its atomic bombs. It was truly the initial stages of the Americanization of the Old World. In view of the United States's vast economic power, it did little good for countries like France to try to outlaw the importation and sale of items such as Coca Cola (Kennedy, 1987:29). Only a few short years before, at the beginning of the war, the United States was producing only about one-third of the world's manufactured good, which at that time was twice that of Nazi Germany and almost ten times that of Japan.

With such immense resources, it is not surprising that after 1945 the United States began to extend military protection (some would say "capitalistic-militaristic imperialism"). By 1970 the United States had more than one million soldiers in 30 countries and was a major supplier of military aid to nearly 100 nations around the world (Kennedy, 1987:29). As the United States' military commitments began to increase after 1945, however, its position in the world manufacturing and world gross national production began to decline, slowly at first and then with increasing speed. For our purposes, it is significant to recognize that while the United States' military expenditures under Presidents Eisenhower and Kennedy were approximately ten percent of the GNP (Gross National Product), the United States' share of global production and wealth was about twice what it is now. Even so, despite today's weakened domestic and international economy, the United States still devotes approximately seven percent of its GNP to defense spending, a percentage that is higher than major economic rivals such as Japan and West Germany.

A glimpse at the precarious nature of the United States' 1980s economic condition and its strong commitment to defense spending can be seen by recognizing, first, that under President Reagan our defense spending increased at least 50 percent more than what was spent under President Carter, Reagan's predecessor. Second, we can examine the growth of our national debt and the interest on the debt. In 1980, for example, the federal deficit was $59.6 billion; in 1985 it was $202.8 billion. Interest on these debts was $52.5 billion and $129 billion respectively in 1980 and 1985 (Kennedy, 1988:33). In 1988 the United States had a $500 billion federal deficit, a far cry from when it owned two-thirds of the world's gold reserves in 1945. Some observers have termed this situation the "Argentining of America" (Newsweek, 1988a:22). Others have predicted that the United States' world economic position will continue to decline, and that the next century belongs not to the United States, but to countries in Asia, especially Japan. This point is made vividly clear by recognizing that by 1995 private Japanese investors will own $1 trillion, or ten percent, of all assets in the United States (Newsweek, 1988a:45).

Other changes in different parts of the world also contributed to the United States' predicament. Over the last two decades, for instance, some foreign countries have increased their world production in areas where the United States once ranked supreme, such as in the production of textiles, iron and steel, shipbuilding, and basic chemicals. In addition, the United States faces stiff international competition in the production and distribution of robotics, aerospace technology, automobiles, machine tools, and computers (Kennedy, 1987:29). And in food production, another area the United States ranked supreme even into the 1970s, Third World countries and the European Economic Community now export food, thus competing with the United States's farm production and sales. Consequently, at least for the time being, some experts say the "world is awash in food" (Kennedy, 1987:29).

The Persistence of Inequality in the United States

Since the 1960s it has become clearer that the roots of inequality run even deeper in the United States than many had suspected. By the 1980s college attendance had become more and more difficult for young people, some feminists were expressing doubts over the meaning of "gender equality," and racism was reappearing in some especially ugly forms. Because of the underlying economic shifts outlined above, the economic pie was no longer as large to the relative number of those hungry for a slice as it had seemed in the 1960s and early 1970s. Because the power of youths had declined as the huge number of "baby boomers" who had fueled the protests of the 1960s moved toward middle age, and perhaps because many of the more energetic, educated, and articulate women and blacks had been successful in obtaining their own slice of the pie, thus becoming a part of the "System," pressure for basic systemic change ebbed. More and more people seemed to focus on their own, personal problems and to seek gratification through attention to their own, intensely personal world. By the end of the 1970s, Lasch (1978) had already cited the rise of a "culture of narcissism," and some were proclaiming the coming of the "Me Decade."

The racism issue may be taken as an example. During the late 1960s, President Lyndon B. Johnson had appointed the Kerner Commission, charging it to investigate the causes of the racial riots of the time. The Commission had concluded that the riots were the result of white racism and cautioned that unless white attitudes and behavior changed, the United States would continue to move toward a system made up of two societies, one black, one white — separate and unequal. Twenty years later it was evident that while some progress had been made, the black community had become comprised of three separate groups (*New York Times*, 1988a:13). One of these contained the black middle class, a group which had relative economic success during the two decades prior to the 1980s. This group also had the most success in the political arena; almost 300 cities in the United States have black mayors, and in 1988 the Rev. Jesse Jackson, a black Christian minister, was a viable candidate for the United States' presidency.

The black working class comprised the second group. These blacks often experienced great difficulty sustaining their economic position, because they were most vulnerable to the effects of modern "de-industrialization."

The "black underclass," the third group, was composed of people who had succumbed to the economic and social strains inherent in slum living (Wilson, 1987). They represented the "miserable human residue, mired in hard-core unemployment, violent crime, drug-use, teen-age pregnancy and one of the world's worst human environments, [which] seems to be a partial, perverse result of the very success of other blacks" (*New York Times*, 1988a:13). The bleakness of the economic situation for black citizens is made more clear by incorporating the following information into our examination of the last decade:

- The black median income was 57 percent that of whites; it declined about 4 percent since the early 1970s as the black-white income gap has continued to widen during the last fifteen years.
- Though blacks represent only 11.7 percent of the total population, three times as many blacks as whites live in poverty.
- The percentage of black high school graduates starting college declined over the last 12 years: In 1976, 34 percent of the black high school graduates entered college, but by the late 1980s this figure and dropped to 26 percent. Of blacks entering college, moreover, only 42 percent graduate. This trend was worse during the 1980s.

- According to the federal government's Office for Civil Rights, minority students were also more likely than whites to be suspended or placed in classes for the handicapped, and they were less likely to graduate from public high schools (*New York Times*, 1988b:16).

These figures lead to an interesting and important question: Did racial hatred and violence directed at minorities increase in the United States in the late 1980s? Unfortunately, no reliable data exist on racial, religious, or ethnic violence for the entire United States (*New York Times*, 1987c:13). Only a few cities, New York, for example, have created special units for crimes motivated by hatred. Nevertheless, several sources show that reports of racial strife and violence are on the increase. In mid-1987 the United States Justice Department's Community Relations Service released information indicating that racial incidents reported to the government rose from 99 in 1980 to 276 in 1986 (*New York Times*, 1987c:13). Corroborative information is present in investigations of arson and cross-burnings that have followed the move of minorities into mostly white neighborhoods. The Klanwatch Project of the Southern Poverty Law Project, Montgomery, Alabama, found that between 1985 and 1986, there were hundreds of acts of vandalism and other incidents directed at members of minority groups who had moved into mostly white areas (*New York Times*, 1987d:22).

Reports such as these were not restricted to the Deep South. In New York City alone the number of reports of incidents of racial assaults in which blacks and whites were injured in the first eight months of 1987 were the highest in the seven-year Investigating Unit. There were 235 incidents in all of 1986, while 301 incidents were reported in the first eight months of 1987. A similar trend was reported by the Mayor's Management Report; it stated that the number of bias incidents doubled between fiscal year 1986 and 1987 (*New York Times*, 1987e:19). Further, the Anti-Defamation League of B'nai B'rith reported that anti-Semitic acts rose 12 percent in 1987. New York, the state with the largest Jewish population, led the nation with vandalism incidents, followed by California, New Jersey, and Florida (*New York Times*, 1987f:13).

The range of racial and ethnic incidents during the 1980s is striking. Students at Dartmouth College, for example, were charged with harassing a black professor (*New York Times,* 1988c:7; *New York Times,* 1988d:3). Cadets at the Citadel, a prestigious military college located in Charleston, South Carolina, were indicted on charges of racial hazing (*New York Times,* 1987g:15). A 37-year-old F.B.I. agent reported that he was the victim of years of harassment by other agents, including having a family photograph on his desk destroyed when someone taped a picture of an ape over his son's face and having his signature forged on two insurance forms, one for death and dismemberment (*New York Time,* 1988e:1,17).

Part of the mood of the 1980s was symbolized by the Bernard Goetz case. Just three days before Christmas 1984, Goetz, a middle-class white, shot four black youths on a New York subway, after one of them had asked for five dollars. In June 1987 a jury acquitted Goetz on the shooting charge. Throughout the proceedings, a debate raged over issues of racial tension, self-defense and the perception that Goetz's acquittal would be interpreted as widening the circumstances justifying deadly force, at least of whites against blacks (*Newsweek,* 1987b:20-21; *New York Time,* 1987h:11).

The Rhetoric of Stability

Those who do not wish to consider fundamental changes in the social order tend to locate the sources of social problems such as crime either in defective individuals or in failures of the institutions of socialization (Rubington and Weinberg, 1971). The increase in racial discrimination and violence outlined above represented but one example, albeit a very important one, of tendencies to see certain *types of people* as the problem. As for the focus upon the alleged *failures of our institutions of socialization,* it amounts to a belief that the "American Way of Life" is either exemplary or at least fundamentally sound, but that the institutions of work, family, education, and religion are somehow failing to integrate potential troublemakers into the "mainstream"; as such, institutions are therefore in need of reaffirmation and strengthening. If the first of these perspectives may be said to characterize President Nixon, the second was well represented by the Democratic successor to the Nixon-Ford years, James Earl

("Jimmy") Carter.

Carter's rise to the United States Presidency is instructive. Long before the underlying problems of the United States's economic decline described earlier were apparent to the mass media or the general public, important American financial interests had responded with the creation in 1973 of the Trilateral Commission, a combined effort of powerful interests in America, Europe, and Japan. The one-time director of the Commission, Zbigniew Brzezinski, summarized public disenchantment over Watergate, Ford's subsequent pardon of Nixon, and a host of related signs of loss of faith in the "system" by writing that "the democratic candidate in 1976 will have to emphasize work, the family, religion, and increasing patriotism to be elected" (Allen, 1977). Partly as one aspect of the "Southern Strategy" to win back the electoral votes of the South, Carter was selected as a Southern governor exemplifying these attributes. Upon his election, Brzezinski, became Carter's National Security Advisor.

President Carter was elected not only because of powerful supports from influential political "kingmakers," however, but also because he symbolized the "mood" of the times better than any other candidate. Indeed, it is important to remember that political figures in America are successful in large part because of their ability to mold themselves to the public mood, to "become what they want." Carter succeeded in reaffirming the work ethic to the extent that he was often called a "workaholic," and he was well-known for his familial affection for wife, daughter, and even his "bad-boy" brother, Billy. As a self-proclaimed "born-again" Christian with evangelicals in his immediate family, he represented some of the longing for a return to more traditional religious values and for moral leadership in the aftermath of the Watergate scandal. His Presidency floundered, however, upon his inability to reaffirm the power of patriotism with a victory over the hostage-holders in Iran, and he was in turn succeeded by Ronald Reagan, who became even more a symbol of America in the 1980s than Carter had been in his time.

During the late 1970s President Carter spoke publicly of surveys showing a pervasive "malaise" in the United States. The public had lost much of the traditional American faith in education as a force for socialization. Many seemed to feel that the changes of the 1960s had destroyed the cohesion of the family and undermined its capacity to socialize and control American citizens. Religion seemed to offer personal solace to an increasing number of citizens, but perhaps it became less of a vehicle for community building and reform as more and more Americans turned to charismatic televangelists for spiritual direction.

By the end of the 1970s, the mood of the American public seemed to fit nicely with candidate Reagan's position that too many "naysayers" were spending too much time criticizing America and focusing on the dark side when what was needed was for a patriotic public to "stand up for America." Society as a whole seemed to be tired of social concerns and eager to turn its back on internal problems of economic decline, racism, poverty, environmental pollution and all the rest, almost as if they did not exist. It was not a time in which strain theories were likely to gain much of a hearing, much less conflict theories. While labeling theory was paid some lip-service in certain quarters, some of the old stereotypes were back in fashion, including racist labeling and the tendency to define social problems by attaching negative labels to troublemakers as if the labels explained everything.

The times were more attuned to theoretical perspectives which located the source of problems in "bad apples," particular types of individuals in need of additional social control. But in a time when faith had been lost in the "containing" and "bonding" power of the family and the school, the two institutions of socialization upon which control theory relied, and when people now seemed unwilling to provide the financial support needed to strengthen them, increased reliance on a "tough" criminal justice system held great appeal for many.

The inauguration of President Reagan suggested to some that the United States public was about to embrace the 1950s spirit once again. The theme of the "Me Decade" that had been proclaimed in the late 1970s began to take on a somewhat different tinge. While the focus was much upon the individual "looking out for Number 1," there was at the same time more and more condemnation of the "permissive society." Thus, for example, the society as a whole seemed to view much more positively the somewhat cynical pursuit of individual, material success in the "rat race," while growing much less tolerant of individualistic pursuits of pleasure in the form of sex and drugs. In fact, it became fashionable to call for surveillance over sexuality and compulsory drug testing on the principle of restriction of individual rights for the protection of society.

The Embrace of Materialism. The America of the 1980s often seemed like a case of "life imitating art," if the mass media portrayals can be called "art." The top-ranked television series in 1981 was the prime-time soap-opera "Dallas," featuring scenes of Texas highrollers led by the conniving Ewing oil baron "J.R." Later in the decade, the real-life Wall Street wheeler-dealer Ivan Boesky, who had summarized the thinking of many in his assertion that "Greed is not a bad thing" (*Newsweek*, 1988b:42), was named by *Fortune* magazine as "Crook of the Year" (*Newsweek*, 1988b:44), after agreeing to relinquish illegal profits of $50 million and indemnify another $50 million, and was later honored with a three-year prison sentence. In 1984, "Lifestyles of the Rich and Famous" was brought to television under the guidance of its aptly named host, Robin Leach (*Newsweek*, 1988b:42), and in that same year *Newsweek* declared the real-life "Year of the Yuppie." In direct contrast to the "Yippies" of the 1960s, the "Yuppies" (Young Upwardly Mobile Urban Professionals) represented a symbol of the times as a demographic cohort of self-centered, materialistic, plastic people bent entirely on "making it" with no social conscience getting in the way.

The Reaffirmation of Traditional Sexual Preachments. The open, hedonistic sexuality which many associated with the rise of the 1960s counterculture was declared a thing of the past in articles with titles such as "Sex in the 80s: The Revolution Is Over" (*Time*, 1984:74-78). A *Newsweek* cover story announced that the "Playboy Party Is Over," and *Time* referred to an era of "Sex Busters." Examples of the new mood abound: Congressional opposition to the Braille editions of *Playboy* magazine that had been published monthly since 1970 under the National Library Service for the Blind and Physically Handicapped; a highly criticized government-sponsored study of how children are portrayed in *Playboy, Penthouse,* and *Hustler*; increased violence against homosexuals; and a hotly disputed Justice Department report on pornography.

The debate over sexual values also reached into the nation's courts. For example, in *Bowers v. Hardwick* (1986), decided in the middle of the decade, the Supreme Court upheld (by the narrowest of margins in a 5-4 split), a Georgia law that made it a felony punishable by 20 years in prison for consenting adults to engage in oral or anal sexual relations. The case developed innocently enough when a police officer went to Hardwick's apartment to serve a warrant for carrying an open container of alcohol in a public place (part of a "crackdown" on drinking). The officer was ushered into the apartment by a guest and told that he could find Hardwick in his bedroom. There the officer discovered Hardwick engaged in oral sex with another man and made an arrest. In effect, the court ruled that individuals under Georgia law had no right to engage in such acts even as consenting adults in a private bedroom, taking the position that the state had a legitimate right to restrict and control such behavior as part of its responsibility for enforcing public morality even in private places.

In a matter also related to balancing privacy versus state interests, the 1980s witnessed the increasingly heated debate on the right of women to terminate pregnancy through abortion. The courts were asked repeatedly to reconsider *Roe v. Wade*, the 1973 Supreme Court case which had declared as unconstitutional laws prohibiting abortion, largely on the judgment that state interests were not compelling enough to justify interference in the personal privacy of women. As a difficult moral dilemma, the stance taken on abortion often cut across usual ideological lines (e.g., liberal Catholics opposing "pro-choice"). Even so, the growing pro-life movement was nourished by America's turn to the right, as conservative politicians, religious leaders, and right-to-life groups played prominent roles in the crusade to overturn *Roe v. Wade*. They argued that the interest of the state in maintaining public morality — represented most fully in the moral choice to protect the lives of the unborn — was more than sufficient to allow state legislatures once again to restrict, if not criminalize, the practice of abortion.

Finally, the 1980s saw the emergence of AIDS as a growing threat. AIDS's mounting toll initiated much discourse in the media and in political forums over existing sexual practices. For liberals, AIDS precipitated a call for more pragmatism in sexual relationships: the prudent selection of partners, the practice of "safe sex," and broader efforts to educate about the transmission of sexual diseases. But for conservatives, the AIDS menace provided incontrovertible evidence of the dire consequences of the breakdown of sexual morality. Ultimately, conservatives warned, the problem of AIDS reflected a moral failing — the result of sex outside the boundaries of marriage — and it could only be eliminated by a reaffirmation of traditional sexual values.

The "War on Drugs." Early in the Reagan administration there had been anti-drug campaigns, and in 1986 the federal government declared a new $250 million "War on Drugs," a "war" that was to extend the compulsory drug testing of employees in the world of business and athletics to federal employees (*Newsweek*, 1986a; *Time*, 1986a:12, 13). The announcement of the new testing policy came after a five-month Congressional study that had concluded that "urinalysis procedures were expensive, 'useless in most cases' and often inaccurate" (*Washington Post*, 1986:15), and was to be implemented despite the lack of any evidence that those to be tested had used illegal drugs or had committed any crime at all. The federal government was described as in a "frenzy" over drugs (*New York Times*, 1986a:25). Despite arguments that what employees do on their "private time" was their "own business" unless it affects job performance and that such testing replaces the due process assumption of innocence with an assumption of guilt until proven otherwise, a White House poll reported that "the public was more concerned about drugs than about such matters as the federal budget deficit and arms control" (*Time*, 1986a:12).

The Department of Justice and the U.S. Supreme Court. While it may not be true that the positions taken by units of the federal government reflect the times exactly, they do provide clues. Thus it is instructive to consider trends in both the United States Department of Justice and the U.S. Supreme Court during the 1980s. In both cases there was increasing reluctance to focus upon possible social conditions underlying crime and a tendency to regard ordinary, street criminals with their impoverished, minority-group backgrounds as deserving a harsher treatment than they were receiving.

At the beginning of President Reagan's second term, his close friend Edwin Meese was appointed Attorney General. From that point, even the decisions of the U.S. Supreme Court came into official question when they seemed to stray beyond the accepted position. Although the court itself was moving in the same direction, it found on occasion that it could not keep up with the pace of the new definitions.

Attorney General Meese, for example, declared in 1986 that

Supreme Court decisions should not necessarily by regarded as the supreme law of the land (*Newsweek*, 1986b:9). He argued that Supreme Court decisions were binding *only* for those involved in a specific case (*New York Times*, 1986b). A similar position was advocated by the chief of the Justice Department's civil-rights division, William Bradford Reynolds. Not only did he publicly criticize the competence of a Supreme Court judge, he also argued that efforts to achieve a radically egalitarian society would, perhaps, pose a major threat to individual liberty (*Newsweek*, 1986c:27). Reynolds was also the leader of assaults on federal civil-rights and school desegregation programs, efforts to enhance equality in women's college athletics, and efforts to halt antidiscrimination in housing. According to Griffin Bell, Attorney General under President Carter, "That's what he was hired to do" (*Newsweek*, 1986c:27).

In matters closely related to criminal justice, the leadership of the Justice Department was equally conservative. Attorney General Meese, for example, advocated overturning the 1966 Miranda decision which required the police to inform criminal suspects of their legal rights. He referred to the decision as "infamous" (*New York Times*, 1987i:13). Chief Justice William H. Rehnquist sounded a similar refrain by calling for a limit on last-minute appeals filed by death row inmates. He argued that such appeals create "chaotic conditions. . . within a day or two before an execution . . ." (*New York Times*, 1988f:7). Unfortunately the "chaotic conditions" which concern Rehnquist resulted in part from the fact that the Supreme Court "made it clear that the constitutional right to assign counsel [did] not apply to litigation beyond the first appeal" (*New York Times*, 1988g:27). Of the nearly 2,000 inmates on death row in 37 states, 99 percent cannot afford a lawyer. Meanwhile, Attorney General Meese advocated execution for teenaged killers (*Cincinnati Enquirer*, 1985a:1,6).

In view of the conservative atmosphere just described for the Justice Department during the Reagan administration, it was not surprising that the Supreme Court, in a 5-4 decision, voted to restudy the *Runyon v. McCrary* (1976) decision which had expanded the rights of minorities to sue private parties for racial discrimination. Three of the five judges voting for the reexamination were appointed to their positions by President Reagan; Chief Justice Rehnquist, who also voted for the restudy, had been elevated to this position by President Reagan (*New York Times*, 1988h:1, 11).

In summary, amid the economic and political turmoil of the 1980s, the mood of the United States also contained the need to reaffirm and perhaps revitalize, faith in "the American way of life." The opportunity to address this need was provided by the 100th birthday of the Statue of Liberty in 1986.

After two years of refurbishing at a cost of $39 million, the Statue of Liberty and all that it symbolizes was celebrated with the most expensive and extravagant party ever held in the world. It was attended by more than 5 million people. And as testimony to the themes of liberty, freedom, and a new life, each central to the core of American values and symbolized by the Statue of Liberty, more than 25,000 immigrants took the citizenship oath on July 4, 1986, in 44 different locations across the United States. The reaffirmation celebration was also attended by foreign dignitaries, and no less than 35 foreign warships stood by in New York Harbor as a symbolic gesture supporting the American way of life. And in true American form, a dance was held on Governors Island . . . at a cost of $10,000 per couple (*Time*, 1986b; *Newsweek*, 1986d).

CONTENT: INDIVIDUALISTIC THEORIES REVITALIZED

Rather than being a period of new theories cut from whole cloth, the 1980s were primarily a time that witnessed the revitalization of old theories. Especially significant for our purposes is recognizing that some of the revitalized theories stressed explanations of crime which focused on the question, "What's wrong with individual criminals?"—a question that directs attention to looking *within* individuals for explanations of their behavior.

The rise in such individualistic thinking comes as little surprise. The 1980s, as we have seen, ushered in a period of rising conservatism — so much so that politicians scurried to avoid the label of "liberal." At its best, conservatism represents a principled defense of individual responsibility, of respect for tradition, and of the need for social order. At its worst, however, conservatism turns a blind eye to the difficult social circumstances endured by many citizens. "Failure" — whether by being poor, or perhaps by being criminal — is seen either as a matter of choosing a profligate lifestyle or as a product of defects in the individual's character or endowment. The danger of this thinking is not only that it erroneously overlooks the social sources of human behavior but also that it eases social conscience: Because individuals are to blame for their actions, no need exists to question the justice of the prevailing social arrangements or to support policies that call on citizens to share their advantages with the less fortunate.

In short, the context of the past decade or so has been fertile soil for the growth of conservative thinking about crime. Sociological explanations of crime still accrue substantial support, but now they face stiff competition from explanations that seek to revitalize the thinking of the early classical and positivist schools of criminology and thus to locate crime's causes within an individual's will, mind, and body (Flanagan, 1987).

Crime and Human Nature: Wilson and Herrnstein

The best publicized example to the return of individualistic explanations of crime appeared in James Q. Wilson and Richard J. Herrnstein's *Crime and Human Nature* (1985). It was greeted by numerous reviews in such well-known publications as *Time, Newsweek, U.S. News and World Report, Vogue, New York Times*, and the *Chronicle of Higher Education*, and it was also treated as a news item by the Associated Press (see *Cincinnati Enquirer*, 1985:C-12). The basic argument offered by Wilson, then a Harvard University political scientist and now at UCLA, and Herrnstein, a psychologist from Harvard, was based on a biosocial explanation of behavior, which focused attention primarily on "constitutional factors" (Wilson and Herrnstein, 1985: Chapter 3). Such factors, some of which are genetic, were treated by Wilson and Herrnstein as predisposing individuals to engage in criminal behavior. In their words, they wanted to explain "why some individuals are more likely than others to commit crime," and "why some persons commit serious crimes at a higher rate and others do not" (Wilson and Herrnstein, 1985:20-21). Their effort was directed toward explaining *criminality* rather than *crime*.

Although the authors did not give their theory a specific label or name, its biosocial focus was clear:

The existence of biological predispositions means that circumstances that activate behavior in one person will not do so in another, that social forces cannot deter criminal behavior in 100 percent of the population, and that the distribution of crime within and across societies may, to some extent, reflect underlying distributions of constitutional factors. Crime cannot be understood without taking into account predispositions and their biological roots. (Wilson and Herrnstein, 1985:103)

In certain respects, Wilson and Herrnstein's (1985:89) perspective harkens back to the theories of Lombroso, Hooton, Sheldon, and the Gluecks (see Chapter 2) and to the positivist school of criminology. Although largely ignored by today's criminologists because of theoretical and methodological problems, Wilson and Herrnstein claim that a distinctive body type exists which distinguishes criminals from noncriminals: "Wherever it has been examined, criminals on the average differ in physique from the population at large. They tend to be more mesomorphic (muscular) and less ectomorphic (linear). . . . A corresponding argument is that the more muscular criminals are more likely to have biological parents who are themselves criminals." On the importance of family and its contribution to crime the authors state "bad families produce bad children" (Wilson and Herrnstein, 1985:215). The authors buttressed this position by an extensive review of the work published on twins and adopted children (1985:69-103).

The major argument here is that if there is a genetic connection to crime, it should show up when identical twins raised in the same environment are compared with fraternal twins also raised in the same environment. The findings suggest that if one identical twin has committed crimes, the other twin is also likely to have also committed crimes. Research does not support this finding for fraternal twins.

Research on adopted children has focused on the criminality of the children compared to the criminality of their biological and adoptive parents. It is argued that children whose biological parents are criminals would engage in crime more than the adoptive parents. If genetics are connected to crime, it would have an influence despite the environment. Some research findings suggest that the criminality of biological parents is more significant in explaining the criminality of children than the criminality of adoptive parents.

Just how constitutional factors influence criminality is a point on which Wilson and Herrnstein express caution. They base their answers on what people consider rewarding, and their ability to postpone gratification until sometime in the future. According to Wilson and Herrnstein, constitutional factors have an impact on the ability to consider future and immediate rewards and punishments. For example, aggressive and impulsive males with low intelligence are at a greater risk of committing crimes than young males who have developed "the bite of conscience," which reflects a higher cognitive and intellectual development.

Gibbs (1985) interpreted an emphasis on rewards and punishments to mean that Wilson and Herrnstein attempted to develop an "operant-utilitarian" theory of criminality, although they did not give it a label at all. Again it is necessary to mention that an emphasis on rewards and punishments was pursued by the scholars in the classical school of criminology. They attempted to deter individual acts of crime by imposing punishments sufficiently severe to outweigh the benefits of illegal conduct.

The evaluations of *Crime and Human Nature* did not heap praise on Wilson and Herrnstein. The reasons were many but they can be divided into two categories: conceptual/empirical and ideological. The conceptual/empirical criticisms focused on the authors' lack of "concern about the empirical applicability of their terms" (Gibbs, 1985:383). They used such concepts as "ratio of rewards," "material and nonmaterial crime," "approval of peers," "sense of inequity," and many other concepts (see Wilson and Herrnstein's Chapter 2—"A Theory of Criminal Behavior"). However, they failed to offer any numerical or operational expressions for the concepts. Consequently there was a lack of clarity about what they were trying communicate, thus creating difficult obstacles to conducting research which would test their theory.

Another troublesome dimension of their work was their claim that they were confining their attention to serious street crimes and predatory crimes such as murder, robbery, and burglary. But their failure to include such offenses as white-collar crimes under the label of predatory crimes, and their failure to explain why burglary should be considered a street crime, raised serious doubt about the generality and conceptual clarity of their theoretical arguments. As Gibbs (1985:382) stated, the relatively loose manner in which Wilson and Herrnstein used labels for crimes "are better suited for journalism than criminology."

An equally troublesome aspect of *Crime and Human Nature* was that while the authors gave the impression that they were objective in the selection and presentation of relevant literature, they may have in fact been highly selective in what they reviewed (Kamin, 1986). The problem here is that while the reader was given the impression that their arguments were based on solid *science* and therefore should be *believed*, in more than one instance their arguments were based on shaky evidence. The reader, however, was not given this information. For example, Wilson and Herrnstein's (1985:418) observation that young people growing up in the 1960s were less willing to delay gratification than young people growing up 15 years earlier, was based on a "single experimental study, [taken] at face value" (Kamin, 1985:22). In addition, the authors failed to cite published research which indicated that noncriminals were found to be *more* mesomorphic in body type than delinquents (Kamin, 1985:24). Apparently Wilson and Herrnstein elected to emphasize resources which supported their arguments for constitutional factors related to crime, rather than address the literature which questioned or confounded this argument.

These criticisms, however serious, did not overshadow the ideological implications of some of Wilson and Herrnstein's arguments, and why their arguments were given wide attention. On this point, Kamin (1985:25) stated:

> The Wilson and Herrnstein work ought not to be judged in isolation. Their selective use of poor data to support a muddled ideology of biological determinism is not unrepresentative of American social science in the sixth year of the Reagan presidency. The political climate of the times makes it easy to understand why social scientists now rush to locate the causes of social tensions in genes and in deep-rooted biological substrata.

To be more specific, Wilson and Herrnstein's work implied that certain biological predispositions, found frequently in the poor may be responsible for excessive criminal behavior. This message, particularly when read by those lacking criminological expertise and who do not pause to read the authors' caveats about their argument, carries disquieting policy implications. We have seen in Chapter 2 that early biological theories were used to justify repressive and physically intrusive policies. Hopefully we have moved beyond such practices. Even so, the historical record teaches that attempts to root crime in human nature exempt the social fabric from blame and lend credence to the idea that offenders are largely beyond reform and in need of punitive control.

Prevalence of Biological Theorizing

Wilson and Herrnstein's work takes on added significance when we realize that it was not an idiosyncratic event, but representative of a growing movement to root crime in human nature. In 1985, for example, a major newspaper reported that the brains of executed prisoners were being studied at the University of Florida (*Cincinnati Enquirer*, 1985b). A study out of the New York University Medical School reported that convicted murderers had once suffered head injuries (*New York Times*, 1986c). Along the same line of reasoning, two medical doctors reported at the 1985 Fourth World Congress of Biological Psychiatry, that 90 percent of the excessively violent people had brain defects (*New York Times*, 1985:17,19).

While the claims of most of this type of research were presented in rather general terms such as "brain damage" or "neurological defects,"' reports identifying a *specific* defect began to appear in 1987. One report which made the front page of the *New York Times*, for instance, linked manic depression to a "specific genetic defect" (*New York Times*, 1987j:1). Perhaps the most important observation here is that while medical scientists claim that a specific genetic structure can explain a specific form of behavior, such claims are only a short step from the creation of policies which would require "special treatment" for people with a particular genetic structure. While this may sound alarmist, we hasten to note that in 1988 the National Research Council, the operating arm of the National Academy of Science which Congress chartered to advise the federal government, called for a 15-year study effort "to diagram the possible 100,000 human genes" (*New York Times*, 1988i:1,13). At an estimated cost of $3 billion, it would "set the stage for constructing the ultimate physical map — the complete DNA sequence of the human genome" (*New York Times*, 1988i:13). No objections to this type of research were reported by the Council.

If this research is completed, it would be a tremendous, almost unimaginable, boost to the theories that claim criminal behavior is based in biological factors. In fact, such a boost may be much closer than we think. Research DNA "finger printing" has already been used to obtain convictions for rape and murder in both the United States and England. It may be only a short step before the DNA structure of convicted criminals is used as the bases of screening the public for potential offenders with similar DNA structures.

These comments are not meant to imply that criminality has no biological determinants, or that biological research cannot be conducted responsibly and illuminate the human condition. Still, the sudden popularity of linking crime to human nature gives us reason to pause. As Gould (1981) points out, historically biological theories have gained advocates by providing scientific legitimacy for racist and class-biased feelings and policies. In a time when it is unfashionable to embrace liberal sympathies for the disadvantaged and racial strife has surfaced more frequently, it seems reasonable to caution that the newsworthiness of reports on offenders' criminogenic nature may be traced less to the quality of the empirical data and more fully to the prevailing social context.

Varieties of Conservative Theory

The emphasis on crime's biological roots represents only one theme found in conservative writings about crime (including Wilson and Herrnstein's *Crime and Human Nature*). At the risk of simplifying complex arguments, three additional types of conservative theorizing can be delineated (Currie, 1985:22-50).

First, by revitalizing classical school principles, some commentators have developed "rational-choice" or "econometric" models of crime. Individuals are conceived as choosing crime when the benefits of illegality exceeds its costs — or, in more colloquial terms, when "crime pays" (van den Haag, 1975). For the most part, these commentators have focused on how increased punishment — scaring people straight — will reduce crime. It is instructive that these theorists have overlooked how increasing the rewards of conformity (e.g., more lucrative employment) can achieve similar gains in crime control.

Second, other commentators have attempted to demonstrate that offenders persist in crime because they think differently. In their popular book *The Criminal Personality*, for example, Samuel Yochelson and Stanton Samenow (1976) argue for the existence of pathological thought patterns, a "criminal mind." Offenders are depicted as manipulative and calculating, and as largely immune to efforts to treat them.

Third, some conservatives have linked crime to a distinctive kind of social influence: the permissive culture in American society. Though minimizing the criminogenic effects of class and social inequality, they argue that family and schools are failing to discipline and punish effectively (see also Hirschi, 1983). Underlying these claims is the notion that unless humans' baser instincts are tamed — "spare the rod, spoil the child" — they will embark on a life of crime.

These observations on crime should not be dismissed out-of-hand: Some offenders do calculate crime's profitability; some think differently; and some become lawbreakers due to lax child rearing. Even so, each of these brands of conservative theorizing falls short as a general model of crime causation. Empirical evidence, for example, is equivocal on the extent to which complex decision-making by offenders can be reduced to a simple model of weighing costs and benefits; simply raising the costs of crime does not seem an effective crime control strategy (Finckenauer, 1982). Similarly, cognitive approaches to understanding offenders' thinking have merit, but simple constructs — such as a "criminal minds" — have not been demonstrated to exist across offenders. Thus Yochelson and Samenow's study was limited to a highly specialized, institutionalized group of offenders; moreover, this research left unexplained the critical causal point: Where do criminal minds come from? (Pfohl, 1985). Further, families and schools clearly have an impact on criminal involvement (Blumstein, Cohen, Roth, and Visher, 1986). But as Elliott Currie (1985) points out, crime is not associated with permissiveness per se, but with child rearing that is overly neglectful or overly harsh — in short, with practices that fail to nurture healthy development.

A more general criticism, however, can be leveled at these types of conservative theorizing: They treat larger social arrangements and forces as inconsequential (Currie, 1985). Even if offenders make decisions on costs and benefits, we are told little of why society is structured in such a way as to make joining a gang "pay" for some youths, and going to college pay for other youths. The existence of criminal minds, as noted, is taken for granted, with little thought given to the social circumstances that may have shaped this unhealthy development. And parents and teachers are warned that tough discipline is a panacea for misbehavior, but we learn little of how poverty, loss of manufacturing jobs in cities, and neighborhood disintegration strain families and schools, and thereby reduce their ability to furnish youth with a nurturant environment (see also W. J. Wilson, 1987). In short, by seeing crime as simply a matter of making bad choices, bad personalities, or the failure to tame bad impulses, attention is deflected away from defects in the social structure that form the wider context of crime causation.

CONSEQUENCES OF CONSERVATIVE THEORY: POLICY IMPLICATIONS

The conservatives' policy agenda is clear: lock offenders up. On this point, they have much to be pleased about. Over the past two decades, prison populations have more than doubled, escalating wildly to unprecedented numbers. But why should conservatives endorse so enthusiastically this policy of filling the nation's prison system to its brim?

Policies, we have argued, must be traced to their theoretical underpinnings. Two aspects of conservative theorizing make incarceration seem a prudent practice. First, in revitalizing classical theory, conservatives emphasize the need to ensure that crime does not pay. Mandating lengthy prison terms increases the cost of offending. Lawbreakers are scared straight by incarceration while those contemplating crime are deterred from acting on these impulses. Second, in revitalizing the pathological brand of Positivist theory, conservatives believe that a proportion of offenders — whether due to a criminal mind or to a criminal nature — are beyond reform and must be incapacitated behind thick walls and sturdy bars. "Wicked people exist," observes James Q. Wilson (1975:235). "Nothing avails except to set them apart from innocent people."

There can be little doubt that such thinking has justified, if not actively encouraged, the ready use of prisons as a solution to crime. If conservatives gain comfort from rising inmate populations, they have far less reason to be sanguine about the effects of this policy. Research on the deterrent effects of imprisonment is equivocal at best; getting tough does not seem to scare past or future offenders straight (Currie, 1985; Finckenauer, 1982). Similarly, though locking up offenders in large numbers reduces crime, its overall effect is modest. A doubling of the prison population, for example, has achieved only a small decrease (less than 10 percent) in crime rates (Visher, 1987). More disturbing, with construction costs of $30,000 to $80,000 a cell and the yearly cost for housing an inmate in excess of $10,000, this modest reduction in crime has been achieved only at substantial drain on state treasuries nationwide (Camp and Camp, 1987).

Biases die hard, and thus it is unlikely that conservatives' faith in imprisonment soon will wane. Even so, the financial burdens of prisons in fiscally tight times have provided ample motivation to search for alternative methods of social control. Still, in turning to community corrections, conservatives have brought a distinctive look. These conservative times have resulted in a redefinition of the meaning and importance of community, public, and privacy. Just a few short years ago it would have been highly offensive to the American public to turn a home into a prison, a bedroom into a cell. But by the mid-1980s, several states followed the lead of Florida and Kentucky in passing laws permitting house arrest and electronic monitoring (see Ball, Huff and Lilly, 1988; Ball and Lilly, 1985; Ball and Lilly, 1986a,b; Lilly, Ball and Lotz, 1986; Lilly, 1988). An equally offensive idea that was rejected in the United States in the 19th century reappeared in the 1980s: charging offenders a daily fee for their supervision and keep. While it has several drawbacks, communities in California, Ohio, Michigan and Maryland now charge inmates between $20 and $85 per day (USA Today, 1987:8A).

With homes being used as prisons and inmates being charged daily fees, it is not surprising that public humiliation or public punishment also has reappeared. In Portland, Oregon, for instance, a sex molester not only received the usual sentence of no alcohol, no drugs, counseling, orders to stay away from parks and school yards, plus a jail sentence, but also upon release from jail he was required to put a sign on his front door which read: "Dangerous Sex Offender, No Children Allowed," (*New York Times*, 1987k:10). A similar form of public humiliation was used in one Oklahoma city in which convicted drunk drivers were required to put bumper stickers on their cars which read, "I am a convicted DWI, driving while intoxicated, DUI, driving under the influence. Report any erratic driving to the Midwest City Police" (*ABC News Nightline*, 1986).

Even when offenders remain in the community, then, conservatives pay little attention to crime's social roots. Instead, assuming that offenders' social circumstances are either unfixable or unimportant in crime causation, they restrict their attention to finding inexpensive ways to incapacitate offenders (e.g., house arrest) or to deter crime by increasing its costs (e.g., public humiliation). The merits of these community punishments are still to be determined, but it seems imprudent to anticipate that they represent a panacea for today's crime problem.

CONCLUSION

The 1980s ushered in ways of thinking abut crime which, though packaged in different language, revitalized the old idea that the sources of lawlessness reside in individuals, not within the social fabric. The rekindling of this type of theorizing, we believe, was no coincidence. Like other theories before it, conservative theory drew its power and popularity from the prevailing social context. And as we have seen, conservative thinking has had its day in influencing the direction of criminal justice policy. Locking people up in unprecedented numbers only makes sense if one believes prisons reduce lawlessness by deterring the calculating and by incapacitating the wicked.

In short, our discussion of conservative theory reflects the central point of this book: ideas about crime — or what we call theories — are a product of society and have consequences for policy. We hope that this theme has served as a useful framework for understanding criminological theory's stages of development and its impact on the criminal justice system. We also hope, however, that our observations on the intimate link among context, theory, and policy will have a personal relevance to readers. A look to the past illuminates the risk of taking for granted one's existing social reality. Whether a criminologist or a citizen, we are enmeshed in a social context that shapes our beliefs about crime and its control. We cannot fully escape this context, but as reflexive creatures we can explore our biases, think more clearly about crime, and embrace policies less contaminated by our prejudices.

References

ABC News Nightline (1986, May 20) "Public humiliation."

AGNEW, ROBERT (1985) "A revised strain theory of delinquency." Social Forces 64 (September):151-167.

AICHHORN, AUGUST (1936) Wayward Youth. New York: Viking.

AKERS, RONALD L. (1977) Deviant Behavior: A Social Learning Approach (2nd ed.). Belmont, CA: Wadsworth.

AKERS, RONALD L., MARVIN D. KROHN, LONN LANZA-KADUCE, and MARCIA RADOSEVICH (1979) "Social learning and deviant behavior: A specific test of a general theory." American Sociological Review 44 (August):636-655.

ALEXANDER, FRANZ and WILLIAM HEALY (1935) Roots of Crime. New York: Knopf.

ALLEN, FRANCIS A. (1973) "Raffaele Garofalo," pp. 318-340 in Herrman Mannheim (ed.), Pioneers in Criminology (2nd ed.). Montclair, NJ: Patterson Smith.

ALLEN, MARK (1977) "James E. Carter and the Trilateral Commission: A southern strategy." Black Scholar 8 (May):2-7.

ARONOWITZ, STANLEY (1973) False Promises: The Shaping of American Working Class Consciousness. New York: McGraw-Hill.

BALL, RICHARD A. (1966) "An empirical exploration of the neutralization hypothesis." Criminologica 4:22-32.

BALL, RICHARD A. (1978) "The dialectical method: Its application to social theory." Social Forces 57:785-798.

BALL, RICHARD A. (1979) "Toward a dialectical criminology," pp. 11-26 in Marvin D. Krohn and Ronald L. Akers (ed.), Crime, Law, and Sanctions. Beverly Hills, CA: Sage.

BALL, RICHARD A., C. RONALD HUFF, and J. ROBERT LILLY (1988) House Arrest and Correctional Policy: Doing Time at Home. Newbury Park, CA: Sage.

BALL, RICHARD A. and J. ROBERT LILLY (1982) "The menace of margarine: The rise and fall of a social problem." Social Problems 29:488-498.

BALL, RICHARD A. and J. ROBERT LILLY (1985) "Home incarceration: An international alternative to institutional incarceration." International Journal of Comparative and Applied Criminal Justice 9 (Winter):85-97.

BALL, RICHARD A. and J. ROBERT LILLY (1986a) "The potential use of home incarceration with drunken drivers." Crime and Delinquency 32:187-196.

BALL, RICHARD A. and J. ROBERT LILLY (1986b) "A theoretical rationale for home incarceration." Federal Probation L, 1 (March):17-24.

BARAN, PAUL A. and PAUL M. SWEEZY (1966) Monopoly Capitalism: An Essay on the American Economic and Social Order. New York: Monthly Review Press.

BARNES, HARRY E. (1930). "Criminology," in Encyclopedia of the Social Sciences (Vol. 4). New York: Macmillan.

BARTOLLAS, CLEMENS (1985) Juvenile Delinquency. New York: John Wiley.

BAYER, RONALD (1981) "Crime punishment, and the decline of liberal optimism." Crime and Delinquency 27 (April):169-190.

BAZEMORE, GORDON (1985) "Delinquency reform and the labeling perspective." Criminal Justice and Behavior 12 (June):131-169.

BECCARIA, CESARE (1963) On Crimes and Punishments. (Henry Paolucci, trans.). Indianapolis: Bobbs-Merrill.

BECKER, HOWARD S. (1963) Outsiders: Studies in the Sociology of Deviance. New York: Free Press.

BECKWITH, JAN (1985) "Social and political uses of genetics in the United States: Past and present," pp. 316-326 in Frank H. Marsh and Janet Katz (eds.), Biology, Crime and Ethics: A Study of Biological Explanations for Criminal Behavior. Cincinnati, OH: Anderson.

BENNETT, GEORGETTE (1987) Crimewarps: The Future of Crime in America. New York: Anchor/Doubleday.

BENTHAM, JEREMY (1948) "An introduction to the principles of morals and legislation," in Laurence J. Lafleur (ed.). New York: Hafner.

BERGER, PETER C. and LUCKMAN, THOMAS (1966) The Social Construction of Reality. Garden City, NY: Anchor.

BERNARD, THOMAS J. (1984) "Control criticisms of strain theories: An assessment of theoretical and empirical adequacy." Journal of Research in Crime and Delinquency 21 (November):353-372.

BINDER, ARNOLD and GILBERT GEIS (1984) "Ad Populum argumentation in criminology: Juvenile diversion as rhetoric." Crime and Delinquency 30 (April):309-333.

BLUMSTEIN, ALFRED, JACQUELINE COHEN, JEFFREY A. ROTH, and CHRISTY A. VISHER (1986) Criminal Careers and "Career Criminals" (Vol. 1). Washington, DC: National Academy Press.

BONGER, WILLEM (1969[1916]) Criminality and Economic Conditions. Bloomington: Indiana University Press.

Bowers v. Hardwick (1986) 478 U.S. 186.

Bureau of Justice Statistics (1988) "Households touched by crime, 1987." Washington, DC: U.S. Department of Justice.

BURGESS, ROBERT L. and RONALD L. AKERS (1966) "A differential association-reinforcement theory of criminal behavior." Social Problems 14 (Fall):128-146.

CAMP, GEORGE M. and CAMILLE GRAHAM CAMP (1987) The Corrections Yearbook. South Salem, NY: Criminal Justice Institute.

CHAMBLISS, WILLIAM J. (1964) "A sociological analysis of the law of vagrancy." Social Problems 12:67-77.

CHAMBLISS, WILLIAM J. (1969) Crime and the Legal Process. New York: McGraw-Hill.

CHAMBLISS, WILLIAM J. (1975) "Toward a political economy of crime." Theory and Society 2:152-153.

CHAMBLISS, WILLIAM J. (1984) "The saints and the roughnecks," pp. 126-135 in W. J. Chambliss (ed.), Criminal Law in Action (2nd ed.). New York: John Wiley.

CHAMBLISS, WILLIAM J. (1987) "I wish I didn't know now what I didn't know then." Criminologist 12:1-9.

CHAMBLISS, WILLIAM and ROBERT T. SEIDMAN (1971) Law, Order, and Power. Reading, MA: Addison-Wesley.

Cincinnati Enquirer (1985a) "Meese: Execute teen-age killers." September 5:1, 6.

Cincinnati Enquirer (1985b) "Officials to probe brain use." October 6.

Cincinnati Enquirer (1985c) [Editorial]. October 28:C-12.

Cincinnati Enquirer (1988) "Random drug testing proposed for agencies." May 4:A4.

CLINARD, MARSHALL (1957) Sociology of Deviant Behavior (3rd ed.). New York: Holt, Rinehart & Winston.

CLOWARD, RICHARD A. (1959) "Illegitimate means, anomie, and deviant behavior." American Sociological Review 24 (April):164-176.

CLOWARD, RICHARD A. and LLOYD E. OHLIN (1960) Delinquency and Opportunity: A Theory of Delinquent Gangs. New York: Free Press.

CLOWARD, RICHARD A. and FRANCES FOX PIVEN (1979) "Hidden protest: The channeling of female innovation and resistance." Signs 4 (Summer):651-669.

COHEN, ALBERT K. (1955) Delinquent Boys: The Culture of the Gang. New York: Free Press.

COHEN, ALBERT K. and JAMES F. SHORT, Jr. (1958) "Research in delinquent sub-cultures." Journal of Social Issues 14:20-37.

COLE, STEPHEN (1975) "The growth of scientific knowledge: Theories of deviance as a case study," pp. 175-200 in Lewis A. Coser (ed.), The Idea of Social Structure: Papers in Honor of Robert K. Merton. New York: Harcourt Brace Jovanovich.

COLVIN, MARK and JOHN PAULY (1983) "A critique of criminology: Toward an integrated structural-Marxist theory of delinquency production." American Journal of Sociology 89:513-551.

COOLEY, CHARLES H. (1902) Human Nature and Social Order. New York: Scribner.

COOLEY, CHARLES H. (1909) Social Organization. New York: Scribner.

COOLEY, CHARLES H. (1922) Human Nature and Social Order (Rev. ed.). New York: Scribner.

Corrections Magazine (1975) "Deinstitutionalization: Special report." 2 (November-December).

CULLEN, FRANCIS T. (1984) Rethinking Crime and Deviance Theory: The Emergence of a Structuring Tradition. Totowa, NJ: Rowman and Allanheld.

CULLEN, FRANCIS T., GREGORY A. CLARK, and JOHN F. WOZNIAK (1985) "Explaining the get tough movement: Can the public be blamed?" Federal Probation 49 (June):16-24.

CULLEN, FRANCIS T. and JOHN B. CULLEN (1978) Toward a Paradigm of Labeling Theory. Lincoln: University of Nebraska.

CULLEN, FRANCIS T. and KAREN GILBERT (1982) Reaffirming Rehabilitation. Cincinnati: Anderson.

CULLEN, FRANCIS T., WILLIAM J. MAAKESTAD, and GRAY CAVENDER (1987) Corporate Crime Under Attack: The Ford Pinto Case and Beyond. Cincinnati: Anderson.

CURRIE, ELLIOTT (1985) Confronting Crime: An American Challenge. New York: Pantheon.

DAHRENDORF, RALF (1958) Class and Class Conflict in Industrial Society. Stanford, CA: Stanford University Press.

DAHRENDORF, RALF (1968) "Toward a theory of social conflict." Journal of Conflict of Resolution 2:170-183.

DAVIS, KINGSLEY (1948) Human Society. New York: Macmillan.

DINITZ, SIMON, WALTER C. RECKLESS and BARBARA KAY (1958) "A self gradient among potential delinquents." Journal of Criminal Law, Criminology and Police Science 49:230-233.

DINITZ, SIMON, FRANK R. SCARPITTI, and WALTER C. RECKLESS (1962) "Delinquency vulnerability: A cross group and longitudinal analysis." American Sociological Review 27:515-517.

DUGDALE, RICHARD L. (1877) The Jukes. New York: Putnam.

DURKHEIM, EMILE (1933) The Division of Labor in Society. Glencoe, IL: Free Press.

DURKHEIM, EMILE (1951) Suicide: A Study in Sociology. (John A. Spaulding and George Simpson, trans.). New York: Free Press. (Original work published 1897)

DURKHEIM, EMILE (1964) The Elementary Forms of the Religious Life. Glencoe, IL: Free Press.

EDWARDS, RICHARD C., MICHAEL REICH, and THOMAS E. WEISSKOPH (1972) The Capitalist System: A Radical Analysis of American Society. Englewood Cliffs, NJ: Prentice-Hall.

ELLIS, HAVELOCK (1913) The Criminal (4th ed.). New York: Scribner.

EMPEY, LAMAR T. (1979) "Foreword — from optimism to despair: New doctrines in juvenile justice," pp. 9-26 in Charles A. Murray and Louis A. Cox, Jr. (eds.), Beyond Probation: Juvenile Corrections and the Chronic Delinquent. Beverly Hills, CA: Sage.

EMPEY, LAMAR T. and LUBEK, STEVEN (1971) The Silverlake Experiment: Testing Delinquency Theory and Community Intervention. Chicago: Aldine.

EMPEY, LAMAR T. (1982) American Delinquency: Its Meaning and Construction (rev. ed.). Homewood, IL: Dorsey.

EMPEY, LAMAR T. and MAYNARD L. ERICKSON (1972) The Provo Experiment: Evaluating Community Control of Delinquency. Lexington, MA: Lexington.

ERIKSON, KAI T. (1966) Wayward Puritans: A Study in Sociology of Deviance. New York: John Wiley.

ESTRABROOK, A. H. (1916) The Jukes in 1915. Washington, DC: Carnegie Institute.

Federal Bureau of Investigation (1988) Uniform Crime Reports: Crime in the United States, 1987. Washington, DC: Government Printing Office.

FINCKENAUER, JAMES O. (1982) Scared Straight! and the Panacea Phenomenon. Englewood Cliffs, NJ: Prentice-Hall.

FLANAGAN, TIMOTHY J. (1987) "Change and influence in popular criminology: Public attributions of crime causation." Journal of Criminal Justice 15 (3):231-243.

FRAZIER, CHARLES E. and JOHN K. COCHRAN (1986) "Official intervention, diversion from the juvenile justice system, and dynamics of human services work: Effects of a reform goal based on labeling theory." Crime and Delinquency 32 (April):157-176.

FREUD, SIGMUND (1920) A General Introduction to Psychoanalysis. New York: Boni and Liveright.

FREUD, SIGMUND (1927) The Ego and the Id. London: Hogarth.

FREUD, SIGMUND (1930) Civilization and Its Discontents. New York: Cape and Smith.

FRIEDAN, BETTY (1963) The Feminine Mystique. New York: Norton.

FRIEDLANDER, KATE (1949) "Latent delinquency and ego development," pp. 205-215 in Kurt R. Eissler (ed.), Searchlights on Delinquency. New York: International University Press.

FRIEDRICHS, DAVID O. (1979) "The law and legitimacy crisis: A critical issue for criminal justice," pp. 290-311 in R. G. Iacovetta and Dae H. Chang (eds.), Critical Issues in Criminal Justice. Durham: Carolina Academic Press.

GALLIHER, JOHN F. and ALLYN WALKER (1977) "The puzzle of the social origins of the Marijuana Tax Act of 1937." Social Problems 24 (February):367-376.

GARFINKEL, HAROLD (1956) "Conditions of successful degradation ceremonies." American Journal of Sociology 61 (March):420-424.

GEIS, GILBERT and COLIN GOFF (1983) "Introduction," pp. ix-xxxiii in Edwin H. Sutherland White Collar Crime: The Uncut Version. New Haven, CT: Yale University Press.

GEIS, GILBERT and COLIN GOFF (1986) "Edwin H. Sutherland's white-collar crime in America: An essay in historical criminology," pp. 1-31 in Criminal Justice History: An International Annual, Vol. 7. Westport, CT: Meckler.

GIBBONS, DON C. (1979) The Criminological Enterprise: Theories and Perspectives. Englewood Cliffs, NJ: Prentice-Hall.

GIBBONS, DON C. and PETER GARABEDIAN (1974) "Conservative, liberal and radical criminology: Some trends and observations," pp. 51-65 in Charles E. Reasons (ed.), The Criminologist: Crime and the Criminal. Pacific Palisades, CA: Goodyear.

GIBBS, JACK P. (1985) "Review essay." Criminology 23 (May):381-388.

GLUECK, SHELDON and ELEANOR GLUECK (1950) Unraveling Juvenile Delinquency. New York: Commonwealth Fund.

GODDARD, H. H. (1914) Feeblemindedness: Its Causes and Consequences. New York: Macmillan.

GODDARD, H. H. (1921) "Feeblemindedness and delinquency." Journal of Psycho-Asthenics 25:168-176.

GODDARD, H. H. (1927) "Who is a moron?" Scientific Monthly 24:41-46.

GORDON, DAVID M. (1971) "Class and the economics of crime." Review of Radical Political Economy 3:51-75.

GORING, CHARLES (1913) The English Convict: A Statistical Study. London: His Majesty's Stationery Office.

GOULD, STEPHEN JAY (1981) The Mismeasure of Man. New York: Norton.

GOVE, WALTER R. [ed.] (1975) The Labeling of Deviance: Evaluating a Perspective. Beverly Hills, CA: Sage.

GOVE, WALTER R. [ed.] (1980) The Labeling of Deviance: Evaluating a Perspective (2nd ed.). Beverly Hills, CA: Sage.

GREENBERG, DAVID (1977) "Delinquency and the age structure of society." Con-

210 Criminological Theory

temporary Crises 1:189-233.

GREENBERG, DAVID F. (1981) "Introduction," pp. 1-35 in David F. Greenberg (ed.), Crime and Capitalism. Palo Alto, CA: Mayfield.

HABERMAS, JURGEN (1970) Knowledge and Human Interests. Boston: Beacon.

HABERMAS, JURGEN (1971) Toward a Rational Society. Boston: Beacon.

HAGAN, JOHN L. (1973) "Labeling and deviance: A case study in the 'Sociology of the Interesting.'" Social Problems 20 (Spring):447-458.

HAWKINS, FRANK H. (1931) "Charles Robert Darwin," pp. 4-5 in Encyclopedia of the Social Sciences, Vol. 5. New York: Macmillan.

HAWKINS, GORDON (1976) The Prison: Policy and Practice. Chicago: University of Chicago Press.

HAWLEY, F. FREDERICK (1987) "The black legend in Southern studies: Violence, ideology, and academe." North America Culture 3 (1):29-52.

HINKLE, ROSCOE C. and GISELA J. HINKLE (1954) The Development of Modern Sociology. New York: Random House.

HIRSCHI, TRAVIS (1969) Causes of Delinquency. Berkeley: University of California Press.

HIRSCHI, TRAVIS (1975) "Labeling theory and juvenile delinquency: An assessment of the evidence," pp. 181-201 in Walter R. Gove (ed.), The Labeling of Deviance: Evaluating a Perspective. Beverly Hills, CA: Sage.

HIRSCHI, TRAVIS (1983) "Crime and the family," pp. 53-68 in James Q. Wilson (ed.), Crime and Public Policy. San Francisco: Institute for Contemporary Studies.

HOFSTADTER, RICHARD (1955a) Age of Reform. New York: Knopf.

HOFSTADTER, RICHARD (1955b) Social Darwinism in American Thought. Boston: Beacon.

HOFSTADTER, RICHARD (1963) The Progressive Movement: 1900 to 1915. New York: Touchstone.

HOOTON, EARNEST A. (1939) Crime and the Man. Cambridge, MA: Harvard University Press.

HOWARD, JOHN (1929) The State of the Prisons. London: J. M. Dent.

HUGHES, EVERETT C. (1945) "Dilemmas and contradictions of statuses." American Journal of Sociology 50 (March):353-359.

HUNT, MORTON M. (1961). "How does it come to be so? Profile of Robert K. Merton." New Yorker 36 (January 28):39-64.

HUSSENSTAMM, F. K. (1975) "Bumper stickers and the cops" pp. 251-255 in Darrell J. Steffensmeier and Robert M. Terry (eds.), Examining Deviance Experimentally: Selected Readings. Port Washington, NY: Alfred.

INCIARDI, JAMES (1986) The War on Drugs: Heroin, Cocaine, Crime, and Public Policy. Palo Alto, CA: Mayfield.

JOSEPHSON, ERIC and MARY JOSEPHSON (1962) Man Alone: Alienation in Modern Society. New York: Dell.

KAMIN, LEON L. (1985) "Is crime in the genes? The answer may depend on who chooses the evidence." Scientific American (April):22-25.

KATZ, JANET and CHARLES F. ABEL (1984) The medicalization of repression: Eugenics and crime." Contemporary Crises 8:227-241.

KENNEDY, PAUL (1987) "The (relative) decline of America." Atlantic 260 (August):29-38

KITSUSE, JOHN I. (1964) "Societal reaction to deviant behavior: Problems of theory and method," pp. 87-102 in Howard Becker (ed.), The Other Side. New York: Free Press.

KLEIN, MALCOLM W. (1979) "Deinstitutionalization and diversion of juvenile offenders: A litany of impediments," pp. 145-201 in Norval Morris and Michael Tonry (eds.), Crime and Justice: An Annual Review of Research, Vol. 1. Chicago: University of Chicago Press.

KLEIN, MALCOLM W. (1986) "Labeling theory and delinquency police: An experimental test." Criminal Justice and Behavior 13 (March):47-79.

KOBRIN, SOLOMON (1959) "The Chicago area project: A 25-year assessment." Annals of the American Academy of Political and Social Sciences 332 (March):19-29.

KORNHAUSER, RUTH ROSNER (1978) Social Sources of Delinquency: An Appraisal of Analytic Models. Chicago: University of Chicago Press.

KRETSCHMER, E. (1925) Physique and Character. Trans. by W. J. Sprott. New York: Harcourt Brace Jovanovich.

KRISBERG, BARRY and JAMES AUSTIN (1978) The Children of Ishmael: Critical Perspectives on Juvenile Justice. Palo Alto, CA: Mayfield.

LASCH, CHRISTOPHER (1978) The Culture of Narcissism. New York: Norton.

LATESSA, EDWARD J. (1987) "The effectiveness of intensive supervision with high risk probationers," pp. 99-112 in Belinda R. McCarthy (ed.), Intermediate Punishments: Intensive Supervision, Home Confinement, and Electronic Surveillance. Monsey, NY: Criminal Justice Press.

LAUB, JOHN H. (1983) Criminology in the Making: An Oral History. Boston: Northeastern University Press.

LEDERER, GEORGE (1961) A Nation of Sheep. New York: Fawcett.

LEMERT, EDWIN M. (1951) Social Pathology. New York: McGraw-Hill.

LEMERT, EDWIN M. (1972) Human Deviance, Social Problems, and Social Control (2nd ed.). Englewood Cliffs, NJ: Prentice-Hall.

LILLY, J. ROBERT (forthcoming) "House arrest and 'tagging': Another fatal remedy?" The Journal of Criminal Justice.

LILLY, J. ROBERT, RICHARD A. BALL, and W. ROBERT LOTZ (1986) "Electronic jails revisited." Justice Quarterly 3 (September):353-361.

LINK, BRUCE G., FRANCIS T. CULLEN, JAMES FRANK, and JOHN F. WOZNIAK (1987) "The social rejection of former mental patients: Understanding why labels matters." American Journal of Sociology 92 (May):1461-1500.

LIPSET, SEYMOUR MARTIN and WILLIAM SCHNEIDER (1983) The Confidence Gap: Business, Labor, and Government in the Public Mind. New York: Free Press.

LISKA, ALLEN E. (1981) Perspectives on Deviance. Englewood Cliffs, NJ: Prentice-Hall.

LOFLAND, LYN H. (1973) A World of Strangers: Order and Action in Urban Public Space. New York: Basic Books.

LOMBROSO-FERRERO, GINA (1972) Criminal Man According to the Classification of Cesare Lombroso. Montclair, NJ: Patterson Smith.

MADGE, JOHN (1962) The Origins of Scientific Sociology. New York: Free Press.

MANKOFF, MILTON (1971) "Societal reaction and career deviance: A critical analysis." Sociological Quarterly 12 (Spring):204-218.

MARCUSE, HERBERT (1960) Reason and Revolution. Boston: Beacon.

MARCUSE, HERBERT (1964) One Dimensional Man. Boston: Beacon.

MARCUSE, HERBERT (1972) Counter-Revolution and Revolt. Boston: Beacon.

MARTINDALE, DON (1960) The Nature and Types of Sociological Theory. Cambridge, MA: Houghton Mifflin.

MARX, KARL and FREDERICK ENGELS (1848) "Manifesto of the Communist Party," pp. 10-17 in Marx-Engels Selected Works, Vol. 1. London: Lawrence and Wishart.

MATHIESEN, THOMAS (1974) The Politics of Abolition. New York: Halstead.

MATZA, DAVID (1964) Delinquency and Drift. New York: John Wiley.

MATZA, DAVID (1969) Becoming Deviant. Englewood Cliffs, NJ: Prentice-Hall.

MEAD, GEORGE H. (1934) "Mind, self, and society," in Charles W. Morris (ed.). Chicago: University of Chicago Press.

MERTON, ROBERT K. (1938) "Social structure and anomie." American Sociological Review 3 (October):672-682.

MERTON, ROBERT K. (1957) "Priorities in scientific discovery: A chapter in the sociology of science." American Sociological Review 22 (December):635-659.

MERTON, ROBERT K. (1959) "Social conformity, deviation, and opportunity structures: A comment on the contributions of Dubin and Cloward." American Sociological Review 24 (April):177-189.

MERTON, ROBERT K. (1964) "Anomie, anomia, and social interaction: Contexts of deviant behavior," pp. 213-242 in Marshall B. Clinard (ed.), Anomie and Deviant Behavior. New York: Free Press.

MERTON, ROBERT K. (1968) Social Theory and Social Structure. New York: Free

Press.

MERTON, ROBERT K. and ASHLEY MONTAGU (1940) "Crime and the anthropologist." American Anthropologist 42 (July-September):384-408.

MESSNER, STEVEN F. (1986) "Merton's 'social structure and anomie': The road not taken." Paper presented at the annual meeting of the American Society of Criminology.

MICHALOWSKI, RAYMOND J. and EDWARD W. BOLANDER (1976) "Repression and criminal justice in capitalist America." Sociological Inquiry 46:95-106.

MILIBRAND, RALPH (1969) The State in Capitalist Society. New York: Basic Books.

MILLER, WALTER (1979) "Lower class culture as a generating milieu of gang delinquency," pp. 155-168 in Joseph E. Jacoby (ed.), Classics of Criminology. Oak Park, IL: Moore.

MILLER, ALDEN D. and LLOYD E. OHLIN (1985) Delinquency and Community: Creating Opportunities and Controls. Beverly Hills, CA: Sage.

MOHR, GEORGE J. and RALPH H. GUNDLACH (1929) "A further study of the relation between physique and performance in criminals." Journal of Abnormal and Social Psychology 24:36-50.

MONACHESI, ELIO (1973) "Cesare Beccaria," in Hermann Mannheim (ed.), Pioneers in Criminology. Montclair, NJ: Patterson Smith.

MORASH, MERRY (1982) "Juvenile reaction to labels: An experiment and an exploratory study." Sociology and Social Research 67 (October):76-88.

MORRIS, NORVAL and GORDON HAWKINS (1970) The Honest Politician's Guide to Crime Control. Chicago: University of Chicago Press.

MOYNIHAN, DANIEL P. (1969) Maximum Feasible Misunderstanding: Community Action in the War on Poverty. New York: Free Press.

MURRAY, CHARLES (1984) Losing Ground: American Social Policy, 1950-1980. New York: Basic Books.

New York Times (1985) "Brain defects seen in those who report violent acts." September 17:17, 19.

New York Times (1986a) "Fighting narcotics is everyone's issue now." (August 10):25.

New York Times (1986b) "Meese says court doesn't make law." October 23.

New York Times (1986c) "A study of 15 convicted murderers shows that all had once suffered head injuries." June 3.

New York Times (1987a) "T.V. evangelist resigns, citing sexual blackmail." March 21.

New York Times (1987b) "U.S. churches gain members slowly: Rate of increase keeps pace with population growth." (June 15):13.

New York Times (1987c) "Lack of figures on racial strife fueling dispute." (April 5):13.

New York Times (1987d) "Report traces 45 cases of attacks on minorities." (February 15):22.

New York Times (1987e) "Reports of bias attacks on the rise in New York." (September 23):19.

New York Times (1987f) "Anti-Semitic acts were up 12 percent in 1987." (January 27):13.

New York Times (1987g) "5 Citadel cadets indicted on minor charges of racial hazing." (October 8):15.

New York Times (1987h) "Goetz case: Commentary on nature of urban life." (June 19):11.

New York Times (1987i) "Meese seen as ready to challenge rule on telling suspects of rights." (January 22):13.

New York Times (1987j) "Defective gene tied to form of manic depression illness." (February 26):1.

New York Times (1987k) "Unusual sentence stirs legal dispute." (August 27):10.

New York Times (1988a) "20 years after the Kerner report: Three societies, all separate." (February 29):13.

New York Times (1988b) "Minority students lag, Education Dept. finds." (January 31):16.

New York Times (1988c) "Dartmouth holds meeting to end racism on campus." (March 5):7.

New York Times (1988d) "Dartmouth punishes four students as harassers of professor." (March 11):13.

New York Times (1988e) "Black F.B.I. agent's ordeal: Meanness that never lets up." (January 25):1, 17.

New York Times (1988f) "Death row appeals assailed." (January 28):7.

New York Times (1988g) "The Gideon case 25 years later." (March 16):27.

New York Times (1988h) "Court, 5-4 votes to restudy rights in minority suits." (April 26):1, 11.

New York Times (1988i) "Scientists urge high project to chart all human genes." (February 12):13.

Newsweek (1986a) "Trying to say no." (August 11):14-19.

Newsweek (1986b) "Edwin Meese lifts his lance." (November 3):9.

Newsweek (1986c) "The president's angry apostle." (October 6):27.

Newsweek (1986d) "Sweet land of liberty." Summer.

Newsweek (1987a) "God and money: Sex scandal, greed and lust for power split the TV preaching world." (April 6):16-22.

Newsweek (1987b) "A trial that wouldn't end." (June 19):20-21.

Newsweek (1988a) "Argentining of America." (February 22):22-45.

Newsweek (1988b) "The eighties are over." (January 4):40-44.

NYE, F. IVAN (1958) Family Relationships and Delinquency Behavior. New York: John Wiley.

PALAMARA, FRANCES, FRANCIS T. CULLEN, and JOANNE C. GERSTEN (1986) "The effect of police and mental health intervention on juvenile deviance: Specifying contingencies in the impact of formal reaction." Journal of Health and Social Behavior 27 (March):90-105.

PALEN, J. JOHN. (1981) The Urban World (3rd ed.). New York: McGraw-Hill.

PEPINSKY, HAROLD (1976) Crime and Conflict: A Study in Law and Society. New York: Academic Press.

PERSELL, CAROLINE HODGES (1984) "An interview with Robert K. Merton." Teaching Sociology 11 (July):355-386.

PFOHL, STEPHEN J. (1977) "The 'discovery of child abuse.'" Social Problems 24 (February):310-323.

PFOHL, STEPHEN J. (1985) Images of Deviance and Social Control: A Sociological History. New York: McGraw-Hill.

PILIAVIN, IRVING and SCOTT BRIAR (1964) "Police encounters with juveniles." American Journal of Sociology 70 (September):206-214.

PIVAR, DAVID J. (1973) Purity Crusade: Sexual Morality and Social Control, 1868-1900. Westport, CT: Greenwood.

PLATT, ANTHONY M. (1969) The Child Savers: The Invention of Delinquency. Chicago: University of Chicago Press.

POUND, ROSCOE (1942) Social Control Through Law. New Haven, CT: Yale University Press.

PROVINE, W. B. (1973) "Geneticists and the biology of race crossing." Science 182: 790.

QUINNEY, RICHARD (1969) Criminal Justice in American Society. Boston: Little, Brown.

QUINNEY, RICHARD (1970a) The Problem of Crime. New York: Dodd, Mead.

QUINNEY, RICHARD (1970b) The Social Reality of Crime. Boston: Little, Brown.

QUINNEY, RICHARD (1974a) Critique of the Legal Order: Crime Control in Capitalist Society. Boston: Little, Brown.

QUINNEY, RICHARD (1974b) Crime and Justice in America: A Critical Understanding. Boston: Little, Brown.

QUINNEY, RICHARD (1977) Class, State, and Crime: On the Theory and Practice of Criminal Justice. New York: McKay.

QUINNEY, RICHARD (1980) Class, State, and Crime: On the Theory and Practice of Criminal Justice (2nd ed.). New York: McKay.

RADZINOWICZ, LEON (1966) Ideology and Crime: A Study of Crime in its Social and Historical Context. New York: Columbia University Press.

RECKLESS, WALTER C. (1943) The Etiology of Criminal and Delinquent Behavior. New York: Social Science Research Council.

RECKLESS, WALTER C. (1961) The Crime Problem (3rd ed.). New York: Appleton-Century-Crofts.

RECKLESS, WALTER C. (1967) The Crime Problem (4th ed.). New York: Meredith.

RECKLESS, WALTER C. and SIMON DINITZ (1967) "Pioneering with self-concept as a vulnerability factor in delinquency." Journal of Criminal Law, Criminology and Police Science 58:515-523.

RECKLESS, WALTER C., SIMON DINITZ, and BARBARA KAY (1957) "The self component in potential delinquency and non-delinquency." American Sociological Review 22:566-570.

RECKLESS, WALTER C., SIMON DINITZ, and ELLEN MURRAY (1956) "Self concept as insulator against delinquency." American Sociological Review 21:744-764.

REDL, FRITZ and DAVID WINEMAN (1951) Children Who Hate. New York: Free Press.

REIMAN, JEFFERY (1979) The Rich Get Richer and the Poor Get Prison. New York: John Wiley.

REISS, ALBERT J. (1949) "The accuracy, efficiency, and validity of a prediction instrument." Ph.D. Dissertation, Department of Sociology, University of Chicago.

REISS, ALBERT J. (1951) "Delinquency as the failure of personal and social controls." American Sociological Review 16:196:207.

RENNIE, YSABEL (1978) The Search for Criminal Man: A Conceptual History of the Dangerous Offender. Lexington, MA: Lexington.

Roe v. Wade (1973) 410 U.S. 113.

ROSENFELD, RICHARD (1986) "Rereading Merton: The strain perspective and contemporary sociological theories of crime." Paper presented at the annual meeting of the American Society of Criminology.

ROTHMAN, DAVID J. (1971) The Discovery of the Asylum: Social Order and Disorder in the New Republic. Boston: Little, Brown.

ROTHMAN, DAVID J. (1978) "The state as parent: Social policy in the Progressive Era," pp. 69-96 in Willard Gaylin, Ira Glasser, Steven Marcus, and David Rothman (eds.), Doing Good: The Limits of Benevolence. New York: Pantheon.

ROTHMAN, DAVID J. (1980) Conscience and Convenience: The Asylum and Its Alternatives in Progressive America. Boston: Little, Brown.

RUBINGTON, EARL and MARTIN S. WEINBERG (1971) The Study of Social Problems. New York: Oxford University Press.

Runyon v. McCrary (1976) 427 U.S. 160 99 S. Ct. 2586.

SAMPSON, ROBERT J. (1986) "Effects of socioeconomic context on official reaction to juvenile delinquency." American Sociological Review 51 (December): 876-885.

SCARPITTI, FRANK R., ELLEN MURRAY, SIMON DINITZ, and WALTER C. RECKLESS (1960) "The good boys in a high delinquency area: Four years later." American Sociological Review 25:922-926.

SCHAFER, STEPHEN (1969) Theories in Criminology: Past and Present Philosophies of the Crime Problem. New York: Random House.

SCHEFF, THOMAS J. (1966) Being Mentally Ill. Chicago: Aldine.

SCHEINGOLD, STUART A. (1984) The Politics of Law and Order: Street Crime and Public Policy. New York: Longman.

SCHLOSSMAN, STEVEN, GAIL ZELLMAN, and RICHARD SHAVELSON, with MICHAEL SEDLAK and JANE COBB (1984) Delinquency Prevention in South Chicago: A Fifty-Year Assessment of the Chicago Area Project. Santa Monica, CA: Rand.

SCHUR, EDWIN M. (1965) Crimes Without Victims: Deviant Behavior and Public Policy. Engle vood Cliffs, NJ: Prentice-Hall.

SCHUR, EDWIN M. (1973) Radical Non-Intervention: Rethinking the Delinquency Problem. Engl ;wood Cliffs, NJ: Prentice-Hall.

SCHUR, EDWIN M. and HUGO ADAM BEDEAU (1974) Victimless Crimes: Two

Sides of a Controversy. Englewood Cliffs, NJ: Prentice-Hall.
SCHUESSLER, KARL [ed.] (1973) "Introduction," pp. ix-xxxvi in Edwin H. Sutherland (ed.), On Analyzing Crime. Chicago: University of Chicago Press.
SCHUTZ, ALFRED (1962) The Problem of Social Reality. The Hague: Martinus Nijhoff.
SELLIN, THORSTEN (1937) Research Memorandum on Crime in the Depression. New York: Social Science Research Council.
SELLIN, THORSTEN (1938) Culture Conflict and Crime. New York: Social Science Research Council.
SELLIN, THORSTEN (1973) "Enrico Ferri," pp. 361-384 in Hermann Mannheim (ed.), Pioneers in Criminology (2nd ed.). Montclair, NJ: Patterson Smith.
SHANNON, LYLE W. (1982) Assessing the Relationship of Adult Criminal Careers to Juvenile Careers: A Summary. Washington, DC: U.S. Department of Justice.
SHAW, CLIFFORD R. (1930) The Jack-Roller: A Delinquent Boy's Own Story. Chicago: University of Chicago Press.
SHAW, CLIFFORD R. and HENRY D. McKAY (1972) Juvenile Delinquency and Urban Areas. Chicago: University of Chicago Press.
SHAW, CLIFFORD R., with the assistance of HENRY D. McKAY and JAMES F. MacDONALD (1938) Brothers in Crime. Chicago: University of Chicago Press.
SHAW CLIFFORD R., in collaboration with MAURICE E. MOORE (1931) The Natural History of a Delinquent Career. Chicago: University of Chicago Press.
SHELDON, WILLIAM H. (1949) Varieties of Delinquent Youth: An Introduction to Constitutional Psychiatry. New York: Harper & Brothers.
SHERMAN, MICHAEL and GORDON HAWKINS (1981) Imprisonment in America: Choosing the Future. Chicago: University of Chicago Press.
SHORT, JAMES F., Jr. and FRED L. STRODTBECK (1965) Group Process and Gang Delinquency. Chicago: University of Chicago Press.
SIMON, DAVID R. and D. STANLEY EITZEN (1986) Elite Deviance (2nd ed.). Boston: Allyn & Bacon.
SINCLAIR, UPTON (1905) The Jungle. New York: Signet.
SMITH, JOAN and WILLIAM FRIED (1974) The Uses of the American Prison: Political Theory and Penal Practice. Lexington, MA: Lexington.
SPITZER, STEPHEN (1976) "Toward a Marxian theory of deviance." Social Problems 22:638-651.
STARR, JEROLD M. (1985) "Cultural politics in the 1960s," pp. 235-294 in Jerold M. Starr (ed.), Cultural Politics: Radical Movements in Modern History. New York: Praeger.
STRAUS, MURRAY, RICHARD J. GELLES, and SUZANNE K. STEINMETZ (1980) Behind Closed Doors: Violence in the American Family. Garden City, NJ: Doubleday.
SUTHERLAND, EDWIN H. (1937) The Professional Thief: By a Professional Thief. Chicago: University of Chicago Press.
SUTHERLAND, EDWIN H. (1939) Principles of Criminology (3rd. ed.). Philadelphia: Lippincott.
SUTHERLAND, EDWIN H. (1940) "White-collar criminality." American Sociological Review 5 (February):1-12.
SUTHERLAND, EDWIN H. (1949) White Collar Crime. New York. Holt, Rinehart & Winston.
SUTHERLAND, EDWIN H. (1973[1942]) "On analyzing crime," in Karl Schuessler (ed.). Chicago: University of Chicago Press.
SUTHERLAND, EDWIN H. (1983[1949]) White Collar Crime: The Uncut Version. New Haven, CT: Yale University Press.
SUTHERLAND, EDWIN H. and DONALD R. CRESSEY (1970) Criminology (8th ed.). Philadelphia: Lippincott.
SYKES, GRESHAM M. (1974) "The rise of critical criminology." Journal of Criminal Law and Criminology 65 (June):206-213.
SYKES, GRESHAM M. (1978) Criminology. New York: Harcourt Brace Jovanovich.
SYKES, GRESHAM and DAVID MATZA (1957) "Techniques of neutralization: A

theory of delinquency." American Sociological Review 22:664-673.
SYMONS, JOSEPH N. (1951) "Discussion." American Sociological Review 16:207-208.
SZASZ, THOMAS (1987) Insanity: The Idea and Its Consequences. New York: John Wiley.
TANNENBAUM, FRANK (1938) Crime and the Community. New York: Columbia University Press.
TAYLOR, IAN, PAUL WALTON, and JOCK YOUNG (1973) The New Criminology: For a Social Theory of Deviance. London: Routledge & Kegan Paul.
THOMAS, CHARLES W. and DONNA M. BISHOP (1984) "The effect of formal and informal sanctions on delinquency: A longitudinal comparison of labeling and deterrence theories." Journal of Criminal Law and Criminology 75 (4):1222-1245.
THOMAS, CHARLES W. and JOHN R. HEPBURN (1983) Crime, Criminal Law, and Criminology. Dubuque, IA: William C Brown.
THRASHER, FREDERICK M. (1963[1927]) The Gang: A Study of 1,313 Gangs in Chicago. Chicago: University of Chicago Press.
TIERNEY, KATHLEEN J. (1982) "The battered women movement and the creation of the wife beating problem." Social Problems 29 (February):207-220.
Time (1984) "Sex in the 80s: The revolution is over." (April 9):74-78.
Time (1986a) "Crack down: Reagan declares war on drugs and proposes tests for key officials." (August 18):12-13.
Time (1986b) "Hail liberty." (July 14).
TITTLE, CHARLES R. (1975a) "Labeling and crime: An empirical evaluation," pp. 157-179 in Walter R. Gove (ed.), The Labelling of Deviance: Evaluating a Perspective. Beverly Hills, CA: Sage.
TITTLE, CHARLES R. (1975b) "Deterrents or labeling?" Social Forces 53:399-410.
TURK, AUSTIN T. (1969a) Criminality and Legal Order. Chicago: Rand McNally.
TURK, AUSTIN T. (1969b) "Introduction," pp. 3-20 in Willem Bonger, Criminality and Economic Conditions. Bloomington: Indiana University Press.
TURK, AUSTIN (1987) "Turk and conflict theory: An autobiographical reflection." Criminologist 12:3-7.
TURNER, JONATHAN H. (1978) The Structure of Sociological Theory. Homewood, IL: Dorsey.
USA Today (1987) "More jails are charging inmates for their stay." (November 19):8A.
VAN DEN HAAG, ERNEST (1975) Punishing Criminals: Concerning a Very Old and Painful Question. New York: Basic Books.
VOLD, GEORGE B. (1958) Theoretical Criminology. New York: Oxford University Press.
VOLD, GEORGE B. and THOMAS J. BERNARD (1986) Theoretical Criminology (3rd. ed.). New York: Oxford University Press.
Washington Post (1986) "Drug test called costly, often useless." (June 21): 15.
WHYTE, LAWRENCE (1957) The Organizational Man. New York: McGraw.
WILSON, JAMES Q. (1975) Thinking About Crime. New York: Vintage.
WILSON, JAMES Q. and RICHARD J. HERRNSTEIN (1985) Crime and Human Nature. New York: Simon & Schuster.
WILSON, WILLIAM JULIUS (1987) The Truly Disadvantaged: The Inner City, the Underclass, and Public Policy. Chicago: University of Chicago Press.
WIRTH, LOUIS (1938) "Urbanism as a way of life." American Journal of Sociology 44:1-24.
WOLFF, KURT H. (1964) The Sociology of George Simmel. New York: Free Press.
WOLFGANG, MARVIN K. (1973) "Cesare Lombroso," pp. 232-291 in Hermann Mannheim (ed.), Pioneers in Criminology (2nd ed). Montclair, NJ: Patterson Smith.
WOLFGANG, MARVIN E. and FRANCO FERRACUTI (1982) The Subculture of Violence: Toward an Integrated Theory in Criminology. Beverly Hills, CA: Sage.
WRIGHT, ERIC OLIN (1973) The Politics of Punishment: A Critical Analysis of Prisons in America. New York: Harper & Row.

WRONG, DENNIS (1961) "The oversocialized conception of man in modern sociology." American Sociological Review 26:187-193.
YOCHELSON, SAMUEL and STANTON SAMENOW (1976) The Criminal Personality. New York: Aronson.
ZINN, HOWARD (1964) SNCC: The New Abolitionists. Boston: Beacon.

Index

About the Authors

J. Robert Lilly is Professor of Criminology and Adjunct Professor of Law at Northern Kentucky University. His research interests include juvenile delinquency, house arrest and electronic monitoring, criminal justice in the People's Republic of China, the sociology of law, and criminological theory. He has published in *Criminology, Crime and Delinquency, Social Problems, Legal Studies Forum, Northern Kentucky Law Review, Journal of Drug Issues, The New Scholar, Adolescence, Qualitative Sociology, Federal Probation, International Journal of Comparative and Applied Criminal Justice,* and *Justice Quarterly.* He has coauthored several articles and book chapters with Richard A. Ball, and he is coauthor of *House Arrest and Correctional Policy: Doing Time at Home* (Sage Publications, 1988). He is also the Treasurer of the American Society of Criminology. In 1988, Professor Lilly was Visiting Professor in the School of Law, Leicester Polytechnic, and Visiting Scholar at All Soul's College, Oxford.

Francis T. Cullen is Professor in the Department of Criminal Justice at the University of Cincinnati, where he also holds a joint appointment in Sociology. After receiving his Ph.D. in 1979 from Columbia University, he was on the faculty of Western Illinois University. He is author of *Rethinking Crime and Deviance Theory: The Emergence of a Structuring Tradition,* and coauthor of *Reaffirming Rehabilitation, Corporate Crime Under Attack: The Ford Pinto Case and Beyond,* and *Criminology* (forthcoming). He has published over 50 articles and book chapters, including contributions to the *American Sociological Review, American Journal of Sociology, Criminology, Justice Quarterly, Crime and Delinquency, Journal of Research in Crime and Delinquency,* and *Journal of Health and Social Behavior.* He has served as editor of *Justice Quarterly* and of the *Journal of Crime and Justice.*

Richard A. Ball is Professor of Sociology at West Virginia University. He received his B.A. from West Virginia University in 1958, his M.A. from that institution in 1960, and his Ph.D. from Ohio State University in 1965. He has authored several monographs and approximately 100 articles and book chapters, including articles in the *American Journal of Corrections, American Sociological Review, The American Sociologist, British Journal of Social Psychiatry, Crime and Delinquency, Criminology, Federal Probation, International Journal of Comparative and Applied Criminal Justice, International Social Science Review, Journal of Communication, Journal of Small Business Management, Journal of Psychohistory, Justice Quarterly, Northern Kentucky Law Review, Qualitative Sociology, Rural Sociology, Social Forces, Social Problems, Sociological Focus, Sociological Symposium, Sociology and Social Welfare, Sociology of Work and Occupations, Urban Life, Victimology,* and *World Futures.* His research and interests include home incarceration, criminological theory, social problems theory, sociology of law, and women inmates. He is coauthor of *House Arrest and Correctional Policy: Doing Time at Home* (Sage Publications, 1988).